COLLISION COURSE

THE OLYMPIC TRAGEDY OF
MARY DECKER AND ZOLA BUDD

JASON HENDERSON

First published in Great Britain in 2016 by
ARENA SPORT
An imprint of Birlinn Limited
West Newington House
10 Newington Road
Edinburgh
EH9 1QS

www.arenasportbooks.co.uk

ISBN: 9781909715363
eBook ISBN: 9780857909022

British Library Cataloguing-in-Publication Data
A catalogue record for this book is available on request from the
British Library.

Designed and typeset by Polaris Publishing, Edinburgh
www.polarispublishing.com

Printed in Great Britain by CPI Group (UK) Ltd, Croydon CR0 4YY

CONTENTS

PREFACE

AS AN ATHLETICS-MAD teenager in 1984, the sudden and unexpected arrival of Zola Budd into my country from South Africa gripped my imagination. Excited by the seventeen-year-old's attempt to gain last-gasp qualification to run for Britain in the Los Angeles Olympics a few months later, I remember keeping for several years afterwards a copy of the *Daily Mail* front page splash that broke the story.

Fascinated by her enormous talent and penchant for racing barefoot, I pestered my father to drive me from our home in north-west England to see her run at venues like Crystal Palace in London and Cwmbran in South Wales. There, I soaked up the atmosphere during a magical period for track and field that was filled with superstars such as Seb Coe, Steve Ovett, Steve Cram, Daley Thompson, Ed Moses, Carl Lewis and many more.

The previous year I had devoured the television coverage of the splendid, inaugural IAAF World Championships from Helsinki and replayed the BBC action on an old VHS video recorder so many times that I was able to recite David Coleman's commentary word for word. Among the great champions at the event was Mary Decker, a sublimely gifted American middle-distance runner, who beat the previously invincible Eastern bloc runners not once but twice in dramatic races as she scored what would go down in history as the 'Decker double'.

Little did anyone realise at the time, but Zola and Mary were destined to clash in sensational style at the 1984 Games. In one of the most controversial moments in Olympic history, they produced an incident which is still debated more than thirty years later.

After being a star-struck young runner in the spectator stands, I later gravitated to the press seats when I joined *Athletics Weekly* as a journalist in 1997. Since then I have covered five Olympics for the magazine and have interviewed everyone from Sir Roger Bannister to Usain Bolt. Yet nothing in the sport has intrigued and entertained me as much as the tale of Zola and Mary.

One reason is because there is so much more to their story than Los Angeles '84. Both athletes were trailblazers for women's running and their record-breaking exploits were ahead of their time. As personalities, they are complex characters with complicated back stories involving divorce, suicide, allegations of doping and even murder.

Then there is the politics. Zola's career was hugely affected by the apartheid system in her native country, while Mary raced throughout a Cold War era that resulted in, among other things, two Olympic boycotts.

Inevitably, this book builds towards the focal point of the infamous clash in Los Angeles. But it also strives to be a definitive, warts-and-all account of the lives of two of the most talented and interesting athletes of all time.

Author's note: Mary raced under the names Decker, Tabb and Slaney. Zola used the names Budd and Pieterse. So in order to avoid confusion I have called them Mary and Zola throughout the book, whereas other characters are referred to by their surnames.

INTRODUCTION

IT IS A warm Friday evening in Los Angeles in the summer of 1984 and two nervous young women arrive at the city's Coliseum for one of the most eagerly-anticipated Olympic races of all time. Joining them in the self-styled 'greatest stadium in the world' are ten fellow competitors and a crowd of 85,109. Elsewhere, millions more settle in front of their television sets for a 3000 metres showdown that has caught everyone's imagination.

The giant, sun-drenched sports arena was modelled on – and named after – the Rome amphitheatre famous for staging chariot races and bloodthirsty battles a couple of thousand years earlier. Yet now, in these Games of the XXIII Olympiad, the gladiatorial duo poised to go head to head are female athletes who share a unique talent, a deep desire to win and a fondness for front-running that will ultimately prove their downfall.

Mary Decker is hot favourite with the partisan home crowd and betting experts. The American won gold medals at 1500m and 3000m in dazzling style at the inaugural World Athletics Championships in Helsinki twelve months earlier and is not so much a record-breaker as a record-wrecker after smashing world bests from 800m to 10,000m over the previous decade.

What's more, the twenty-seven-year-old is desperate to make an impact in the Olympics after being thwarted by the US boycott of Moscow 1980, injury before Montreal 1976 and being too young for Munich 1972. Home support is not simply because she is American either. She grew up in nearby southern California and has raced in LA many times.

Pitted against her is Zola Budd, a prodigious teenage waif from South Africa who is wearing a hastily-organised British flag on her vest and, unusually, no shoes on her feet. Only eighteen, Zola is a reluctant runner who has been hustled into international athletics amid a media frenzy of publicity. She looks overwhelmed by the occasion and beneath her shy exterior she carries a deep resentment after being used as a pawn in a political chess game in the run-up to the Games.

Eight months earlier, she was living on a farm in Bloemfontein with a poster of Mary on her bedroom wall and resigned to competing only on South African soil because of her country's exile from global sport due to its apartheid system of racial segregation. Yet after breaking Mary's world 5000m record in Stellenbosch in January 1984 aged just seventeen, the *Daily Mail* newspaper in England dramatically engineered a British passport for her on the grounds that her grandfather was British and whisked her to the UK in time for the LA Games much to the annoyance of established British runners and anti-apartheid campaigners.

As the athletes prepare to step onto the track, officials check their shoes. Mary lifts her Nike spikes and looks confident ahead of the seven-and-a-half-lap test that lies in front of her. Dressed in blood-red kit, she is the glamour girl of American sport and has a decade worth of experience over her younger rival.

Zola, meanwhile, wears the red, white and blue colours of her new country and tentatively lifts her bare feet to show the bemused organisers, who smile in amusement and wave her on. The skin on her soles is tough after covering countless miles on the dry African veldt, yet she wears plasters over her toes to prevent sustaining blisters on the hot, synthetic oval that awaits her.

Despite these Games being blighted by an Eastern bloc boycott, the big danger to Mary and Zola is an athlete from the communist European nation of Romania. Maricica Puică is the reigning world cross country champion and the thirty-four-year-old does not face the same pressure as Mary and Zola. Instead, she looks focused and with bleached-blonde hair to match her yellow vest and spikes she cuts a striking figure.

In total, thirty-one women from twenty countries took part in the heats of the 3000m a couple of days earlier. Now, twelve finalists prepare to take to their marks at 6.40pm on the penultimate day of the track and field programme at these Games.

All of them are pioneers of women's distance running and female sport. Although many of the spectators in Los Angeles do not realise it, they are about to witness the first Olympic women's 3000m, while the 1984 Games also see the inaugural women's marathon.

It is all a far cry from the 1932 Olympics held in the same LA Coliseum fifty-two years earlier. Back then, women were only able to compete in a paltry five individual events – the 100m, 80m hurdles, high jump, discus and javelin – plus the 4x100m relay.

The 1928 Olympics in Amsterdam had featured a women's 800m, but when some of the competitors collapsed at the finish it was scrapped and the longest footrace for women at the Olympics remained a mere 200m until the 800m was finally reintroduced in 1960.

Given this, women's races at many athletics meetings in the 1980s were treated as a quirky sideshow to the men's events. This 3000m in Los Angeles is different, though, because for once a women's race is generating as much interest as a men's event. It is the glamour event of the Games with Mary and Zola its main protagonists.

The period is notable for great sporting head-to-heads. Tennis clashes include Chris Evert versus Martina Navratilova and John McEnroe against Björn Borg. Cyclists Bernard Hinault and Greg LeMond battle it out in the Tour de France. In boxing, Sugar Ray Leonard and Marvin Hagler dominate the middleweight division. Triathlon witnesses the 'iron war' between Mark Allen and Dave Scott. Athletics is enjoying the great rivalry of Sebastian Coe and Steve Ovett, not to mention Carl Lewis taking on Ben Johnson in the notorious Seoul Olympic 100m sprint final.

As Mary and Zola stride out onto the track in Los Angeles, their duel is equally intriguing. Like Coe and Ovett, the two women are contrasting characters yet with richer and more colourful backgrounds. With her tousled hair and good looks, Mary is a marketing executive's dream. She is also articulate and emotional, wearing her heart on her sleeve.

In this regard, Zola cannot be more different. Not only is the tomboyish youngster painfully introverted, but she is uncomfortable speaking English ahead of her native Afrikaans language. All of which makes her an easy target for anti-apartheid campaigners firing political potshots at her.

Not surprisingly, Mary receives the biggest cheer as the athletes are introduced to the crowd. This has been a great Games for the hosts and they expect their 3000m runner to deliver another gold.

Already, Lewis has won the men's 100m, 200m and long jump titles for the United States and only needs victory in the 4x100m to match Jesse Owens' 1936 achievement of winning four gold medals at the same Games. In the women's sprints, Valerie Brisco-Hooks has almost matched Lewis with 200m,

400m and 4x400m golds. In the inaugural Olympic marathon, the diminutive Joan Benoit produces a giant-killing run to beat Norwegian favourites Grete Waitz and Ingrid Kristiansen.

In the absence of Russia and East Germany, the Americans are on course to top the medals table in emphatic fashion. The host nation aside, these are the Games of decathlete Daley Thompson, Portuguese marathoner Carlos Lopes and one of the great British supermilers of the era, Coe, who is poised to successfully defend his 1500m title the day after Mary's and Zola's 3000m race.

This is a golden era for athletics and for the Olympics itself. After Munich was marred by terrorist killings in 1972 and Montreal had been forced into debt to pay for its 1976 Games, the Los Angeles Olympics is proving a huge commercial success.

Under the leadership of its main organiser, Peter Ueberroth, the Games are ahead of their time when it comes to attracting sponsors and on course to make a substantial profit. The athletics action is not the only hit either. Outside the Coliseum, the 1984 Games are lit up by the exploits of American gymnast Mary Lou Retton and a US basketball team led by Michael Jordan, while a young British rower called Steve Redgrave wins the first of his five Olympic medals.

Initially embarrassed by the Eastern bloc boycott, US President Ronald Reagan looks proudly on as his country – and its athletes – rise to the occasion. Nothing ever goes perfectly, however, and Mary and Zola are oblivious to their destiny as key characters in what will soon become one of the most controversial races in Olympic history.

The impending disaster in this 3000m race will be talked about – and fiercely debated – for decades to come. In fact it will follow a script that even Hollywood movie producers in nearby Tinseltown would struggle to dream up.

In the realm of Olympic controversies, it will be placed on a par with the drug-infested 1988 Olympic 100m final, the black power salute by Tommie Smith and John Carlos at the 1968 Games, the shock Soviet basketball win over the United States in 1972 and the Winter Olympics conflict between Tonya Harding and Nancy Kerrigan in 1994. Not only will it haunt Mary and Zola for the rest of their lives but it will come to define athletics careers that were otherwise filled with record-breaking and championship-winning performances.

As the athletes stand behind a curved white line that marks the start at the end of the back straight, Puică is on the inside, Zola near the middle and Mary towards the outside. An official in an orange blazer and white hat summons them forward by waving a small flag, before shouting: "On your marks!"

A moment later and the runners sprint into the bend, jostling for position, unaware they are on a collision course that will change their lives forever. The crowd is going to be cheated, Mary's Olympic curse will continue and Zola's nightmare is set to deepen in the most spectacular of circumstances.

PART ONE

THE EARLY DAYS

CHAPTER ONE

CHILDHOOD PRODIGIES

"Zola Budd has the legs of an antelope,
the face of an angel and the luck of a leper."
William Oscar Johnson, *Sports Illustrated*

BORN ON 4 August 1958, Mary Teresa Decker had a head start of almost eight years in life over Zola Budd, who was born on 26 May 1966. The two were also separated by around 8000 miles as they were raised in very different parts of the world.

Mary grew up in Bunnvale, New Jersey, a small community on the eastern side of the United States, while Zola was brought up on the other side of the Atlantic Ocean in the South African city of Bloemfontein. Bunnvale is a relatively nondescript place but is little over an hour outside the vibrant metropolis of New York City, whereas Zola's home town is known as the 'city of roses' or, in the South African language of Afrikaans, the 'fountain of flowers'.

Despite its colourful name, Bloemfontein rests on an expanse of dry grassland. The capital of the Orange Free State, an area famous for its gold and diamond mines, the town is also the birthplace of Lord of the Rings author JRR Tolkien and sits at 1395 metres (more than 4500ft) above sea level, although this is significantly lower than the highlands of Kenya and Ethiopia that produce so many world-class endurance runners.

Mary and Zola would become known for the extraordinary race at the Los Angeles Olympics, but their early years were not without drama either.

Naturally, they enjoyed many memorable moments during their childhood, but these were interspersed with a number of upsetting experiences.

It began for Zola before she even appeared into the world as she endured a difficult birth that almost killed her thirty-eight-year-old mother. During a marathon labour in Bloemfontein Hospital, the infant Zola had turned the wrong way around in the womb and after doctors and nurses managed to get her out via an emergency Caesarean they set about trying to save the life of a mother who was haemorrhaging blood and would subsequently spend the next three days drifting in and out of consciousness.

Zola's mother was christened Hendrina Wilhelmina de Swardt but became known to everyone as 'Tossie', while Zola's father was called Frank Budd. Their daughter, Zola, would be born as a citizen of the Republic of South Africa, but Tossie's family were Dutch and Frank's relatives came from London, the latter being a vital factor in helping Zola switch countries to run for Great Britain in the Olympics eighteen years later.

It was Tossie's sixth child as she had previously given birth to Jenny in 1955, followed by Estelle in 1957, Frankie in 1960 and twins Cara and Quintus in 1961. Tragically, however, Frankie was born with a liver disorder and died from a viral infection aged just eleven months, while Jenny passed away in 1980 from an allergic reaction to chemotherapy following an operation for a melanoma on her arm aged only twenty-five.

Before Zola was born, Frank was convinced she would be a boy and was prepared to use the unusual name 'Zero'. On hearing the baby was a girl, though, he kept the letter 'Z' and instead named the tiny infant – she was only 7lb in weight – after the French novelist Émile Zola. "The nurses told me the kid's a stayer," said Frank. "For a while we didn't think she'd survive. But the little bugger pulled through." As a sign of the times, doctors left the space in Zola's birth certificate for race as blank, signifying she was white.

Mary's birth in the United States a few years earlier was not so eventful, but the two girls shared one unfortunate aspect during their youth. Neither Zola nor Mary's parents were a match made in heaven and both children endured family squabbles and domestic turmoil and tension.

Mary spent the first decade of her life in Bunnvale and, like Zola, had several siblings and grew up with an older brother, John, and two sisters, Denise and Christine. Her mother, Jackie, would go on to play a prominent and supportive role in the early part of her running career, while Mary's father, John, was a tool and die maker and private pilot and engineer.

He was also a minor daredevil and once crashed a home-made helicopter, escaping with just a broken rib, and later crashed a motorbike when the twelve-year-old Mary was riding on the machine at the same time. Luckily she emerged with a fractured skull and no other serious damage.

As Zola enjoyed an innocent childhood on the veldt in South Africa, Mary moved from New Jersey to southern California when she was aged ten. First, Mary lived in Santa Ana, then Huntington Beach and Garden Grove, just a short drive down the freeway from the Los Angeles Coliseum, although her parents continued to endure a fractious relationship and by this stage they were on the brink of a divorce.

Mary's first experience of running came quite by accident, too, when she saw a flyer for a local cross country race organised by the parks and recreation department in November 1969 and decided, out of pure boredom, to check it out with a friend. At the time, they did not even know what 'cross country' was but curiosity led them to go anyway.

Showing her talent, the eleven-year-old Mary won the three-quarter-mile race easily as her friend failed to finish. "I don't remember it being very hard," she would later recall. "It was fun and I would have still enjoyed it if I had not won. After that, all I wanted to do was run. I just loved the freedom it gave me."

Before long, Mary was racing frequently and sometimes over extreme distances. In May 1971, for example, aged just twelve she tackled the Palos Verdes Marathon and clocked 3hr 9min 27sec for the hilly, 26.2-mile course despite her previous longest training run having been only 12 miles, which in itself is much longer than most youngsters that age are recommended to run.

New to the sport and brimming with innocence, Mary did not even know how long a marathon was. The world of running was new to her and, while the four-year-old Zola was toddling around her farm on the other side of the world, Mary began to make a name for herself as a runner of exceptional talent. "Even when we played kiss chase with the boys at school when I was very young," Mary would later remember, "I always used to out-run them."

Initially, she was coached by Don DeNoon, a race walker and track and field coach with the Long Beach Comets. DeNoon was not the kind of coach to wrap his athletes in cotton wool either as Mary turned into a prolific racer, even racing on the track the weekend after the Palos Verdes Marathon.

Young athletes often feel indestructible and at the end of this gruelling week Mary had her appendix out and the doctor, sensing something was not quite right with the youngster, asked her if she had been under a lot of stress lately.

Influenced by the coaching methods of Mihály Iglói, a Hungarian who helped popularise the art of interval training, DeNoon fed Mary a diet of track repetitions, partly because the nearby roads in their southern California area were so dangerous that one of his young athletes had been hit by a car out training. History somewhat unfairly paints DeNoon as an overenthusiastic and demanding coach who gave the young Mary too much work to do, but he always denied pushing his athletes too hard and even Mary has said that she drove herself and no one forced her to run.

"People think DeNoon pushed me," Mary later told *The Runner* magazine as her senior career was starting to take off. "They think my mother pushed me, but I can't honestly say I was ever pushed. I trained and raced hard because that was me. It was something within myself."

"Somehow I come off as the villain," an exasperated DeNoon reflected in a letter to *Athletics Weekly* in December 1983. "My life was devoted to Mary and the many other fine athletes that I coached in those days. I have no regrets about the programme that gave her and others the taste of success and the thrill of victory."

Explaining that his athletes never ran more than thirty-five miles per week, he continued: "No one knows Mary like I knew her in those days. She ran only what she wanted to run and when she wanted to run. She loved the excitement, the spotlight and the rewards. Ultimately, Mary was the driving force. I gave direction, encouragement and held the watch."

Under DeNoon's guidance, Mary's performances certainly began to catch the eye. In 1972, aged thirteen, she clocked 2min 12.7sec for 880 yards and was good enough to challenge senior athletes at the US Olympic Trials but the rules decreed that she was too young to compete. Mary and her mother Jackie, who accompanied her to most races, did not realise it at the time, but it was the start of a lifelong Olympic curse that would haunt the young runner.

Mary was soon moving so fast that friends and family following her career could barely catch their breath. That year, fuelled by one of mum Jackie's by now habitual pre-race spaghetti meals, she ran inside five minutes for the mile for the first time with 4:55.0, a world age thirteen best. It was a historic performance for an athlete so young if you consider the first-ever sub-five-minute mile for women had taken place only eighteen years earlier when Diane Leather, a twenty-one-year-old British runner, broke the barrier in the same month that Roger Bannister ran the world's first sub-four-minute mile for men.

Mary's performances continued to gather pace and her improvement showed little sign of hitting a plateau. The following year, aged fourteen, she ran 4:40.1, finishing just over a second behind Lyudmila Bragina, the 1972 Olympic 1500m champion, in an indoor one mile race for the United States versus the Soviet Union in Richmond, Virginia, and later in the year, still aged fourteen, she clocked 2:02.43 for 800 metres and 53.84 for 400 metres – world-class times that athletes a decade older would have been proud of.

If there was one event that propelled Mary to the forefront of the sport and even the attention of the general public, though, it was a match between the United States and the Soviet Union in Minsk in July 1973. There, racing over 800m, she beat Nijolė Sabaitė, a Lithuanian runner representing the Soviet Union who was eight years older than Mary and who had won the silver medal behind Hildegard Falck of West Germany at the Munich Olympics the previous year.

This eleventh US vs USSR match in Minsk featured a number of Olympic champions and world record-holders. "But the athlete who made the most vivid impression was the youngest and smallest one there," reported *Athletics Weekly*.

The British magazine continued: "Mary ran as though she had never heard of Sabaitė (and she probably hadn't, considering she didn't even known that Hildegard Falck was Olympic champion!). Last at the bell, she moved up into third at 600m, second around the last turn and ahead in the final straight. Sabaitė chased after the skinny Californian, all arms and legs and forward lean, but Mary actually accelerated briskly over the final 15 metres to win by a couple of metres in 2:02.9."

At only 5ft tall and weighing 89lb, Mary was definitely punching above her weight and in an amusing moment she was picked to carry the US flag at the meeting but had to be given a miniature one to parade around because the proper flag was too heavy for her. A few days later, she celebrated her fifteenth birthday at a USA versus Africa match in Dakar, Senegal, and blushed with embarrassment when a team gathering was suddenly interrupted so that the prime minister of Senegal, Abdou Diouf, could give her roses and a special gift as the US team sang 'Happy Birthday'.

The birthday present from Diouf was an African warrior on horseback and Mary cried with emotion. It was an ironic gesture given that thirteen years later Zola would find herself snubbed at the World Cross Country Championships by a high-profile athletics administrator from the same country of Senegal called Lamine Diack because she came from a country that practised an apartheid policy that kept black and white people separate.

Mary's international tour during the summer of 1973 was a huge success. After finishing third in an 800m race in Munich (behind Olympic champion Falck), she won similar events over two laps of the track in Turin, against the Soviet runners in Minsk and also Dakar.

The early 1970s was the height of the Cold War. So victory by a pig-tailed, teenage Californian girl against the top Eastern bloc runners – on Soviet soil to boot – was a coup for the United States. Smiling through her braces and gliding her way to triumph after triumph, Mary was American athletics' answer to Olga Korbut, the Soviet gymnast who had starred at the 1972 Olympics. Tiny, brilliant and adored, Mary soon earned the affectionate nickname 'little Mary Decker'.

Even the Soviet Union spectators warmed to her. "The Russian crowd loved Mary's spectacular style," wrote Linda Jacobs in a 1975 book on Mary's early career called *Speed Records and Spaghetti*. "They went wild, cheering for her. In the stands people talked about how tiny she looked, how frail, to run so well and so fast. They liked to see her speeding down the track, twin ponytails flying. She looked more like a kid at recess than a world-class athlete. The Russian fans saw that and loved her for it."

Her victory over the Soviet athletes was not a one-off either. Whereas American chess legend Bobby Fischer beat Russian master Boris Spassky for the world chess title during the Cold War era in 1972 and then promptly retired, Mary had no intention of quitting. In fact, she was just getting warmed up.

During the following winter's indoor season, at the start of 1974 and aged only fifteen, she repeated her win over much older Soviet athletes at 800m, again on Russian soil in Moscow. What's more, she began breaking world senior indoor records at 800m (2:01.8) plus 880 (2:02.4) and 1000 yards (2:26.7).

Victory in Moscow did not come without incident, though. After the 800m she took part in a medley relay and during the anchor leg she was cut up by the Soviet athlete, Sarmite Shtula, who chopped in front of her too early, elbowing her in the process and causing her to lose her stride as she was sent staggering across the track.

A similar incident would take place under a far larger spotlight in the Los Angeles Olympics ten years later and Mary's reaction in Moscow in 1974 was perhaps a sign of things to come. Full of anger, Mary stopped, threw her relay baton angrily at Shtula and broke down in a flood of tears. She then appeared to compose herself and picked up the baton before a cacophony of boos triggered a second outburst and she threw the stick at her rival for a second time, although fortunately her aim was as bad as her self-control as she missed Shtula and was swiftly led away by US team-mates.

The epitaph to the incident was that both teams were disqualified, with the judges penalising Mary for "unethical conduct", although there was an amicable ending that saw the fifteen-year-old politely applauded during the final presentations despite her earlier petulance.

"Mary Decker is either the enfant terrible or the coming star of women's track – or both," wrote Anita Verschoth in *Sports Illustrated*, an American weekly magazine that was beginning to take a big interest in the runner and would go on to feature her several times on its cover.

History shows Mary was not only a rising force but would emerge as the number one trailblazer in a pioneering wave of female runners who would help popularise women's running. In her own country, runners like 1968 Olympic 800m gold medallist Madeline Manning, five-time world cross country champion Doris Brown and multiple US and world record-breaker Francie Larrieu, were setting the pace in style and Mary took the baton with aplomb.

As athletics rolled into the 1970s, it was very much a male-dominated sport. Women runners were considered a novelty in the United States and they were judged as much for their looks as their speed and stamina. Track and field was not viewed as very 'ladylike' and the lack of encouragement and support meant that standards were modest. The first sub-three-hour marathon by a woman, for example, did not take place until 1971 whereas nowadays it is a barrier that hundreds of women routinely break every year.

Enjoying a honeymoon period with the press and public, 'little Mary Decker' was developing into a bona fide athletics star and starting to generate more column inches than some of the leading male athletes. Plenty of problems and challenges were just about to surface, though, testing her mental and physical ability to the limit.

These would include injuries that would become the bane of Mary's life and she suffered an early major one soon after her splendid international tour of 1973. Surprisingly, it did not happen while running, but instead she caught her foot in spokes in her bicycle and fractured a bone.

A cast was placed on her foot for six weeks and she recovered in time to enjoy a great indoor season at the start of 1974. It would prove to be the first of many injuries, though, and Mary would later say: "My body was changing so much at that age. I was ripe to get hurt. I grew several inches taller in a year or two and gained weight. My stride changed and I was awkward – there was all of this extra 'me' and I didn't know what to do with it."

Looking for someone to blame, the sport pointed the finger at her coach during her early years in athletics, but DeNoon has always insisted her only interruptions during the four-plus years he oversaw her training were from the motorcycle accident with her father, a bout of Sever's disease – the inflammation of the bone in the heel in children – and the removal of her appendix. "Surely her routine with me was not the cause of her cycle accident, childhood inflammation and the appendectomy," he said.

At home, Mary's parents finally split up in the summer of 1974 with her father moving out of the family home. "It's their business," said Mary, "if they're not happy together, then why shouldn't they get a divorce?"

When it came to coaching relationships, Mary had an amicable split with DeNoon in March 1974 and began a spell under the wing of Ted Devian and then Bob Glazier as she began a habit of switching coaches almost as regularly as her running shoes when results did not go her way.

Athletics aside, Mary was a typical teenage girl with her mouth full of braces, a habit of plucking her eyebrows and replacing them with a line drawn with a pencil and the occasional boyfriend, the most prominent of whom during high school was a tall and slightly older fellow runner called Bill Graves.

At school, Mary was not a fan of English and maths and definitely did not enjoy doing homework. Despite this, she earned As and Bs for most subjects. As for hobbies, she became so good at sewing, she made her own school clothes. When it came to pocket money, regular stints of babysitting earned the teenager a little spare cash from time to time.

After her indoor 800m win and relay histrionics in Moscow in early 1974, Mary enjoyed another big win in a US v USSR match over 800m in Durham, North Carolina, in July 1974 in 2:02.29 but she then suffered from another broken bone, this time a stress fracture in her right ankle, as her career became increasingly peppered with injury-related interruptions.

It even prompted the late, great Steve Prefontaine, a runner who held US records from 2000m to 10,000m and who was renowned for pushing himself to the limit, to intervene with some words of warning. "Her future could go up in smoke if she's pushed too hard," he said. "I couldn't believe her training schedule when I saw it. She could become so sick of running that she'll want to retire at eighteen.

"She is the greatest female 800m runner in the world right now at fifteen. She can be the greatest for quite a few years but she's not going to make it if she keeps going like she is now."

Prefontaine, who sadly did not live to see Mary's career develop as he died in a car accident in 1975 aged twenty-four, was prophetic with his predictions as well. Unfortunately Mary's injury woes only became worse, too, as she barely raced in 1975 and 1976 due to crippling shin pains and this, of course, ruled out her chance of running at the Montreal Games, which she watched at home on television, her eyes full of tears as she watched athletes she had beaten make the Olympic podium.

When the Montreal Games took place, Zola was only ten years old and beginning to run competitively. Her parents nicknamed her Laatlammethie, which is Afrikaans for 'late lamb', but Zola was growing up fast. Despite her traumatic birth, which saw her placed in an incubator by doctors worried about her health, she swiftly made progress – physically and mentally.

At school, Zola was a good student and a natural when it came to sport. In her first year at Onze Rust primary school in Bloemfontein she won the 60m sprint race on sports day against children in her age group. Outside athletics, she also developed a love for netball, a fast-paced ball game derived from basketball which is popular in British Commonwealth countries. Like basketball, in netball it helps if you are tall but height was not a quality Zola was particularly blessed with and later, during her running career, sports physiologists would put her success down to the fact that her lightweight frame housed a 'Rolls Royce engine'.

So while Zola struggled to make an impact on the netball courts, she was unwittingly building this formidable cardiovascular engine back home on her family farm as she played for hours on end outdoors. Tossie worked in catering and Frank helped run a process engraving business in Bloemfontein, but the family moved around a succession of smallholdings in the area with the only consistent factor being that they were surrounded by animals, all of which Zola adored.

The creatures ranged from chickens to ostriches. Her first pet was a cat that had mysteriously lost its tail. She called it Stompie and spent most of her time keeping it away from the large number of mice and rats which she also kept. In addition, the family owned a Doberman called Dobie, there was a wire-haired terrier called Fraaier (which means 'prettier than anyone else' in Afrikaans), a poodle called Natasha and there were also cows and ducks in the Budd-owned menagerie.

Amusingly, Zola would later be photographed running alongside the ostriches, helping create a myth that she trained with them, although in reality she simply led a very active life as a child and spent most of her time whizzing around her farm and the surrounding area.

It was the lifestyle of a typical tomboy and her neighbours nicknamed her 'Boetie', which is the Afrikaans equivalent of 'son' in English. Zola even enjoyed acting the part of Tarzan when playing in the countryside during long, hot weekends or school holidays.

Not that Zola was alone with nothing more than a farmyard of animals. She enjoyed a tight-knit relationship with her siblings, especially her eldest sister Jenny, and one of the local children whom she was inseparable from for a time was a boy called Thipe.

Her friend Thipe was the son of local farm workers and his skin colour was black. Not that Zola cared, because she simply treated him as her best friend and played outdoor games with him for hours on end.

Sometimes they played hide and seek or went mining for imaginary diamonds in the ground. On other occasions their games were rather more gruesome as they caught flying insects and tied their legs together so they would buzz around their heads like helicopters.

The irony was so thick, you could choke on it. Here was the young Zola, playing happily with someone whose skin colour was irrelevant to her. Yet a few years later she would be castigated for her links to a country that was divided by its policy of racial segregation.

Of more concern to Zola during her youth was her parents' increasingly distant relationship – one that would eventually end in divorce. Tossie's side of the family had fought for the Afrikaans-speaking settlers in the Boer War, with Frank's forefathers having battled for the British in the same dispute. This naturally led to a culture clash in Zola's house and her parents gradually drifted apart.

There was even a mild language barrier as Tossie, Zola and her siblings spoke in Afrikaans while Frank's first language was English. In fact, Zola grew up talking in Afrikaans so much that she would later have difficulty speaking English on the international athletics circuit. She understood the language perfectly but had problems articulating herself.

As the family moved around the area, Zola shifted from school to school. At one point she had a brief, miserable spell in a well-to-do, all-girls school called Oranje Meisies. Zola felt uncomfortable alongside richer children from upper-class families and to make matters worse she was forced to have a small operation aged thirteen to take out a small bone from both of her arches, which had been causing her to run and walk in a pigeon-toed fashion and, post-surgery, required her feet to be put into plaster. Clearly unhappy, she moved to Hoërskool Sentraal school in the Dan Pienaar suburb of Bloemfontein where her running continued to prosper.

By now, Zola carried her first running-related wound. It was a scar on her neck sustained when the tough nylon tape at the finish line cut her during one of her growing number of school sprint races. The tough, tomboyish Zola brushed it off, though, and began toying with longer distances – the events that would ultimately become her forte.

After a few years of sprint races at primary school, she ran her first longer distance event over 1200m in junior school. At the time, three laps of the track seemed like a long way, but she laid down her first serious marker as a distance-running talent as she won with ease in just inside five minutes.

As Zola was enjoying her first strides in the sport, over in the United States the older Mary was enduring a tough few years in her mid to late teens. Yet determined to fulfil her potential, she was keen to fight through her injury problems and make her debut at the elusive Olympic Games.

In 1976 she graduated from Orange High School and was reunited for a brief, unproductive period with DeNoon. A fresh new chapter in her life was about to begin, though, as she moved briefly to Denver and then in spring 1977 enrolled at the nearby University of Colorado in the foothills of the Rocky Mountains of the western United States and started working in a running shoe store owned by Frank Shorter, the 1972 Olympic marathon gold medallist. There, in the city of Boulder, she soaked up the running culture and in addition benefited from living at altitude of 1650m, which would boost her number of red blood cells and help her endurance ability despite the fact that she was unable to train much.

Finally, her bad luck with injuries began to turn. On the advice of Dick Quax, a New Zealand runner who set a world 5000m record and won Olympic silver in the 1970s, Mary was examined for possible compartment syndrome in her shins and tests showed she needed surgery. "She is a physical genius," said Quax, who now began to have a hand in coaching Mary. "All that speed and she seems to be able to run all day as well."

Her problem was due to the sheath around the muscle being too tight, so when she tried to run and the muscle filled with blood and expanded, it caused cramps and a painful, numbing tightness. The hard part was diagnosing the problem, but the solution was not as difficult. In July 1977, back home in California, an old physician friend, Dr Glen Almquist, slit the sheath around the muscle to release the pressure and to allow it to grow back to a more natural size. Finally, Mary's 'shin splints', as it was called, was cured.

It is to the credit of coach Rich Castro at the University of Colorado that he had the vision to give Mary a scholarship despite her injuries. Similarly, Shorter saw her world-beating potential and was supportive and fiercely protective of a runner who was in danger of being exploited by sponsors and universities keen to lure Mary into their world.

Mary's period in Colorado saw her get back on track and she did not waste any time getting stuck into races again. In January 1978 she raced several times in Australia and New Zealand following a training and racing schedule written for her by Quax and returned for the indoor season in the United States and smashed the world record for 1000 yards at the *Los Angeles Times* meeting with 2:23.8. "No more injuries and no more losses. I'm only looking upwards," she said after receiving a standing ovation from the 16,000 crowd. "It almost seems like the faster I go, the easier it is."

For Mary, though, it was often a case of taking one step back for every two steps forward and the summer seasons of 1978 and 1979 were not outstanding for Mary due to tendonitis, sciatica and calf problems. She also had a second operation on her peanut brittle shins in August 1978 but she was slowly rebuilding her body and confidence.

Team-mates in Colorado gave Mary a nickname – 'Eek' – due to her habit of shrieking out suddenly on the team bus. Mary also enjoyed soaking in hot baths after training and secretly yearned for the warm climate of California as opposed to the chilly and often snowy area of Boulder.

Given this, her time at Colorado was short-lived and she stayed there just two seasons, quitting her course and moving to Oregon, an athletics-mad area steeped in running history, in May 1979. Juggling her training with a part-time job in a Nike retail outlet in downtown Eugene, Mary was poised to enjoy a fresh surge of improvements and in 1980, by which time she was twenty-one, she enjoyed a streak of victories and record-breaking performances.

Starting in Australia and New Zealand again during the southern hemisphere's summer track and field season, she ran her first outdoor world record – a one mile best of 4:21.68 in Auckland – which was followed by an impressive 2:01.1 for 800m on a grass track in Sydney during an Oceanic tour that saw her win five races.

On returning to America in February 1980 she ran a world indoor 1500m record of 4:00.8 in front of a large, noisy crowd at the Millrose Games in New York's Madison Square Garden followed by an indoor mile record of 4:17.55 on an over-sized, 352 yards track in the giant Houston Astrodome and then world bests of 1:58.9 and 1:59.7 for 800m and 880y in the same race in San Diego. They were exceptional performances and Mary had become the first American woman to break world records at distances further than 400 yards, but the races that gave her most pleasure were over the magical distance of the mile.

Mary had grown up reading about the exploits of the world's first sub-four-minute miler Bannister, not to mention the American miler Jim Ryun, who broke four minutes at high school before breaking world senior records for the distance in the late 1960s. With the beautiful synchrony of four laps to the mile on an outdoor track, it was a race that captured the imagination of many athletes and Mary was among them.

Mary's run in Auckland on 26 January 1980, beat the previous outdoor one mile record held by Natalia Mărăşescu of Romania by four tenths of a second. What's more, Mary was breaking US records for 800m and 1500m en route during these races and there was more to come during the summer.

In July and August of 1980, Mary set four American records for 1500m, gradually improving from 4:01.17 in Stuttgart to 3:59.43 in Zürich as she consigned Jan Merrill's four-year-old national best for the metric mile to the history books. In addition, she smashed her national record for 3000m with 8:38.73 in Oslo. Yet frustratingly these performances were little more than a consolation prize for an athlete who was forced to sit out her third consecutive Olympic Games.

Mary won the US Olympic Trials over 1500m in 1980 but did not travel to the Moscow Games due to the American boycott. After the Soviet Union invaded Afghanistan in 1979, the United States vowed to pull out of Moscow in protest and President Jimmy Carter remained true to his word, which left Mary as one of many athletes innocently drawn into the political crossfire. "Each time," Mary rued, "I just said to myself, 'My time will come.'"

Saying this, Mary would have had her work cut out to beat Tatyana Kazankina in Moscow. For not only did the Russian win 1500m gold at the Games for the host nation with an Olympic record of 3:56.56, but she beat Mary easily in races straight after the Games. First, Kazankina finished four seconds ahead of Mary over 1500m in Rome – 3:58.96 to 4:03.15. Then the Olympic champion annihilated Mary by seven seconds at the big Weltklasse Grand Prix meeting in Zürich by clocking a time of 3:52.47 that survived as the world record for 13 years and still stands as the European record today.

Passing through the 800m mark in a blistering 2:04, Mary could not stay with Kazankina as the Soviet runner strode away like a machine to run even faster for the metric mile than the legendary Paavo Nurmi had managed in the 1920s during a period that saw the flying Finn break twenty-two men's world records and win nine Olympic gold medals.

Four years earlier, in 1976, Kazankina had won the 800m and 1500m double at the Montreal Games, too, which included an 800m world record of 1:54.94. All of which was an amazing – some would say suspicious – improvement from a couple of years earlier when, in 1974 aged twenty-two, the Leningrad-based runner had finished fourth and last in the 800m indoor race that the teenage Mary had won in the US v USSR match in Moscow.

From that humbling defeat in 1974, Kazankina rose to become the first woman to run inside 1:55 for 800m and 4:00 for 1500m. Fast times aside, her withering sprint finish brought her three Olympic titles by 1980.

"She was a standard bearer for the totalitarian East and an affront to Western democracies," wrote Frank Murphy in *The Silence of Great Distance*, a book charting the growth of women's distance running. "She was an uncommon individual crafted to perfection by her regime . . . a mighty atom, the Russian dragonfly, the mouse that roared, the original large engine in a small frame, the keeper of extraordinary calm, a confident woman bent on survival, the master kicker."

Even Mary bowed to Kazankina's superiority, saying at the time: "I don't think I would have won gold at the 1980 Olympics, because 3:56 is a bit quick for me," she said, adding: "But I would have won a medal."

Back in South Africa, 1980 was an important year for Zola as well, in more ways than one. On the good side, she met Pieter Labuschagne for the first time. A history teacher at Hoërskool Sentraal school, Labuschagne doubled up as the institution's athletics coach and was destined to guide Zola into the 1984 Olympics.

On the bad side, Zola's eldest sister Jenny died in September. Worse than bad, it was truly tragic for the youngster because Jenny had been a close friend and mentor in a household that was slowly being torn apart by parental bickering.

In addition, Tossie suffered bouts of sickness which meant Jenny turned into a maternal figure for the young Zola. It's even been suggested that Jenny was the first person she called 'mum'.

Such was Zola's bond with Jenny, it took her seven years before she could bring herself to visit her sister's grave. Aged thirteen, Zola had barely even considered the concept of death. She was in denial and her solution was to retreat into her new world of running.

The phrase 'raw talent' is something of a cliché, but Zola was exactly that. She wore running shoes on the roads, but on the track, turf and trails she ran barefoot and loved the feeling of freedom it gave her as she began to build stamina to accompany the speed she had already demonstrated at primary school level.

Plus, good running shoes or racing spikes were not cheap and the Budd household was not rich. So there was probably an element of Zola preferring to keep the family expenses as low as possible. Also, Zola was hardly alone and many children in South Africa ran around without shoes.

This meant athletics aficionados would later draw comparisons with the 1962 European 5000m champion Bruce Tulloh of Great Britain. Nicknamed "Barefoot Bruce" due to his preference of racing shoeless, Tulloh had a similar wide-armed action and light stride to the young Zola.

From those early races against children in the same school, Zola progressed from local to regional to national level and increasingly found a natural target in the shape of Stephanie Gerber, who was three months older. To begin with, Gerber was so superior she was relaxing at the finish line in her tracksuit when Zola finished the same race some distance behind. Great distance runners are never short of perseverance, however, and Zola won the South African schools cross country title in Bloemfontein in July 1980 and in November smashed through the 4min 30sec barrier for 1500m with 4:24.3 during one of several defeats at the hands of Gerber.

The following April saw Zola make a further breakthrough as she took the South African under-16 800m title, again in Bloemfontein. After having lost to Gerber by less than a second over 1500m at the same championships the previous day, Zola went into the shorter event with a 'nothing to lose' mentality and ran 2:11.9 to win.

Racing on the eve of her fifteenth birthday, it was Zola's first big victory and she would later rank it among the most pleasing performances of her career. Her sister Jenny was no longer with her, but Zola immersed herself in the world of athletics and now, under the guidance of Labuschagne, was running up to sixty miles per week in training – a significant amount for a girl in her mid-teens.

The hard work paid off. In November 1981 Gerber set a South African record of 4:18.8 for 1500m, but this time Zola's friend and nemesis had no time to put her tracksuit on before Zola finished because only two tenths of a second separated the two runners and it proved to be Zola's last defeat by a South African until 1983, when she was narrowly out-sprinted over 1000m by Ilze Venter.

The "bullet from Bloemfontein", as the local press dubbed her, was beginning to fly and in February 1982, still only fifteen, she set a South African under-19 1500m record of 4:09.1 – a performance that led to her earning her first Springbok colours – followed by a national under-16 record of 2:06.5 the following month and then a South African under-19 3000m record of 9:05.7 in April before improving to 9:03.5 in October.

Still no one predicted Zola's amazing breakthrough onto the world stage two years later. Her eventual clash with Mary, who was now establishing herself as the golden girl of American athletics and global middle-distance running, was also unimaginable.

Mary and Zola had enjoyed – and sometimes endured – contrasting childhoods. Yet they emerged into the early 1980s with one key element in common. Both were prodigious running talents with a natural and merciless instinct to run the legs off their rivals from the front of the field by setting a blistering pace.

CHAPTER TWO

DOUBLE DECKER

"From the knees up, she's world class.
From the knees down, we live from day to day."
Dick Brown, Mary's coach 1980-84

ELITE ATHLETES ARE often compared to Formula One racing cars. Their finely-tuned engines and mechanics are capable of amazing speed, but in turn they are delicate machines and more prone to breakdowns than slower, reliable family vehicles or shuffling, recreational joggers.

To many observers, Mary is the classic example. In full flight and free of injury, she was beautiful to watch as she gracefully glided around the track at a pace most of her rivals could only dream of following. Yet her body was also fragile and her biomechanics often betrayed her as she was rarely without a niggling pain of some kind. Usually these were in her lower legs but it seemed Mary suffered from every athletics ailment imaginable, from problems in her back down to plantar fasciitis in the arches of her feet.

Her successful European tour of 1980 ended in typical injury-related frustration. After smashing the four-minute barrier for 1500m for the first time during her heavy defeat at the hands of Olympic champion Kazankina in Zürich, Mary took on one race too many when she tackled a 3000m in Brussels. Despite her left Achilles tendon being sore, she blasted off at world record pace but was forced to withdraw after 2000m of the race when feeling a sharp pain in her heel.

It was her sixth race in just eighteen days and her body failed to handle the stress as she suffered a minor tear to the Achilles. Surgery followed and after resuming training her old shin soreness re-emerged, requiring yet another session under the surgeon's knife.

The 1981 season was a write-off for Mary and she was accruing a bewildering number of scars on her legs. In total, she would ultimately endure around thirty surgical operations, primarily below the knees, during her career. It is a statistic that few other world-class athletes can match and a testament to her talent is that she was able to run as fast as she did with so many setbacks.

"Every injury, every operation, has taken its toll, physically, mentally and emotionally," Mary told the *New York Times* in 1983. "But each time I've been hurt, it's just made me more determined to come back again."

She added: "People have always described me as 'the perfect runner from the head to the knees – and glass from there on down'. "I've got rabbits' feet, with very high arches and narrow heels. They make me an efficient runner, because only my toes and heels strike the surface and very little of my foot hits the ground. But that's also the problem; because my arch isn't absorbing any of the shock, my heels and shins take all the punishment."

Writing in *The Runner* magazine, Eric Olsen described how, during Mary's lowest moments, she went on "a pilgrimage from doctor to doctor to doctor". On Mary's nomadic quest for a cure to her injury nightmare, he added: "They tried everything: acupressure, acupuncture, orthotics. They injected her with radio-opaque and radioactive dyes and took X-rays by the score, stuck her legs in casts, cut the casts off, stuck her legs back in, and gave her drugs – cortisone, of course, and every other anti-inflammatory drug you can think of, drugs that are legal, drugs they give to horses, drugs that made Decker's hair fall out in clumps and her legs swell up."

A prolific chronicler of Mary's career in the 1980s, Olsen continued: "That Decker survived all these years of medical experimentation unscathed says something about her enormous reserves of strength and vitality, and through it all she never lost hope. Or almost never."

Despite this, Mary was poised to enjoy her greatest period on the track. In 1982 and 1983 she went on an unbeaten, record-breaking spree that culminated in her finest moment at the inaugural World Athletics Championships in Helsinki. During these two magnificent seasons she won thirty-eight races and set eight world records before ending the period with two global gold medals in the Finnish capital – an achievement that became known in athletics folklore as the 'Decker double'.

Amazingly, not only did Mary manage this off a background of endless sessions with physiotherapists and surgeons, but it happened in the midst of a brief and unhappy first marriage. Ron Tabb was a fellow international runner who had moved to Eugene as an adidas representative and it seemed like an ideal match. Two years older than Mary, he finished third in the Boston Marathon in 1980 and went on to place runner-up to Greg Meyer in the same Boston race in 1983 before joining Mary in the US team for the World Championships in Helsinki, where he would place eighteenth in the marathon. Yet after a wedding in September 1981, they swiftly grew apart and their divorce was finalised in December 1983.

Perhaps, with hindsight, the foundations for marriage were not ideal. Earlier in 1981, Mary had been engaged to Brent James, a production line manager for Nike, with a wedding due to take place in Eugene in September. Ultimately, Mary would get married in Eugene in September, but to Tabb rather than James. In fact, during a whirlwind romance, Mary came within a couple of hours of marrying Tabb in Hawaii in June of 1981 but was persuaded by friends to wait until September. "We went to the beach instead," smiled Mary.

On 12 September they enjoyed a quiet ceremony attended by fifty or so guests. Mary was given away by her friend John Gregorio and subsequent coverage in *The Runner* magazine described the occasion as "our royal wedding". Straight after the reception the newlyweds drove to the airport to catch an overnight flight to Montreal so Tabb could run the Canadian city's marathon the next day at 9am – a race he finished in an under par 2:27.

Kenny Moore, an Olympic marathon runner in 1968 and 1972 and journalist with *Sports Illustrated*, described Tabb as "a patient and selfless man, who has been instrumental in gently guiding his sometimes over-spirited wife through a gradual return to her extraordinary form".

Mary briefly ran under the surname Decker-Tabb and, while it appeared an ideal partnership as they enjoyed the same love of competitive running, in reality they began to frustrate and annoy each other. The duo even shared the same coach, Dick Brown, who Mary moved to after having spent brief periods being advised by New Zealand runner Quax and the renowned Oregon-based coaching guru Bill Bowerman.

Maybe part of the reason for the marriage break-up is that world-class athletes, by their nature, must be more than a little selfish if they are to attain their goals and the husband-and-wife team was torn between supporting each other and focusing on their own career. Tabb, after all, was no mean runner himself. He won marathons in five different continents, with twenty of his races faster than 2hr 20min and qualified for the 1980 Olympics for the United States, although was thwarted by the boycott. "I will go to my grave and be bitter about it because it completely changes your life," he said in 2013.

A training partner of Alberto Salazar, the No.1 American distance runner in the 1980s, Tabb met Mary through a mutual friend and fellow runner Alex Kasich and then knocked on her door late one night and persuaded her to go out with him. Looking back, he says he has few regrets in life and after getting remarried he went on to own a sports bar and diner in Cornelius, Oregon.

"He was unhappy with me if I ran well because I got so much attention," said Mary on her ill-fated first marriage. "And he was unhappy if I ran poorly, because I ran poorly. I felt I couldn't win." A few years later in another interview, she added: "It was the pits. We'd go out for training runs and it would end up as some sort of competition."

Mary's marriage and new coaching set-up happened after she had moved to Eugene, Oregon, where Brown worked as an exercise physiologist and administrator for an organisation called Athletics West that had been created by Nike in 1977 to nurture American athletes ahead of the Olympics. The mild and damp climate in the north-west state of America is very different to the warmth of southern California or the chilly mountains of Colorado, but this, together with the coaching inconsistency and ill-fated marriage, formed the platform for Mary's brilliant 1982 and 1983 seasons.

The athlete was no longer 'little Mary Decker' either. By now she had emerged from adolescence and was a headstrong young woman with a reputation for being demanding and sometimes hot-headed. Journalists covering her career recognised this as well and the word 'spunky' crops up frequently to describe her during articles from the period. In this regard, Brown was the perfect foil to Mary's fiery personality as he was well known for his calm, soothing personality and an emphasis on caution when it came to setting training schedules. Mary even described Brown as a 'father figure' in interviews.

"I moved to Eugene because Pre always said I should," said Mary, a few years later, referring to Prefontaine, who had been coached by Bowerman at the University of Oregon. There, Mary benefited from the expertise of Bowerman and Brown as they limited the amount of mileage and tough track sessions she would do. Initially Bowerman oversaw Mary's training, but she increasingly moved under the wing of Brown from 1981 onwards, although Bowerman's wisdom and input was never far away.

"She's genetically gifted," said Brown. "God went zap and her genes came together. After that, it's a matter of not allowing her to over-train and get hurt. From the knees up, she's world class. From the knees down, we live from day to day."

The cautious routine paid off and at the start of 1982 Mary set four world indoor records. It was the first time Mary had raced on the track in almost a year and a half as she ran a world mile record of 4:24.6 in Los Angeles followed by 8:47.3 for 3000m in Inglewood, California, then 4:21.47 for the mile at the Millrose Games in New York and 4:20.5 back on the west coast in San Diego.

"At fourteen, Mary Decker was a track prodigy," wrote the *New York Times*. "At twenty-three, Mary Decker-Tabb is running better than ever, with world indoor bests at four distances."

In trademark style, Mary led all of those indoor events and in the New York race, which was held on a tight 160-yard banked track in the city's Madison Square Garden, she finished half a lap ahead of a quality field as a capacity crowd of more than 18,000 spectators cheered her home.

It was a golden era for indoor athletics in the United States with American middle-distance greats such as Steve Scott, Don Paige and Doug Padilla thrilling the packed crowds at Madison Square Garden and elsewhere. The biggest draw, though, was Eamonn Coghlan, an Irish miler who earned the nickname 'the chairman of the boards' due to his record-breaking form on the tight, wooden indoor tracks of the period.

Like Mary, Coghlan was unlucky at the Olympic Games, finishing fourth in the 1500m at the 1976 Games and fourth in the 5000m at the 1980 Games. But on the indoor boards he was virtually unbeatable and became the first man to break 3:50 for the mile indoors in 1983 with 3:49.78.

If Coghlan was the most popular and dominant men's runner on the US indoor circuit, then Mary was the female equivalent. Her mile best of 4:20.5 set in San Diego on 19 February 1982, still stands as a US indoor record today, while one of her six victories at the Millrose Games – her 4:00.8 1500m from 1980 – has survived many years as a meeting record.

"Everywhere she went, crowds flocked to see her run," wrote Matthew Newman in a short book about Mary which was published in 1986. "More than ever, Mary prided herself on looking great when she ran. She always wore make-up and jewellery. Her showmanship was even more polished. She loved to have the crowd on her side and she knew how to win them over."

Mary did not deny it, telling the *New York Times*: "I do have a touch of the ham in me. I always shave my legs and spruce up before a meet. And when I go out onto the track, I try to get a sense of the crowd. I love to have a good crowd and be accepted by them."

Charisma and showmanship aside, Mary's attractive features turned heads and features on her during the 1980s are peppered with references to her good looks by journalists who could not help mentioning it. One article went as far as to mention the "slobbering, schoolboy crushes" that many people in the sport harboured, while Simon Barnes, the long-time chief sports writer at *The Times*, dubbed her "the world's sexiest athlete".

Mary carried her great form into the outdoor season in 1982 and showed she did not always have to lead from the front as she followed British runner Paula Fudge through the first couple of miles of a 5000m race in Eugene before cruising clear to set an outdoor world record of 15:08.26, beating New Zealander Anne Audain's previous mark by five seconds. Fudge, a former holder of the record, finished 70m adrift and Mary enjoyed the experience, saying: "I let someone else lead and I was surprised I felt as good as I did – nice and relaxed for a change."

Traditionally, Europe is the focal point of world athletics during the outdoor season. Most of the biggest and most lucrative grand prix meetings are held in countries such as Switzerland, Belgium, Germany and England and every summer the top athletes on the planet ply their trade at these premier events in cities like Zürich, Brussels and London. So even in a relatively quiet season that did not feature a major championship, athletes like Mary would travel over to Europe for a succession of competitions.

After her 5000m world record, Mary opened her European campaign for 1982 with an American mile record of 4:21.46 in Oslo in late June before returning to the Norwegian city to win a 3000m at the Bislett Games – one of the most historic meetings on the calendar – in 8:29.71. The world record of 8:27.12 was held by Lyudmila Bragina, the 1972 Olympic 1500m champion from Russia, but Mary fell just short of the mark on a night dominated by British runner David Moorcroft's near-six-second demolition of Kenyan Henry Rono's world 5000m record.

In Oslo, Mary became only the second woman in history to break 8:30 for 3000m and a couple of days later she smashed the world mile record in Paris with 4:18.08. "I was tired," she said. "The 3000m in Oslo took a lot out of me." Nevertheless, she took more than two-and-a-half seconds off the previous mark held by Lyudmila Veselkova of Russia as the American waged a one-woman assault on the Soviet stranglehold on women's middle-distance running. Then, showing no sign of slowing down, Mary ended her European tour with a personal best for 800m of 1:58.33 in Lausanne as she narrowly missed the US record.

The best was arguably yet to come, though. On returning to the United States, Mary heard about a 10,000m race at home in Hayward Field in Eugene and despite suffering from jetlag after a 16-hour journey she began making enquiries to run on the day of the race itself. The idea worried her coach, Brown, as Mary had raced five times in Europe during the previous three weeks. Also, 10,000m was 6.2 miles and 25 laps on an unforgiving synthetic track. So Brown gave his blessing as long as Mary wore road racing shoes – or 'flats' as they are known – which have greater support and cushioning than the flimsier spiked shoes that most athletes wear in track races. Brown added that Mary should drop out if she felt bad and it would be her last outing on a track for at least a week in order to let her body recover.

Mary agreed and with no specific preparation for a race this far, she ran 31:35.3 to beat the world record – held by another Soviet athlete, this time Yelena Sipatova – by 42 seconds and the US record by a whopping 77 seconds. For women, 10,000m races on the track, not to mention 5000m events, were still in their infancy and the records were not as tough as they are today. Still, Mary obliterated the old mark after entering on a whim and treating it almost like a training run with racing flats that she described as "cloddy" after the race. "It just proves the records aren't that stiff yet," she said, after her sixth world record of 1982, "and they'll be running 30 minutes (dead) before too much longer."

At the end of 1982, Mary held every American record from 800m to 10,000m. As the end of season honours were dished out, she became the first woman to win the prestigious Jesse Owens award, a prize that had gone to Carl Lewis and Ed Moses over the previous two seasons, while *Runner's World* magazine described her as "the greatest female middle-distance runner the United States has ever produced".

Olympic marathon legend Shorter said: "Generally, the track world breaks down into form runners and strength runners. Mary is that remarkable combination of form and strength."

Brooks Johnson, head coach of the US Olympic team in 1984, was another coach who cooed over Mary's formidable running technique. "It is like watching a symphony in motion," he said. "She has the best biomechanics of anyone I've seen."

Tabb, meanwhile, was developing a reputation for accurately predicting his wife's times despite their crumbling relationship and suggested she could be the first woman to break 2hr 20min for the marathon. This was a time when the world record was held by Grete Waitz of Norway with 2:25:42 and it would be another nineteen years before the world would see the first sub-2:20 marathon by a woman.

At one stage, Mary even considered an audacious 3000m and marathon double at the Los Angeles Olympics. Speaking to Ted Tedeschi of *New York Running Times* before the 1983 season, she said she was toying with the idea of tackling "the 3000m and a longer race", although it became a moot point when Olympic organisers scheduled the marathon before the 3000m.

Such was Mary's range of ability, it was hard to choose her strongest distance. Her potential to run a great marathon was a mouthwatering prospect, especially given the mystique and glamour associated with the 26.2-mile event, but at the opposite end of the spectrum she demonstrated fearsome speed as well. Over 200 metres, for example, Mary was once timed at 23.7 seconds from a standing start on a dirt track compared to the 21.83 best of Evelyn Ashford, the US record-holder over the distance in addition to being a world 100m record-holder and 1984 Olympic 100m champion.

Yet Mary's Formula One-style engine was incredibly delicate and Brown's main challenge was helping her avoid injury-enforced lay-offs. For one, she was rarely allowed to run more than sixty miles per week in training, which is probably the bare minimum that an athlete should tackle if they want to fulfil their potential and become competitive on the global stage. Weekly sessions with a chiropractor became the norm for an athlete whose back was so tight she was often unable to do a full sit-up. Similarly, massage sessions under the healing hands of Rich Phaigh were a daily occurrence and the therapist always knew he had his work cut out to iron out the knots and scar tissue in Mary's legs.

Much of this work was done at the Athletics West headquarters in Oregon. Athletics West had been set up by Bowerman and Nike co-founder Phil Knight and initially included male athletes like Craig Virgin, the 1980 and 1981 world cross country champion, plus Boston and New York City marathon winner Salazar. But the early 1980s saw female runners such as Mary and Joan Benoit signed by Athletics West as the distinctive red and white colours of the team became increasingly prevalent. "They kind of bent the rules for me," said Mary, after joining what had previously been seen as an all boys' club. "It was a test to see how women would work in a team situation with men and I was only let in after a meeting where the team's members and their wives voted on whether to let me in."

Athletics West not only offered top coaching knowledge from the likes of Bowerman and Brown and medical back-up from therapists like Phaigh, but it provided a structure for American athletes to survive financially after their life at university ended. Student athletes were relatively well looked after in the United States, but once their education ended they entered an athletics environment which was, in some quarters, reluctant to ditch its amateur ethos. These were changing times for the sport as it struggled to embrace professionalism and Mary's emergence as the world's premier female middle-distance runner coincided with it.

Older officials zealously guarded the Corinthian principles and amateurism despite the increasing monetisation of athletics. The result was an uneasy period that was described as 'shamateurism', where unofficial payments in brown envelopes were secretly given to athletes behind the scenes at athletics events.

The Kiwi runner Audain, for example, whose 5000m world record Mary had beaten in 1982, was temporarily banned from athletics in 1981 for openly accepting prize money at a road race. Consequently, athletes such as Mary were forced to wrestle with this problem as they pursued their sport and tried to make a living from it.

The answer, for a short period at least, came in the form of trust funds, whereby earnings were placed in a bank for safekeeping until the athlete retired. These trust funds were the brainchild of the International Amateur Athletic Federation, or IAAF, the global governing body of the sport which would finally – and belatedly – lose the word amateur from its title in 2001 as it became the International Association of Athletics Federations. In Mary's case, her earnings in the 1982 season went into a bank in Indianapolis, although Athletics West covered most of her living and travel expenses, plus medical back-up and negotiations with race organisers.

"I have to live with this system for the same reason every other amateur athlete does – so I can compete in the Olympics," said Mary. "I think it's wrong, of course. I think every athlete, pro and amateur, ought to be able to participate. The Olympics should be made an open competition, like tennis at Wimbledon. But for now, we have no choice but to retain our amateur standing for the Olympics."

The period also saw the growth of sponsorship in sport and particularly athletics and Mary's growing status as the golden girl of American athletics meant she would have been foolish not to investigate such opportunities. As well as Nike, Mary endorsed companies such as Timex and Kodak, bringing in an estimated $300,000 a year by 1984 – the equivalent to almost $1 million today. Financially, it was a big change for a runner who had spent spells working in McDonald's and Jack in the Box fast food outlets to earn money.

To help her seal these deals was the International Management Group, known as IMG for short. Founded by lawyer Mark McCormack a few years earlier, IMG initially helped golfers such as Arnold Palmer, Jack Nicklaus and Gary Player, but it soon began to expand to look after the interests of track and field stars such as Sebastian Coe, who signed with IMG after breaking world records for 800m, 1500m and the mile. Today, every elite athlete worth their salt is represented by a management agency to look after their commercial interests, but Mary was among the first back in the early 1980s.

While Mary's athletics endeavours were supported by Athletics West and Nike, her biggest rivals from Eastern Europe were backed by a state-sponsored system. Desperate to use the global sporting stage to prove their political superiority, socialist nations such as the Soviet Union and East Germany ploughed money into helping their athletes, gymnasts, swimmers, wrestlers and rowers succeed at the Olympics.

There was also a dark side to the efforts of the Eastern bloc nations that came in the shape of performance-enhancing drugs. History now tells us that East Germany, in particular, employed a state-supported system of doping, while Soviet and Romanian athletes were hardly innocent either.

Romania's Mărăşescu, for example, the world mile record-holder prior to Mary, was banned for eighteen months in 1979 for steroid abuse, while Kazankina, the Soviet Union's three-time Olympic gold medallist at the 1976 and 1980 Games, served a similar ban in 1984 after refusing to take a drugs test.

It was against this backdrop of suspicion that Mary entered the 1983 season. The pinnacle of the campaign would be the inaugural IAAF World Championships in Helsinki and her main rivals would be athletes from behind the Iron Curtain. After the boycott of the Moscow Olympics and President Reagan's denouncement of the Union of Soviet Socialist Republics as "an evil empire", Cold War tensions showed little sign of disappearing in the early 1980s and America's No.1 female runner was heading for a showdown with the all-conquering Soviet athletes on neutral territory in Finland.

Never afraid to be outspoken, Mary had no qualms about giving her opinion on the doping suspicions. Speaking to *Track & Field News* magazine after her heavy defeat at the hands of Kazankina over 1500m in Zürich at the end of the 1980 season, Mary said: "I was psychologically beaten before the race started. I looked at the Soviet women and literally could not believe it. They didn't look like women I had ever seen before. Their muscle definition was so pronounced.

"I don't doubt that they are females biologically speaking," she continued, "but, shall we say, chemically I am not so sure."

If such comments made their way back to the Soviet Union then they only served to heighten the anticipation – and potential animosity – ahead of the World Championships. Kazankina would head into 1983 as world 1500m record-holder and three-time Olympic champion and she would be joined at the World Championships in Helsinki by a strong contingent of Soviet middle-distance runners.

Mary knew anything other than her best would not be good enough to beat her Soviet rivals and she wintered well with a rare injury-free period of training. Sensibly, she kept her indoor season at the start of 1983 to a minimum and raced just three times with a couple of one mile victories at New York's Millrose Games and in Dallas together with a world best for two miles of 9:31.7 at the Sunkist Invitational in Los Angeles.

Inevitably, it wouldn't be Mary without the odd hiccup. The Millrose Games mile saw her embroiled in a brief controversy when she pushed a lapped runner, Angelita Lind, out of the way when the Puerto Rican failed to move out to let her pass. In March she separated from her husband as her short marriage to Tabb drew to a close and in April she hurt her neck in a car crash, although she recovered from the whiplash to form part of a US record-breaking Athletics West 4x800m quartet at the Mt Sac Relays.

There, running in Walnut, California, she bashed out a swift split of 2:01.5 as she joined Sue Addison, Lee Arbogast and Chris Mullen in setting a national best mark that would survive for thirty years, when it was eventually beaten at the Penn Relays in 2013.

After this, Mary stretched her legs on the roads with a US 10km record of 31:52 at home in Eugene. Her winning streak continued in June with victories over 1500m in Berkeley (4:04.5), the mile in Westwood (4:21.65) and at 3000m in San Jose (8:42.48) and at the Prefontaine Classic in Eugene (8:42.38). All of which set her up perfectly for the US Championships and World Championships trials in Indianapolis.

The event at Indiana University was dominated by Carl Lewis with brilliant performances in the 100m, 200m and long jump. Ed Moses was also in terrific form as he romped to his seventy-fifth consecutive victory over 400m hurdles. Mary also impressed, though, as she first took the 1500m title in 4:03.50 and just 55 minutes later lined up for the 3000m final and cruised home first again in 8:38.36.

"I wanted to see how I could run the 3000m when I was tired," she said. "But the 1500m really didn't make me that tired."

As always at the US Championships, the timetable replicated the major international championship schedule that would face the athletes later in the season. So Mary had the additional challenge of navigating heats in Indianapolis and it proved the ideal preparation for Helsinki.

Six days after her double at the US trials, Mary gained a psychological edge over her East German rivals when she won the 1500m at a United States versus German Democratic Republic (GDR) match in Los Angeles. Not only did she break four minutes with 3:59.93 but she covered the last lap in a brisk 60.3 seconds.

Moving over to Europe, she showed no sign of jetlag as she set a US 1500m record of 3:57.12 in Stockholm as the United States took on a combined Nordic nations' team. It was a tremendous run and it would remain the national best for thirty-two years until Shannon Rowbury finally improved it to 3:56.29 in 2015 in a Monaco race that saw Genzebe Dibaba of Ethiopia set a world record of 3:50.07.

"On the track," wrote Tedeschi in *New York Running Times*, "Mary is a cheetah with staying power. When she is healthy, the records fall like a house of cards."

Mary was producing performances that would stand the test of time. Her 1500m in Stockholm saw her pass through 400m in 62.6, 800m in 2:06.9 and 1200m in 3:10 before she sliced two seconds off her own American record to win by 11 seconds. As a bonus, it was the quickest ever seen by a non-Soviet runner.

Such performances sometimes come at a price, though, and after her race in Stockholm, Mary came down with a mild head cold and inflamed a tendon in her right leg after being persuaded, against her better judgement, to jog a lap of honour in the Swedish capital's Olympic Stadium in bare feet. Yet Mary had the Midas touch during her 1983 season and headed straight across to the north-east of England and a Rank Xerox Games in Gateshead where she concluded her preparations for Helsinki with another American record. This time racing over 800m in windy conditions on the final day of July, she went through halfway in 57.0 before coming home in 1:57.6 to break Madeline Manning's seven-year-old US best of 1:57.9. "I feel so bad I'll take any time under Madeline's record," Mary coughed, as the cold she had contracted in Sweden was still stubbornly hanging around.

At the US Championships earlier in the season, Mary was not planning to double up in Helsinki. But the races in Stockholm and Gateshead convinced her to tackle the 1500m as well as the 3000m at the biggest event of the year. Still, the general feeling was that no matter how hard Mary pushed the pace, it seemed inevitable that one of the Soviet athletes would storm past her in the closing stages and many experts gave her little chance of victory. "I'll have to push the pace from the start," Mary confidently predicted, speaking after her US record in Stockholm, "but even when they start to kick I don't think they'll run away from me. I'm looking forward to having someone with me on the last lap. Then I'll really have to run. It'll be fun."

Until 1983, the Olympic Games had been the only truly global gathering of elite athletes. Held once every four years, it represented the pinnacle of sporting success with track and field being the showpiece event. This changed, though, when the IAAF staged its inaugural World Championships with the initial plan to hold it every four years and never in the same year as the Olympics. Featuring exactly the same quality and quantity of athletes that would take part in the Olympics, the idea immediately gained kudos with athletes and fans and it provided the perfect platform for Mary to shine.

These inaugural World Championships were hardly a hesitant, humdrum affair either. Instead they were a roaring success. "Take a bow, IAAF," wrote Mel Watman in *Athletics Weekly*'s coverage from Helsinki. "For my money, this was better than any Olympic Games. The standard of competition was higher even than at the Olympic Games; the number of countries represented (more than 150) easily outstripped any previous international gathering; the stadium was completely sold out on four of the seven days; while an immense number of televiewers throughout the world caught the athletics bug as the dramas of the week were played out on their screens."

American sprints and long jump legend Lewis led the long list of star performers in Helsinki with three gold medals. British decathlete Daley Thompson excelled throughout his ten events to beat his big rival, Jürgen Hingsen of West Germany. One year before the first Olympic marathon for women, the great Norwegian runner Waitz took the world title, while Australian Rob de Castella took the men's marathon crown. Middle-distance greats Steve Cram of Great Britain, Joaquim Cruz of Brazil and Jarmila Kratochvilová of Czechoslovakia triumphed on the track. A young Sergey Bubka took the first of six outdoor world pole vault titles. In the javelin, the home crowd went crazy when Tiina Lillak produced an inspired, last-round throw to beat Fatima Whitbread of Britain.

Amid this feast of athletics, Mary's performances are remembered as one of the highlights of the championships. First came the 3000m final on Wednesday, 10 August, where opposition included the fearsome Kazankina and her Soviet team-mate and world record-holder for the distance with a best of 8:26.78, Svetlana Ulmasova.

Now aged thirty-one, reports prior to Helsinki suggested that Kazankina had retired. The fact she had skipped the 1982 European Championships the previous year fuelled the rumours. As it turned out, though, she had been injured and taken time out to have her second child.

In the 3000m heats, held two days before the final, Mary was drawn in the same race as Kazankina and they cruised home first in exactly the same time of 8:44.72, while Ulmasova was a couple of seconds slower when winning the other heat. For the final, a sizeable field of fifteen women lined up and the scene was set for a classic encounter as the front-running Mary attempted to blunt the sting of Kazankina's and Ulmasova's finishing sprint.

Predictably, the race followed the script in the early stages with Mary setting the pace from the front as Kazankina and Ulmasova settled in behind as the third Soviet runner in the final, Natalya Artyomova, was never a factor as she faded to finish eighth and would later, like so many Russians, fail a drugs test for steroids in 1992.

The contrast between Mary and the older Kazankina was striking. The American glided around the track in graceful fashion with a long, smooth stride and her wavy hair bobbing up and down on the back of her neck, whereas Kazankina ran in a choppier, staccato style with her short hair and pale, gaunt features giving her a faintly vampiric and ghoulish appearance.

Kazankina was also the athlete with the superior CV, which included a world 1500m record five seconds quicker than Mary's US record mark. The Soviets enjoyed strength in numbers as well, because if Kazankina faltered then Ulmasova was waiting in the wings.

Mary was confident of her own strategy, though. Because many of her races had virtually turned into solo time trials, she was not used to jostling with rivals in a pack, so before the final Bowerman and Brown felt her best chance was to get out in front and gradually wind the pace up.

Halfway through the seven-and-a-half-lap race, Mary's strong tempo had whittled the lead group down to five athletes. Mary led from Kazankina and Ulmasova, both Russians hugging the kerb on the inside lane as they stalked the leader, with Wendy Sly of Great Britain running slightly wide and challenging Kazankina for pole position on Mary's right shoulder. The Italian Agnese Possamai completed the lead quintet as Brigitte Kraus, a West German who would later feature in the closing stages, was surprisingly a few metres adrift and seemingly struggling.

Somewhat prophetically, in view of what would happen in Los Angeles twelve months later, marathon legend Shorter discussed Mary's front-running tactics during NBC's commentary, saying: "It keeps her out of trouble. She's not going to get tripped. She's not going to fall down. She's not going to get boxed. But she is vulnerable out front because she's putting in more effort."

Out of trouble and laying down the gauntlet to Soviet athletes who were hitherto considered invincible, Mary was running with freedom and confidence despite failing to shake off the small pack of runners following in her slipstream. Likewise, Sly was running boldly as the twenty-three-year-old, who had won silver in the Commonwealth Games at 3000m behind Audain the previous year, moved alongside Kazankina, which among other things effectively boxed in the Soviet No.1 on the inside, trapping her on the kerb.

"It was a good feeling, compared to being way out in front," said Mary. "You can't make mistakes and you sure keep alert. It seemed no time at all until we were coming up to the last lap."

As the bell rang for the start of the final 400m, Kazankina discovered a Western wall of Mary and Sly in front of her. Pulling out wide to overtake Sly was an option, but the wily Russian held her ground down the back straight to conserve her energy as the tall Kraus, the European indoor 1500m champion, came into contention, surging through on the inside and snapping at Mary's heels as the six women jostled for position with little over half a minute's worth of racing to go.

Suddenly, small gaps began to open and Kazankina wriggled through a space between Mary and Sly and as the runners rounded the final bend the Russian had finally found the perfect position and was poised on Mary's shoulder, ready to strike. Behind, Kraus was running strongly in third, Sly was fading and Ulmasova desperately swung out wide to attack with a belated attempt to challenge. For the world record-holder, it was too late, though, as the battle for gold was now between two athletes in the home straight as Kazankina and Mary slugged it out neck and neck.

Then, with 50m to go, Mary found an inspirational final burst of energy. Nodding her head slightly, pumping her arms furiously and lengthening her stride, she drew away with an emphatic and decisive surge to win in 8:34.62. "I took a deep breath, relaxed and went," she later explained.

A broken figure, Kazankina suffered the indignity of being pipped for silver on the line by another Western athlete as Kraus finished half a second behind Mary. "I had every chance, but my final sprint failed," said Kazankina, who was unable to live with Mary's last lap of 60 seconds. Neither was Ulmasova, who came in fourth, while the plucky Sly ran 8:37.06 to beat Audain's Commonwealth record by more than eight seconds in fifth as Possamai was sixth.

"She ran that race from the front," said legendary commentator David Coleman on BBC television. "When the gun went, she went and she never, ever lost the lead."

Cliff Temple in *The Sunday Times* wrote: "To Deckerologists it was Minsk 1973 all over again. That day, the pig-tailed 14-year-old outsprinted the Russians to win an 800m match race against even greater odds; comic strip stuff."

Watman reported in *Athletics Weekly*: "What an inspiration the twenty-five-year-old American is to Western girls who for so long have suffered from an inferiority complex towards the Eastern Europeans – and what a marvellous advertisement she is for the sport."

Yet Mary was only halfway through her attempt to win double global gold. Two days later, she took to the Helsinki track again for the 1500m rounds and similarly to the 3000m she was drawn in the same heat as her biggest rival, Zamira Zaytseva of the Soviet Union, plus the in-form Sly. Qualifying for the final was a formality, though, and on Sunday, 14 August, Mary lined up against a Soviet Union triumvirate of Zaytseva, Yekaterina Podkopayeva and Ravilya Agletdinova – all of whom had fresher legs than the American and were determined to get revenge following the 3000m.

After having run 3:56.14 for 1500m in Kiev in 1982, Zaytseva was faster on paper than Mary. Indeed, such was the strength of the Soviet squad, in 1980 Zaytseva ran 3:56.9 – again, quicker than Mary's US record – but it was only good enough for fourth at the Russian Championships in Moscow and she failed to make the cut for the Olympics on home soil. Similarly, Podkopayeva was another runner in that super-fast Olympic trials race in 1980 and clocked 3:57.4 in fifth – only a fraction slower than Mary's best. Ominously, the Soviet Union's 1500m trio in Helsinki were all significantly quicker than Mary over 800m, too, which would make them strong favourites if the race boiled down to a sprint.

Nerves were evident on the start line as the twelve-strong field suffered a faulty start when Zaytseva twitched too early. As in the 3000m four days earlier, Mary hit the front straight away and went through the first 400m in 64.04 seconds – which was quicker than the slow, cagey men's final at the same championships won by Cram. Unlike Kazankina, however, Zaytseva ran more aggressively, going straight onto Mary's shoulder and avoiding the inside kerb position that her team-mate had got trapped in.

Passing 800m in 2:10.9 and mimicking her tactics from the 3000m, Mary still led from the combative Zaytseva as Sly was tucked on the inside in third followed by Gabriella Dorio of Italy and Doina Melinte of Romania. Refusing to get flustered by the nagging presence of Zaytseva poised on her shoulder, the American continued to set a strong but far from suicidal tempo, which was similar in style to the pace of the 3000m a few days earlier.

Then, with 200m to go, the race exploded into action as Zaytseva challenged Mary for the lead, sprinting past and swiftly cutting back into the inside lane, while simultaneously Podkopayeva and Agletdinova surged past Sly and Dorio into third and fourth positions as the Soviet Union athletes sprang into life.

Shocked by Zaytseva's dramatic injection of speed, Mary was forced to concede the lead for the first time in the race and the Soviet runner from Uzbekistan built up a lead of two metres as she entered the home straight with her head rocking from side to side as Mary, refusing to panic, maintained her usual fluid stride.

"It was a mistake, letting her cut me off," said Mary. "But I didn't want to have to make a sudden move. I stay more relaxed if I move into my sprint gradually. So I had to let her get a little lead."

With 50m to go, victory looked certain to go to the Russian. Yet with a final effort that was even more inspired and dramatic than her finishing flourish in the 3000m, Mary dug deep into her reserves, pulled out into lane two and lifted her pace.

"The tables were being turned in the most dramatic manner," wrote Watman in *Athletics Weekly*. "Zaytseva was now the prey; Decker the hunter."

Entering the final ten metres, Mary drew level with her rival. By this stage, she had superior momentum to carry her into the lead and in desperation the exhausted Zaytseva hurled herself at the finish line in an anguished and futile attempt to rescue the race. The Decker double was complete and the United States basked in a glorious victory over their deadly rivals.

Clocking 4:00.9 to Zaytseva's 4:01.19, Mary's winning margin was not as great as the 3000m, but who cared? A final lap of 60.2 seconds once again carried her to the gold as she earned the admiration of the sports world with not only her athleticism but her gritty, never-say-die attitude.

For the record, Podkopayeva's and Agletdinova's third and fourth positions meant the Soviet athletes filled the three places behind Mary. In fifth, Sly ran another personal best of 4:04.14, while Melinte and Dorio in sixth and seventh were destined for greater things 12 months later when they won Olympic titles at 800m and 1500m.

"I lost a lot of space on the final turn and was lucky to make it up," Mary told NBC after the race, diplomatically pointing out that Zaytseva's sharp overtaking manoeuvre caused her to chop her stride.

Weeks later and enjoying an end-of-season awards period that included being named *Sports Illustrated* sportsperson of the year, she went further, saying: "She hit me practically every stride the whole way. Not obviously, but just brushing elbows, touching shoes. I thought about taking a swing at her, but then I worried about being disqualified, too. I was conscious of the US versus USSR thing there a little. But it's lucky I didn't have a relay baton this time. I might have thrown it again.

"I lost my temper. I caught her because I was so angry," Mary continued, admitting that she had not noticed Zaytseva fall during the melee of the final, frantic metres. "My eyes had been shut. I didn't know I'd won until I saw the replay on the scoreboard. The only way of getting back at her was to win."

Toni Reavis, an American athletics commentator in Helsinki, described the races as "Pulse-pounding stuff", adding: "She was hanging on for one, coming from behind for the other, against the big, bad Russians. I think they were the two best races I've ever seen."

Carrying her form into some post-championships grand prix races, Mary won 3000m races in Zürich and Koblenz in 8:36.51 and 8:36.77, an 800m in Berlin in 1:59.14, a fast 3:59.8 1500m in Cologne and wrapped up her 1983 campaign with a UK all-comers' one mile record of 4:22.66 at the Coca-Cola International Athletes' Club meeting at Crystal Palace. As well as holding every US record from 800m to 10,000m, she had also broken seven world records over the previous two seasons and had built up an unbeaten streak of twenty races.

"The sight of Mary Decker in action generates the kind of delicious anxiety that once came from a new Alfred Hitchcock film," wrote the US magazine *Newsweek*. "She is the queen of middle-distances."

What a summer it had been for the twenty-five-year-old and as she headed into Olympic year she was on top of the world. What's more, the greatest show on earth was being held at home in Los Angeles.

"It's just perfect," she said, painfully oblivious to the fact that an unknown, waif-like, barefoot teenager from the sporting pariah of South Africa was destined to scupper her Olympic dreams once again in the most dramatic fashion imaginable.

CHAPTER THREE

BUDD'S BREAKTHROUGH

"Zola is a running machine. All I'm doing is improving the infrastructure, the capacity of her lungs and the efficiency of her body."
Pieter Labuschagne, Zola's coach

WHEN MARY WAS completing her majestic Decker double in Helsinki, Zola had only just turned seventeen. Training and racing in relative anonymity in Bloemfontein, the bespectacled South African student was still largely taking part in junior competitions against fellow teenagers. So the possibility of her being one of Mary's main challengers at the following year's Olympics seemed unlikely, to put it mildly.

Zola was not so much a rival as a fan. A poster of Mary dominated her bedroom wall. Alongside the picture of the American middle-distance star were smaller photographs of Allison Roe, the 1981 Boston and New York City marathon winner from New Zealand, together with British supermilers Coe and Ovett, plus various pictures of animals, especially horses. Scattered on the floor, stuffed toys were strewn around. On her door, a quote from AA Milne read: "One of the advantages of being disorderly is that one is constantly making exciting discoveries," which apart from anything else gave her a good excuse to have a typically messy teenage bedroom.

One area where Zola was organised was in the compilation of her training diaries. There she meticulously logged her relentless progression with ever-improving training sessions and a growing list of record-breaking track performances. Going into the 1983 season with personal best times of 2:06.5 for 800m, 4:09.1 for 1500m and 8:59.2 for 3000m, Zola was still some way short of Mary's best marks. Nevertheless, the youngster was on a steep upward curve and in 1982 had ambitiously set herself targets of 4:05 for 1500m and 8:45 for 3000m for the next season.

Breaking 4:05 would not happen until 1984, but in Durban on April 2, 1983, she smashed the 8:45 barrier for the longer distance by six seconds with 8:39.00. A couple of months earlier, Zola had set her first world junior record of 15:35.67 for 5000m in Durban followed by an 8:46.41 world junior 3000m best in Stellenbosch. But these were merely an appetizer to her 8:39.00 effort in Durban, which not only broke her world junior best by more than seven seconds but was a South African senior record and a national under-19 title.

Still only sixteen, the time would have been good enough to place her seventh in the world 3000m final in Helsinki later that same year. Given this, Zola has always ranked it as one of the top three or four performances of her entire career.

A few days later, the youngster captured the 1500m and 3000m titles at her national senior championships in Bloemfontein. She then improved her world junior 5000m mark by nine seconds to 15:24.08 in Stellenbosch in late April and then, following the southern hemisphere winter break, clocked 15:10.65 in Port Elizabeth in October aged seventeen before ending the year with a 4:06.87 South African 1500m record in Bloemfontein.

Many modern-day recreational runners consider it a triumph if they can get close to twenty minutes for 5000m. Yet here was a teenage waif of a girl racing without shoes not only making a mockery of that kind of time but coming within two seconds of Mary's world record of 15:08.26 from 1982. In all, 1983 saw Zola win six national titles, set five world junior records, an all-African record, five South African senior records and she was named as her country's sportswoman of the year.

Not that many from outside South Africa were even vaguely aware of Zola's exploits. Because of its apartheid policy of excluding black people from sections of its society, the global sporting community punished South Africa by excluding the country from international sport. Consequently, South Africa did not take part in the Olympic Games from 1964 to 1988 and of course this meant there was definitely no team at the IAAF World Championships in Helsinki.

For many years, no 'mixed sport' was allowed by officials in South Africa and in the stands there was strict segregation with black spectators kept separate from white fans. Sports arenas even went so far as to have different entrances and toilet facilities for black and white people. The word 'apartheid' itself is translated as 'separateness' and when spoken in Afrikaans is pronounced 'apart-hate'.

The Olympic ban started at the Tokyo Games in 1964 when the International Olympic Committee withdrew its invitation to South Africa after it insisted its team would not be racially integrated. Four years later, the IOC was ready to welcome South Africa back after assurances that its team would be multi-racial but the plan fell apart when other African nations threatened to boycott the Games. Then, in 1970, South Africa was formally expelled by the IOC.

Predictably, some athletes grew frustrated by their inability to compete on the world stage and among these Sydney Maree was perhaps the best known runner. Ten years older than Zola, he was born in South Africa but moved to the United States, initially to study at Villanova University, where he lived for eighteen years before moving back to South Africa when the apartheid system had been dismantled.

Unlike Zola, he had black skin and therefore little hope of seeing his athletics potential fulfilled in his native country. South Africa's loss was America's gain as he went on to set a world 1500m record in 1983 and a US record for 5000m in 1985 in addition to finishing fifth in the 1988 Olympic 5000m final. Even now, he still holds the course record for New York City's Fifth Avenue Mile – 3:47.52 from 1981.

Similarly, Marcello Fiasconaro was born in Cape Town in 1949 but moved to Italy in 1970 and set a world 800m record of 1:43.7 in Milan in 1973. The son of a South African woman and Italian fighter pilot from Sicily who had been shot down over East Africa during the Second World War, Fiasconaro's 800m best still stands as the Italian record today.

Not so lucky was Johan Fourie, a white South African middle-distance runner who was seven years older than Zola and unlike Maree and Fiasconaro he remained trapped in his own country. In 1987, Fourie ran 3:33.87 for 1500m and 3:50.82 for the mile – world-class times achieved without any great competition – and the legendary South African ultra-distance runner Bruce Fordyce is among those who believe Fourie could have run around 3:30

and 3:50 and challenged Coe, Ovett and Cram if he had been able to race internationally.

Away from the middle-distance events, there was the fascinating case of sprinter Paul Nash, who equalled the world record for 100m of 10.0 seconds four times in 1968, once in front of a 16,000 crowd at the Krugersdorp Stadium in South Africa. The son of a British couple, Nash was born in London in 1947 and won Amateur Athletic Association (AAA) of England sprint titles during his career at London's White City, but he was a white man living in South Africa and denied the chance to race at the Olympics due to his nation's sporting ban.

British athletics officials considered him for the GB team for the Mexico Games in 1968 but decided he was "a British citizen but not a British athlete". Today, Nash believes he could have beaten Jim Hines of America to the Olympic 100m in 1968 but the world was denied the clash and Nash – who was dubbed "the fastest white man in the world" – retired prematurely due to arthritis.

Set against this complicated backdrop, young Zola was attempting to make a name for herself as a runner. Politics and sport have always had an uneasy relationship, but while Mary's clashes against the Eastern Europeans had Cold War connotations and her hopes of racing in the Moscow Olympics had been dashed by a political boycott, Zola was similarly finding her career complicated by her country's social system and the negative international reaction to it.

Like Maree, Zola was beginning to receive offers to study at universities in the United States. The young runner also yearned to test her ability against runners from other countries. Certainly, her performances in 1983 helped her get noticed by athletics aficionados outside South Africa, not to mention talent scouts from US colleges. She even popped up briefly in *The Times* of London in October 1983 when the newspaper ran a small Associated Press agency news item a couple of days after her 5000m in Port Elizabeth.

It read: "A white South African woman athlete, Zola Budd, who runs barefoot, has come within 2.39 seconds of the women's world record for the 5000 metres (established by Mary Decker) and is now considering a scholarship to the University of California. Her time of 15 minutes 10.65 seconds was set at the University of Port Elizabeth on Monday. Unless she changes nationality, Miss Budd will find American college athletics the only opportunity for serious competition."

Despite this, Zola was barely on Mary's radar. At the end of 1983 the American was basking in the end-of-season glory of having twice beaten the best that the mighty Soviet Union could throw at her at the World Championships. So a relative novice from a country that was banned from the international sporting scene was hardly likely to worry her.

Zola had other ideas, though. The youngster concealed an inner yearning to one day race outside South Africa. She had no idea how she would do it. Merely that she would find a way.

Meanwhile, she immersed herself in her training and racing. Ever since her elder sister Jenny had died three years earlier she had buried herself in running. It was her escape from the real world and the skilful coaching of Labuschagne was helping her fulfil her potential.

If Mary had been reared on a diet of speed work and interval sessions by her first coach DeNoon in California, Zola's training consisted of a background of steady distance running. Labuschagne was influenced by the theories of Arthur Lydiard, the New Zealander who coached Peter Snell, among others, to Olympic titles in the 1960s by firstly building an endurance base with long, steady running before adding faster-paced efforts closer to the main races of the season.

To Labuschagne, though, there was no need to complicate things and in a biography of Zola published by the *Daily Mail* in 1984, he said: "Zola is a running machine. All I'm doing is improving the infrastructure, the capacity of her lungs and the efficiency of her body. Really, all I've been doing is improving the roads and rails within her."

He added: "Once she realised the improvement training was having on her, there wasn't any stopping her. Now, if I tell her to rest for two weeks, she's ringing me after three days, begging to run again. After a week, her mother is ringing, too. Zola's impossible to live with if she's not running.

"I have been holding her back. If I'm not with her in a car or running alongside, she trains too hard. If I tell her to do another two kilometres, she'll want to do five. If I say six sets of 800 metres, she'll do eight. If she ever did any real track training, she would improve enormously. She broke the South African 1500m record (in 1983) without doing any track training.

"Much of her success is down to her mum's cooking and dad's physique," he continued. "The only supplement I give her is iron tablets each day. We have success, so why change it? Perhaps when she is older we can be more scientific.

"What bothers her most right now is putting on weight, but I tell her she's like her dad and will be skinny all her life. I try not to interfere with what nature has given her. I try to understand her, how she's behaving and thinking and between those narrow lines I'm coaching her."

As the 1984 season was about to begin, Labuschagne had been coaching Zola for almost four years and felt the world 3000m record was within reach – albeit an unofficial world record due to their South African status. After running 8:39 in 1983, Labuschagne's target for Zola was 8:32 in 1984 before a tilt at Ulmasova's world record of 8:26.78 in 1985. "Her big future," he added, "lies in the marathon. Before she's twenty-four, she'll be doing a marathon in 2:22."

A 6ft 1in mustached man in his early 30s, Labuschagne had a French background and was a decent club level runner himself with bests ranging from 1:56 for 800m through to 2:45 for the marathon. Married to a fellow teacher, he was known simply as 'Lappies' and when it came to coaching Zola he did far more than give her sessions and pre-race pep-talks. "She believes in him like she believes in the Bible," said Frank Budd about his daughter's relationship with the coach.

As Zola's running progressed, Labuschagne became like a father figure to the young runner. "Her parents haven't the contact with her that they had with their older children," Labuschagne explained. "I live in her world of athletics and education. I know how she's thinking, her feelings and what she wants."

History was the subject Labuschagne taught in schools during the period but he had graduated in political science and it was perhaps no coincidence that Zola chose the same topic to study at the Orange Free State University. Coach, friend and confidant, Labuschagne seemed the ideal man to guide Zola as she reached a crucial part of her career.

"I think running is Zola's way of expressing herself," Labuschagne said. "She doesn't want to be a star. Promoters used to want her to wave to the crowd but she says it isn't necessary. That's how she is – independent-minded. She will do it her way."

On her quiet personality, he added: "She didn't smile much, or joke with the other kids. When she began to run, she took on that great frown of concentration from start to finish. Her determination came across like an army of safari ants on the march. She was the most dedicated runner I had ever seen."

One newspaper described Labuschagne memorably as "an archetypal

Corinthian . . . unlike the nicotine-stained coach played by Ian Holm in *Chariots of Fire*, Pieter is a total amateur who didn't get an extra cent for turning the giggly schoolgirls of Bloemfontein Central High into running machines".

In stark contrast to Mary, Zola hardly ever suffered from running injuries during her teenage years. Apart from the minor operation on her arches when she was thirteen to remove a bone and the occasional day off with a cold, her athletics career had barely suffered any setbacks. Outside sport, she graduated from high school in Bloemfontein in 1983 with multiple distinctions before beginning her course in political science, history, the South Sotho language, ethnology and psychology at university.

Going into 1984, Zola was in great shape – physically and mentally – and poised to enjoy further improvements on the track. Yet little did she know just how much of an impact her first race of the year was going to make. It was a performance that would bring her to the attention of the world and one that would change her life forever.

Stellenbosch was the scene on the Western Cape of South Africa. It was 5 January and Coetzenburg Stadium on the city's university campus grounds had drawn a sizeable crowd to watch the action. It was also the start of another Olympic year, although this meant little to a South African sporting community that was barred from competing there.

Zola was racing in the 5000m, which was a rarely run event for women in 1984. Men had tackled the distance in the Olympics since 1912, for example, but the first women's 5000m at the Games would not take place until 1996. Consequently, the event was in its infancy and developing at a quick rate. In 1981, Ingrid Kristiansen of Norway had become the first woman to break the 15:30 barrier and since then the record had been improved by Mary to 15:08.26 in 1982. To illustrate the primitive nature of those marks, Tirunesh Dibaba of Ethiopia brought the world record down to 14:11.15 in 2008.

Zola had already shown her promise in 1983 by coming within two seconds of Mary's mark for the distance, but in Stellenbosch she smashed the world record by almost six-and-a-half seconds to clock 15:01.83. What made it all the more remarkable was the fact that Zola had been buffeted by wind on a particularly blustery night and she had only completed one track session before the race – a session of 5x1km with a two-minute rest between each effort seven days earlier.

That workout had gone so well that in the race she felt comfortable during the opening stages in Stellenbosch that saw her pass 1500m in 4:21.1 and 3000m in 8:55.9 – averaging well inside three minutes for each kilometre and a metronomic 72 seconds per lap. "Zo-la! Zo-la!" the crowd chanted, sensing something special as the elfin-like runner strode around the track, barefoot and wearing the colours of her old school in Bloemfontein, Hoërskool Sentraal, as she steadily lapped the entire field.

"Zola's stride, her hallmark, saved her. It never changed," Amby Burfoot, the 1968 Boston Marathon winner, wrote in *Runner's World*. "She runs with a distinct forward lean and with an undistinguished knee lift, but her kickback could rival that of the finest quarter-miler. As the fatigue began to show, thick creases formed across her forehead, above the soft contact lenses she wears when racing and her mouth gasped for air with little goldfish gulps."

Burfoot added: "Her heels fairly graze her derriere and hamstring muscles, if indeed there is any muscle below the surface of her remarkably long, thin legs. The force behind her stride cannot be explained, merely marvelled at."

"At the bell I was gasping for breath, thinking only of the finish and wishing the torture was at an end," said Zola in her autobiography, which was written in 1989 with South African journalist Hugh Eley. "I couldn't allow myself to slacken off. 'Keep going, push yourself, you can do it' – those were the thoughts that flashed through my mind on the final lap and I had difficulty comprehending my achievement when I saw the time.

"At seventeen I was the fastest woman in the world and as the news flashed around the globe I was to become one of the most sought-after women in the world."

Long before the age of the internet and social media, journalists relied on phone calls and fax machines and dictating their words to copytakers in their offices. Nevertheless the news quickly began to spread around the world and *The Times* of London carried a *Reuters* news agency item on 6 January which read: "Zola Budd of South Africa clipped more than six seconds off the American Mary Decker's women's 5000-metre world record".

It was only the start. *Sports Illustrated* described Zola as "a prodigy even among prodigies," adding: "She is six years younger than was Decker when she set the record."

Athletics Weekly, a publication with a reputation for avoiding hyperbole, described Zola's run in Stellenbosch as "fantastic", while the British coach, Wilf Paish, who had witnessed Zola's record first-hand, said: "It was one of the finest I have seen. She is frail but battled against the wind and with runners who were much stronger, but she kept going. There is no doubt she will run under 15 minutes before long."

There were some early comparisons with a certain Stateside future rival as well when *Athletics Weekly* wrote: "Not since the days when little Mary Decker was taking on and beating the might of the Soviet Union as a fourteen and fifteen-year-old has such a young runner as Zola captured the world's imagination. There is no doubt she is the most phenomenally gifted teenage middle/long distance runner in women's athletics history."

For Zola, the experience was bittersweet. As an athlete she was constantly trying to improve and breaking Mary's world record brought much satisfaction. On the flipside, it was a life-changing episode and there were moments in the coming months and years where she would look back on her 5000m record in Stellenbosch in January 1984 and wish it had never happened.

"I became a superstar overnight," she said in her autobiography, "and although I was unaware at the time, my father was the referee of the international race to get the Budd signature. Everyone wanted a slice of Zola in action and while I continued to run and to run well, there was a flurry of activity behind the scenes.

"As wave after wave of publicity threatened to drown me, I was fighting off a bout of extreme exhaustion. I couldn't train for a week after breaking the record and kept crying. There was none of the exultation I thought I would experience after breaking the world record and I was surprised when the offers poured in."

Universities in America had already courted Zola's attention. "Too loud and brash for a shy kiddie like her," said Frank, who soon became overwhelmed with options after the world 5000m record opened a floodgate of further interest. The same IMG marketing agency that Mary had become associated with began to look into making the most of the Budd brand and Frank even met the company's founder in Johannesburg while he was visiting for a golf event. There were enquiries from Rome about giving the athlete Italian citizenship. Bill Muirhead, a no-nonsense businessman who was group marketing director of Defy, a UK-owned electrical company with offices in South Africa, was appointed as an advisor on commercial matters as Zola's life became more complex and complicated.

There was even a marriage proposal from a sixty-five-year-old man in Birmingham, England, called Henry Allen. Contacting Zola via a newspaper, Allen was sufficiently wowed by her performances that he dropped down on one knee, figuratively speaking, and popped the question.

"I would just like to offer her the chance she deserves so much to compete in the Olympics and other international events," said Allen, explaining that his wedding plan was a novel ruse to circumvent the sporting boycott of South Africa. "I found that very embarrassing as any girl would," Zola blushed. "I think I'm too young to get married."

Whereas wild ideas of marrying a pensioner were easily laughed off, a far more serious offer soon emerged from the same country. The *Daily Mail* newspaper started to take a serious interest in Zola and began to concoct a plan to get her a British passport in time to compete for Great Britain in the Los Angeles Olympics a few months later.

John Bryant, features editor at the *Daily Mail* and a former captain of the Oxford University cross country team, dispatched his newspaper's South African correspondent, Peter Younghusband, to investigate further and suggested to his editor, Sir David English, that the newspaper ran an article on Zola. Meanwhile the well-known columnist at the paper, Ian Wooldridge, mentioned in passing that the South African had a British grandfather.

Smelling a huge potential story and spotting a loophole that would eventually get Zola into a British vest, English pounced on the idea. Writing in 2003, Wooldridge remembered the incident as English shouted: "Brilliant! Because of the British family connection, she shall run for us. I can pick up the phone and get her a British passport in two days."

During the period, English was masterminding a renaissance at the *Daily Mail*. When he took over as editor in 1971, the newspaper was a struggling broadsheet aimed at the middle-market and being consistently out-sold by its chief rival, the *Daily Express*. But after turning his paper into a tabloid and employing some of the best writers in the country, such as Wooldridge, he turned the tables on the *Daily Express* in style.

"English was brilliant, ruthless and charming – a fantastically gifted leader, who could be wickedly impish," the *Independent* newspaper described him in his obituary in 1998. "He was the outstanding editor of his generation."

He was certainly at his devilish best when he got wind of Zola's precocious talent and British links and he dispatched two of his sports writers, Neil Wilson and Brian Vine, to South Africa to whisk the wunderkind back to Britain. The country would have a potential Olympic champion to celebrate and the *Daily Mail* would soak up the credit, not to mention newspaper sales for breaking the story. It had the makings of a massive publicity coup on the eve of the Olympics.

As Bryant later recalled on BBC radio: "You have to give credit to Sir David for a story that would run and run. It turned into one of the longest running and most headline-grabbing news stories of all time. He spotted that story from a distance of 3,000 miles and saw its potential."

So began a frenetic period as the newspaper acted swiftly and stealthily to mount its clandestine operation. Before long, Wilson and Vine had the ear of Zola's father, Frank, and were camped out in Bloemfontein. It was a situation that was both unsettling and irritating for Zola.

A quiet soul whose main language was Afrikaans, Zola would usually let her father or coach do the talking for her while she sat back and listened. Such was her lack of confidence when it came to speaking English.

So imagine how she felt when two tabloid newspaper men from Fleet Street barged into her life offering her family large sums of money, a passport of convenience and the chance to run at the Olympic Games. She could tolerate Wilson, the newspaper's athletics correspondent, as he earned respect with his knowledge of the sport. But she found Vine overbearing and annoying.

A rotund character with a booming voice and a habit of wearing Savile Row suits and a monocle, Vine was the polar opposite of the shy South African introvert. A decade earlier, he had been at the heart of one of Fleet Street's biggest scoops when he helped track down Ronnie Biggs, 'Britain's most wanted man', to his hideaway in Brazil and now Vine saw a similarly spectacular story involving Zola.

Among other things, Vine had the job of writing her official biography, a hastily-produced publication full of gushing comments about the athlete and her family. Naturally, this included the details of her British background.

Zola's paternal grandfather was Frank George Budd, a Londoner born in Hackney in 1886, while her maternal great grandmother, Janet McGibbon, was the daughter of a Scottish couple from Falkirk. Janet travelled by boat to South Africa to nurse her sick sister, Margaret, who was married to an English soldier, Captain William Harding of the Royal Dragoons. When Margaret died, Janet married Captain Harding and in 1926 their daughter, Joyce, married Zola's London-born grandfather, who had come to Bloemfontein to work on a local newspaper called *The Friend*. Later, he started a printing and engraving business that Zola's father would inherit. Frank would live to see the birth of his granddaughter, Zola, but died in 1968 aged eighty-two.

"Tenuous" is how Watman described Zola's relationship with Britain in *Athletics Weekly*. "It would be political dynamite if Zola were to appear in British colours," he added. "For Zola to suddenly become internationally eligible for a country to which she has only the remotest of links would surely precipitate a storm of protest which could have disastrous effects for Britain's other athletes. The British athletics authorities' first consideration must be to genuine British athletes and it would be a disgrace if such fine runners as Chris Boxer, Wendy Sly, Jane Furniss and Chris Benning were to lose their Olympic chance in favour of a foreign athlete, no matter how talented she is."

Not surprisingly, it was not easy for Zola to come to adjust to her new-found notoriety. "One day nobody had heard of her; next day reporters from all over the world were at her doorstep," said Labuschagne. "It would be difficult for any young person to cope. But Zola is holding up well.

"It bothers her but she is not letting it show. We have had to think of ways of escaping autograph hunters. We were planning to have autographed postcards of Zola printed and instead of her having to stand and sign for hours on end we'd just hand out these cards."

In January 1984, Zola hinted at moving abroad when she told the *Los Angeles Times*: "Sometimes I feel it might be necessary to go overseas, but I won't leave permanently. If I had to choose between running and staying, I'd probably stay."

Fat chance, for Zola's world was changing fast. Sparked by English's nous for a story, the race was underway to rush through a British passport for her. The *Daily Mail* editor wielded enormous power and his close contacts included none other than the Prime Minister of the United Kingdom, Margaret Thatcher. Before long, the corridors and meeting rooms of Downing Street, Whitehall and Fleet Street were buzzing with activity as English prepared to pay £100,000 for the exclusive rights to her story, together with a job for her father and rent-free house for the family if they went along with the deal. In addition, Labuschagne and his wife, Carin, would be flown over to Britain and the athlete would be given the opportunity to write a lucrative series of Olympic diary columns in the *Daily Mail*.

Largely oblivious to much of this, Zola carried on running and raced a further twelve times in January, February and March during the busy South African athletics season. These included world junior and national senior records of 4:01.81 for 1500m in Port Elizabeth and 8:37.5 for 3000m in Stellenbosch. Displaying the kind of form that simply whet the appetite of the *Daily Mail* even further, Zola also showed impressive speed by threatening the two-minute barrier for 800m with a 2:00.9 win in Kroonstad and at the opposite end of the spectrum again showed her endurance with a 15:09.86 5000m win in Port Elizabeth.

"Zola is the hottest property in world athletics," wrote Wooldridge in the *Daily Mail* on 6 March, as speculation mounted over the athlete's future. "The last place on earth you are likely to hear a rendering of 'God Save the Queen' is Bloemfontein, the epicentre of unforgiving Afrikaanerdom. Yet in a homestead ten miles out into the red dust beyond the city, there hangs a perversely patriotic picture. It is an old nostalgic print of London Bridge and it provides a vital clue to an intriguing sports mystery of this Olympic year."

The award-winning sports writer continued: "Millions, understandably, will ask who is Zola Budd and what – apart from an exotic name with undertones of French romantic literature and English opera – she has to offer. The answer is, minimally, £1 million-worth of sporting talent and possibly an Olympic gold medal in Los Angeles."

Towards the end of this intense period of racing in the early months of the year, Zola began to get wind of the discussions that were taking place behind her back between her father and the *Daily Mail* journalists. Finally, in late March, Frank told his daughter about the plan for her to get a British passport, move to England and run in the Olympics. It was as simple as that. Or so they thought.

Seduced by the idea of breaking a huge exclusive and the chance to be at the centre of the biggest sports event of the year, the *Daily Mail* charged on with its mission to bring the Budds to Britain without giving much thought to some of the more negative consequences. For starters, Zola did not even speak fluent English. How would others react to a South African being given preferential treatment in the British citizenship process? Then there was the thorny topic of apartheid politics and how people would view Britain's attempts to sidestep the international sporting ban on South Africa.

Always a perceptive writer, Wooldridge flagged it up in one of his early columns on the topic when he asked: "If Zola burned her bridges in South Africa, could she survive the so-far unknown pressures of celebrity?"

Wooldridge's colleague, Bryant, also began to feel uncomfortable. "When I heard of the way she was being whisked off to Britain," he wrote in *Runner's World* in 2009, "together with the cloak-and-dagger nature of a secret airlift, I was more than a bit sniffy. 'Leave me out of it,' I said to the editor, 'I think it's a stunt – and not much to do with athletics'."

Marketing guru McCormack from the IMG agency that had signed Zola, voiced further concerns. "Her talent is vast but there could be a lot of personal tragedy on the horizon," he said prophetically. "My hunch is the *Mail* is not doing this for totally philanthropic reasons. They are pretty commercial about the whole thing and their approach is all about fast headlines."

Initially, Zola felt the scheme was a daft idea that would never happen. As the days wore on, though, she began to view it as a way to escape a university course that she was so far not enjoying. Most of all, the chance to race at the Olympic Games was an athlete's ultimate dream.

English's prediction that he could get her a passport within three days ended up taking a little longer – ten days, in fact – although that was still far quicker than the usual 12 months or so that it took under normal circumstances. The speed at which the citizenship was rushed through was impressive, but behind the scenes there was considerable debate.

English arranged a meeting in early March with Neil Macfarlane, the sports minister under Thatcher's ruling Conservative Party, where he floated the idea and began to apply intense pressure, arguing that his newspaper hoped to be able to run a positive story on how the Government had helped enable Zola to come to Britain and win a medal in the Olympics.

Macfarlane reported to the foreign secretary, Leon Brittan, "David English left me in no doubt last night that he is prepared to use all his contacts to secure entry for Zola Budd and we can anticipate a *Daily Mail* crusade."

Geoffrey Howe, the foreign secretary, warned that giving Zola a passport in such speedy fashion would be "unseemly" and annoy governments around the world. "The whole question of sport and South Africa is a political minefield," he said.

Malcolm Rifkind, a junior foreign office minister at the time who would later become foreign secretary and defence secretary, was similarly cautious, saying: "This problem gives considerable scope for embarrassment to Her Majesty's Government and that it will be particularly important to show that we are not singling out the Budd family for any special treatment."

Ewen Fergusson, the British ambassador to South Africa, also thought it a bad idea and Howe wrote to tell him about "strong domestic political considerations which have influenced ministers".

Naturally, politicians from the opposition party Labour attacked the plan to fast-track a passport for Zola. One of the chief critics was Denis Howell, although the Labour MP was accused of hypocrisy. Back in the 1960s, Howell had used his role as sports minister to rush through a British passport for South African-born weightlifter Precious McKenzie in 1965 so he could compete for England in the Commonwealth Games and GB in the Olympics.

Howell said: "It seems to follow directly from the pressure from Sir David English that the Home Office has been used to facilitate a disgraceful newspaper stunt and an obscene marketing operation. None of this sordid commercialism has got much to do with the Olympic ethic."

Fellow Labour MP, Doug Hoyle, went further when he asked: "I just wonder if she would have had the same treatment if her skin had been black."

Never a newspaper to mince its words, the *Daily Mail* hit back, describing Labour's "sour smear campaign" on its front cover as a "twisted reaction … a shoddy, contemptible and worthless case . . . Labour stands indicted itself for petty-mindedness, hypocrisy and a spirit so narrowly partisan that it reveals itself as a party not fit to be given power over sporting matters, or indeed anything else".

Again on its front page and illustrating the bitterness and bad feeling that was swirling around Zola's move to the UK, it added: "Instead of rejoicing as most people have done, that Britain has acquired a middle-distance runner of near genius who is sure to bring honour to this country, they (Labour) react with abuse and snarls of rage. What a sanctimonious bunch of creeps they are."

Even the Conservatives were divided within their own party. Clashing with Howe, Brittan disagreed with his Conservative Party colleague and overruled him in favour of giving Zola a passport. In Brittan's view, the best decision was to cut through the red tape as soon as possible and engineer the relevant documents for the runner. By 26 March, the passport application was lodged and the Budds were told it would be considered "sympathetically".

Part of the reason for the rush was due to Zola's eighteenth birthday being on 26 May. Once that date passed, she would be classed as an adult and the rules would change to mean she would have to be a resident in the UK for at least five years before gaining citizenship. Due to this, Zola was more surprised when her father's passport arrived so swiftly. Passport application timescales aside, Olympic fever was inevitably influencing the politicians' decision-making skills.

"It would be very difficult to defend a delay which led to her being unable to attempt to qualify for the United Kingdom for this Olympics," Brittan wrote to Howe. "I am not sure what could be construed as an unseemly rush, but it would certainly be unsatisfactory if we were to allow its consideration to drag on while speculation as to its outcome mounted."

So it was, under considerable pressure from the *Daily Mail*, the home office granted Zola a British passport on 5 April 1984. "She is an exceptional girl and we gave her exceptional treatment," said immigration minister David Waddington.

Zola had been made a naturalised British citizen under section 3(1) of the British Nationality Act, which gives the home secretary blanket discretion to make anyone aged under eighteen a British citizen, regardless of ancestry. With near-perfect timing, the Olympic 3000m final in Los Angeles was little more than four months later.

Not surprisingly, the head coach of the British athletics team, Frank Dick, was delighted at the prospect of her wearing the British vest in Los Angeles. "For her age, she is one of the most remarkable athletes of all time," said Dick, as Nigel Cooper, the British Amateur Athletic Board (BAAB) secretary, added: "It is marvellous that this raw talent is coming here."

Urged by Labuschagne to banish her last-minute doubts and with the *Daily Mail* confident the passport application would be a formality, Zola packed her belongings and with a mixture of excitement and trepidation headed to the Jan Smuts Airport in Johannesburg on 24 March for a flight to England. To maintain the secrecy, Zola's family told friends they were going on holiday. Privately, she described it to herself as 'the great escape'.

"For all her shyness and humility," Vine wrote in the runner's biography, "Zola is a pragmatist. She had long ago decided that she must leave South Africa to fulfil all her dreams."

Describing his newspaper as having "extended the hand of friendship", he continued: "Zola made up her mind that she was in the hands of people who were on a crusade to achieve her destiny."

Boarding KLM flight 594 to Nairobi, the journey would then see them catch an eleven-and-a-half-hour flight to Amsterdam in the Netherlands via business class in a Boeing 747 before catching a private ten-seater plane, which had been chartered by the *Daily Mail*, for the short trip across the English Channel to Southampton. From there, they were taken to a safe house in Brook, a small hamlet on the edge of the New Forest in Hampshire, to avoid the attention of reporters from rival newspapers. Such was the secrecy the Budd family had even travelled part of the way using the false name of Hamilton.

To say it was an adventure for Zola would be an understatement. At this stage in her life, two months before her eighteenth birthday, it was the first time she had ever travelled outside South Africa.

PART TWO

SHOWDOWN IN LOS ANGELES

CHAPTER FOUR

PRE-GAMES BUILD-UP

"Blaming Zola Budd for apartheid is like blaming
Shirley Temple for the Jonestown massacre."
Los Angeles Times

"MAIL BRINGS WONDER GIRL ZOLA TO BRITAIN," blasted the *Daily Mail* on its cover on Tuesday 27 March 1984. Describing Zola as "the most exciting girl runner in the world" the newspaper's "world exclusive on an athletics sensation" sat alongside a rather awkward-looking photograph of her sitting nervously on the aeroplane bound for England.

With appropriately patriotic quotes, Zola proclaimed on the front page splash: "I have been brought up through my family to know about British history and when I run in the Olympics I want to run for the country I feel is mine. I want to adopt Britain as my country and I would be proud to run for it."

"ZOLA GO HOME!" screamed the Daily Express, as the rival newspaper retaliated by doing its best to pour scorn on the *Mail*'s initiative. In spring 1984 the news in the UK was dominated by the miners' strike but the tiny athlete was giving the National Union of Mineworkers' leader, Arthur Scargill, a run for his money when it came to front page headlines.

It was the beginning of a traumatic period for Zola as her quiet, rural existence in sleepy Bloemfontein was replaced by a deeply distressing new life in the media spotlight, involving huge expectations to deliver an Olympic gold and with the British public and media divided over whether they actually wanted her or not.

Given this, she would not surprisingly look back on 5 January 1984, the day she broke Mary's 5000m record, with huge regret. "It was the worst day of my life," she said, adding that the moment she received her British passport was a close runner-up.

On 16 April Zola briefly lost her now regular slot in the prime position on the *Daily Mail* front page when the paper reported the death of Tommy Cooper, the red fez-wearing comedian and magician, who collapsed with a heart attack performing live on stage. Although even then there was a sidebar on the *Mail's* front page alongside the news of Cooper's demise with the headline: "It's time to stop knocking Zola".

The seventeen-year-old only had to blow her nose, so to speak, to make front page news. "Zola goes for a run . . . in shoes!" screamed another Mail headline alongside a picture of her wearing trainers. "Zola will run her heart out for Britain," another cover headline read, next to an image of her with British citizenship documents which had been presented to her by English at a dinner that was attended by Nigel Cooper from the BAAB and Marea Hartman, the long-time secretary of the Women's Amateur Athletic Association.

The hype whipped up by the *Mail* was relentless. Writing in the *Daily Mail*, the paper's athletics correspondent, Wilson, compared his first sighting of Zola to watching Seb Coe race indoors seven years earlier. Zola shared the same "lightness of foot, that floating movement, that long stride on slim, sinewy legs". He added: "To say Zola Budd could be good is like saying Steve Cram has promise."

In one of several publicity stunts, Zola was taken to the house in the London Borough of Hackney where her grandfather used to live. The paper wrote a feature on what happened when the athlete knocked on the door and told the surprised resident that her long-dead relative used to live there. "Fancy your family coming from round here," said Alf Rogers, who now lived in the small house on Rushmore Road with his three Collie dogs. "Blimey, you're famous, you are! You've got to come in."

Readers of the *Daily Mail* reacted and the paper's letters page was full of opinion. "Congratulations to the *Mail* on getting Zola to come to Britain and become a British citizen," wrote Mrs BJ Pierce from Bognor Regis in Sussex.

"This will cut out a lot of red tape and I am sure America would have got her if it hadn't been for your newspaper. I only hope she can stand our weather and I'm glad South African sport has suffered because of apartheid. Thanks again, for Britain's sake."

Tony Davis, of Haslemere in Surrey, added: "The only problem I can see is the embarrassment to other athletes who are not up to Zola's high standards. I raised money for the British Olympic Appeal recently but I will withhold that money if the BAAB does not send her to LA. It seems a great pity that some people do not care about putting some pride back into British sport."

Not everyone agreed, though, even in the *Daily Mail* letters page. "The Government acted in almost indecent haste in making it possible for Zola to run for us," wrote John Timmings from Morden in south-west London. "The girls in this country should be given the money and chance to represent us at the Olympic Games."

The letters columns in *Athletics Weekly* were also busy with remarks about Zola. "It is sad to see our sport being manipulated for the political interests of this Government and, among others, the *Daily Mail*," wrote Philip Shiner from Sparkhill Harriers.

"People should stop carping and welcome Zola," wrote Michael Caudwell of Croydon Harriers. "I hope some of our ladies stop bitching about her. One has a sneaking feeling that they are frightened of being beaten."

David Eveleigh of Exeter Harriers wrote: "We seem to be acting like a soccer team desperate to sign the best talent before the transfer deadline," while Allan Webb from Swindon added: "She must reside in this country for between five and ten years before she can qualify to wear the British vest."

The political rumblings did not stop either. Gerald Kaufman, the shadow home secretary in the UK, demanded an inquiry into what he called the "scandal" of her getting British citizenship in 10 days. Sir Arthur Gold, one of athletics' longest-serving and prominent officials, had "grave misgivings" about the possible inclusion of Zola into the GB team in LA. It was a cutting comment from a respected figure who held, at various times, key roles at the British Olympic Association, European Athletics Association, Amateur Athletic Association, BAAB and UK Sports Council.

The *Daily Mail* did not view it that way. The newspaper felt it was doing the country a favour. "Were she a prodigy with a violin or a piano, she would be free to go as high and as far as her talent could take her," it argued in one of its columns.

Outside the *Daily Mail*, there was notable support from Chris Brasher, the 1956 Olympic steeplechase champion, co-founder of the London Marathon and sports editor at the *Observer* newspaper in London. "To me, the issue is simple," wrote Brasher, who was also well known for helping Bannister to run the first sub-four-minute mile in 1954. "Here is a girl of wondrous talent; sport provides an arena in which talent can flourish; so let us help bring that talent to its rightful place in the world and that place is the Olympic Stadium."

Inevitably, the anti-apartheid rumblings soon began in earnest. The Anti-Apartheid Movement (AAM) had been created in Britain back in 1959 and was dedicated to opposing South Africa's system and to many of its members Zola represented the white minority rulers of a racist state.

In coming months and years, Zola's races in Britain would be accompanied by the dark cloud of a possible anti-apartheid demonstration. Outraged by her presence on British soil, the campaigners carried placards with slogans such as "If Zola runs, apartheid wins", "Zola represents apartheid not Britain" and "apartheid on the run". Such was the determination to scupper her attempts to race outside South Africa, protesters even tried to interrupt her races by gate-crashing the course and charging in front of her.

"British or not, Zola remains a symbol and product of South African society and athletics," wrote Watman in *Athletics Weekly*, "and as such the wider political considerations come into play."

Of course, Zola was not the first sportsperson to become embroiled in an apartheid-related controversy. Perhaps the best known was Basil D'Oliveira, whose role in a doomed England cricket tour to South Africa in 1968 shone a light on the nation's system of racial injustice.

Born in Cape Town, D'Oliveira left South Africa in 1960 and gained British citizenship. From there, the mixed-race player began to represent England and was caught in a storm of debate eight years later when South Africa cancelled a visit by England because it wanted to include him in the game against their all-white team. Following this, South Africa did not play another international cricket match until 1991 and Nelson Mandela, who led the fight against apartheid, described "the D'Oliveira affair", as it became known, as a vital moment in his movement's eventual triumph.

Now, Zola found herself in a similar storm. Anti-apartheid protestors viewed her as a prime target and did not care that the object of their fury was a vulnerable, quiet teenage girl who had not even heard of the imprisoned Mandela until she saw his name written on a protestor's placard. "I asked my coach, 'who is Nelson Mandela?'" Zola later recalled. "He was imprisoned in 1962 and I was born in 1966 and we were so protected from international news and even what was happening in our own country."

Showing their naivety, the Budd family did not seem to anticipate the problems either. "Zola doesn't even have the vote until she's eighteen, so how is she supposed to take responsibility for the things that South Africa is criticised for?" said Zola's father, Frank. "She hasn't done anything wrong," he added. "Why should she be penalised like this? Half the people who shut her off from the world think that there are lions and tigers roaming the streets here (in South Africa). What do they know of our life? What do they know how we and Zola feel about it? And do they care? Some of Zola's running friends were black and our two black servants are devoted to her."

Adding insult to injury, Zola's native South African press began to turn on her. Previously she had been the golden girl of South African sport but after moving to England they accused her of "defecting" and of being a "traitor". Although the South African public perhaps held a different view to the newspaper columnists because when The Star newspaper in Johannesburg held a poll about Zola's move to England, 97 of 101 callers within the first two hours agreed her actions were justified.

Hurt by the criticisms but stubbornly reluctant to get drawn into the apartheid debate, Zola made it clear she just wanted to focus on her athletics. "Apartheid and the other things began before I was born and will probably be resolved long before I die," she said, in a rare comment on the topic. "In the meantime, I want to run – and I will run with or against anyone, of any colour, anywhere, at any time and may the fastest win."

Only 6st 2lb in weight and standing 5ft 2in tall, Zola cut a frail figure during interviews. Her lack of English and painfully-shy personality merely compounded the problems and she looked overwhelmed by the attention that was now being heaped on her. She was, as one journalist cruelly wrote, "Eighteen going on twelve".

Mark Plaatjes, a South African-born runner who went on to win the world marathon title for the United States in 1993, said: "Zola is very shy and bashful. When she accepted awards (in South Africa) she couldn't say anything but 'thank you' and would sit down and blush from head to toe."

Throughout most of her young life so far, Zola had been the polar opposite of a party animal and far more likely to be seen curling up quietly with an Alistair MacLean or Dick Francis book and one of her many animals on her lap. Running was her silent release and the main way she could express herself, but she ran for pleasure, not money, and did not care about the politics that were now threatening to derail her athletics ambitions.

"Blaming Zola Budd for apartheid is like blaming Shirley Temple for the Jonestown massacre," wrote the *Los Angeles Times*, adding of the teenager: "She's a farm girl, not an activist, an athlete, not a provocateur. She happens to be a great runner who chanced to be born in South Africa. So is a zebra. Do we hold it responsible for the excesses of its Government? Maybe Zola should grow some stripes."

Observer writer and athletics legend Brasher captured the essence of her personality when he wrote: "Her voice is so small that you have to bend your ear to her lips; her complexion is as delicate as the proverbial English rose; her spirit is still and quiet. You feel the need to cocoon her from the world, to wrap her in care and love. And then you see her on the track – purposeful, remorseless and toweringly talented."

In *Runner's World*, Burfoot described her voice as "barely an audible squeak, her lips immobile so that the listener glances around for the source of the thin sounds, believing her a ventriloquist."

Added to this there were growing tensions within her family. Her father, Frank, was enjoying returning to his roots, his new-found place in the spotlight and lucrative deal with the *Daily Mail*. He was spending much of his time chewing the cud over fine food, drink and cigarettes in the Savoy and other five-star hotels with men from the *Daily Mail*. But her mother, Tossie, was unhappy in England and literally counting down the days on her calendar until the 3000m final in Los Angeles and the date when, surely, she could return home. Combined with this, Frank and Tossie were not enjoying a pleasant marriage and there was much antagonism, none of which was apparent in the *Daily Mail*'s sanitised stories about their supposedly amazing new life in England.

To its belated credit, years later the *Daily Mail* at least set the record straight when Wooldridge admitted there had been "tears, tantrums, tensions, fierce rows, sulky silences and threats to flee home" in a column full of regret. It did not help that the family was shunted from one house to another to avoid attention from rival newspapers. When their location at the original safe house in the New Forest was rumbled, they were moved into hotels for a period before settling in Guildford, Surrey, which was hardly conducive to creating a serene family life.

Then there was the weather. When the Budd family left South Africa in late March the country had been in the middle of a drought, but on arriving in England they were met by day after day of rain. To Zola, it was cold, misty and bleak and she yearned to run barefoot back on the veldt with the sun beating down on her slim shoulders. Like the anti-apartheid attacks, it came as a shock as well.

"None of the photographs of England had ever shown the rain," Zola later recalled. "I was struck by the dullness, the greyness, the dampness. Coming from South Africa, where the sun is shining for 320 days per year, that was probably the biggest contrast for me."

Given all this, Zola felt exploited and generally miserable with the whole experience. With her father giving her short shrift when she complained, she turned to Labuschagne for solace and implored him to let her return home.

The coach, who was now in England to oversee her training, was more sympathetic than her father. Ultimately, though, he suggested she gritted it out. One small consolation was when she received two pets – a cat and a canary for company – although while the cat was called Johnny, the bird she was given ironically shared the same name, Brian, as the *Mail* hack Vine.

Reminiscing four years later in the *Independent* newspaper, Wilson wrote: "When the news was telephoned to her that the Home Office had issued her a certificate of registration as a British citizen, she showed not the slightest emotion. Her concern at that turning point was only for the welfare of a pet canary which had become 'lost' amid the confusion created by the *Daily Mail's* desperate desire to keep her whereabouts secret from their Fleet Street rivals."

He continued: "Budd, let us remember, was the creation of a newspaper editor's imagination. Had she not been white, so child-like and run barefoot she would have been running still on the veldt. What followed was in the worst traditions of Fleet Street's circulation war: secret hideaways, car chases through Hampshire lanes, roads blocked to prevent pursuit and, ultimately, a distraught Budd pleading not to be treated any more 'like some criminal'.

"Twice in her first week she had to be talked out of taking the next plane 'home'. In hindsight, perhaps the most unfortunate piece of advice she was given was to 'give it another three weeks and all the fuss will have died down', but that first act set the scene for the pantomime that followed."

Animals aside, there was another way to improve her mood – to let her race. Zola was born to run and deeply motivated by fulfilling her potential. The athletics season in the northern hemisphere that she had just moved to was looming and she still had to qualify for the Olympics.

First she needed to join a British club and there was no shortage of options. Eric Hughes of Sale Harriers in Manchester said: "We could do a lot for Zola. She's light, small and not had that much competition. Quite frankly, she needs toughening up and we could do that for her." Borough of Hounslow in London was similarly keen, with club representative Brendan Cupps saying: "Zola would be welcome here."

Faced with the various choices, Zola plumped for Aldershot, Farnham and District Athletics Club in Hampshire. On 10 April, the club voted Zola in as a member and George Aston, spokesman of AFD, said: "We're delighted to have her as a member."

Four days later, on 14 April, Zola's first race on British soil – her first race outside South Africa for that matter – was due to take place in Dartford over 3000m. Her modest target at this Southern Women's League event would be a qualifying time so she could run at the UK Championships the following month. Yet any hopes for a low-key return to racing were scuppered when the scene turned into an extraordinary spectacle as spectators and media piled into the venue and the *Mail* conjured up a grandiose plan to airlift her into the centre of the arena in a helicopter. By now, Britain was well and truly gripped by Buddmania.

In South Africa, Zola had been used to racing on synthetic, all-weather surfaces, but the track in Dartford's Central Park was a humble, old-fashioned dirt track made of cinders. "Zola to face hell track," said one South African newspaper headline. This made racing with spikes necessary, which meant the so-called barefoot wonder girl would complete her opening event in England in shoes.

In selling the TV rights for the meeting, the host club, Dartford Harriers, raised enough money to turn their track into a synthetic surface a couple of years later. They probably boosted their funds with food and drink on the day as well as the arena was flooded with about 6,500 spectators and 100 reporters which included television crews from NBC in America, Japan and the BBC, the latter of which broadcast Zola's race live at just after 3pm on Grandstand.

It was not as if British athletics was bereft of talent or talking points. Coe, Ovett, Cram and Peter Elliott were at the height of their powers. In women's middle-distance events, Sly showed in Helsinki in 1983 that she was a potential Olympic medal winner. Daley Thompson dominated the decathlon. The javelin rivalry between Tessa Sanderson and Fatima Whitbread was at its peak. Dave Moorcroft, Steve Jones, Mike McLeod, Eamonn Martin and many others made Britain a force to be reckoned with in men's distance running. It was a golden era for the country and Zola's arrival and debut race at Dartford made things even spicier.

"For a month I've looked forward to this day," Zola said in one of her Mail columns. "I know there will be stronger opposition in the races ahead but there will not be a harder race for me. All the pressure is on me in this race. Everybody will be expecting so much and I feel I owe everybody it. I just don't want to let them down. But don't expect anything fantastic as I am just running for the qualifying time for the British Championships."

Geoff Wightman, an international marathon runner from the host club Dartford Harriers remembers the efforts to get the track into shape. "By the morning of the race, you could have eaten your dinner off it," he recalled.

After finding a secluded field to warm up, Zola was given a police escort into the venue and amid the glare of TV cameras and the fascinated fans she sped around in 9:02.6 for the seven-and-a-half-lap distance. It was a track record, took five seconds off Yvonne Murray's UK junior record and was inside the 9:05 qualifying standard for the Olympics. Officially, at any rate, because she had of course run much faster in unofficial races in South Africa a few weeks earlier.

Years later Wightman would act as stadium announcer at the London 2012 Olympics, but Dartford in 1984 was one of his early experiences calling a race. "I struggled to make myself heard due to the wave of cheering that followed her around. It was fantastic and the following day the South African newspaper headlines read: 'Zola tames hell track'," he added.

Flanked by Labuschagne, Bryant from the *Mail* and Wightman, Zola looked like a frightened fawn at the post-race press conference which was set up trackside on a small table surrounded by eager onlookers and photographers. Bewildered by the attention and struggling with the language, she deferred to Labuschagne most of the time as the duo looked towards their next races.

At this point, uncertainty still surrounded Zola's chances of representing Britain. Despite having a British passport and qualifying time for the Games, the IOC let it be known that it reserved the right to decide whether Zola's participation in Los Angeles was "in the interests of the Olympic movement".

A spokesman cited a bylaw to Rule 8 of the Olympic Charter, which stated "a naturalised competitor . . . may not participate in the Olympic Games to represent his new country until three years after his naturalisation". But it added: "The period following naturalisation may be reduced or even cancelled with the agreement of the National Olympic Committee and International Federations concerned and the final approval of the IOC executive board."

When quizzed about Zola's status, Sir Arthur Gold said: "We don't want this hanging over the kiddie the whole of the summer, or over the sport for that matter. It is a difficult one and you have to put yourself in the shoes of IOC president Juan Antonio Samaranch. If he says 'no', he will be looked upon as a spoilsport who won't help a young athlete. If he says 'yes', the Third World will attack him for allowing a white South African to come into the Olympics via a side door."

The presence of Zola was dividing opinion among British athletes, too, especially potential rivals in the middle-distance events. Debbie Peel, an 8:50 3000m runner from Crawley, said: "I'm looking forward to the challenge and beating her. She may raise the standard of running in Britain."

Joyce Smith, winner of the inaugural London Marathon in 1981, gave an open-minded assessment: "A lot of athletes born in other countries have competed for Britain. She still has to prove herself here, though."

Other members of the GB team chipped in as well. Shirley Strong, a sprint hurdler from Manchester who was destined to win silver in Los Angeles, enthused: "I'm all for her and good luck to the youngster. I hope she makes the Olympic team. Britain needs somebody like her. Let's face it, there's a lot of scope at that distance."

Kathy Cook, a Wolverhampton sprinter who set long-standing UK sprints records in 1984, said: "I'm pleased Zola will get an opportunity to run, yet I can't help feeling sorry for some of the other athletes who have trained so hard and might now lose their place."

Others were not so enthusiastic. "It would be sad if one of the girls, after doing so much hard training to get to the Olympics, was left behind," said Christina Boxer, the 1982 Commonwealth 1500m champion for England.

British No.1 Sly went further when she told Neil Allen of the London *Evening Standard* she might skip the British Olympic trials in protest. "It's got to be unfair and so discouraging if Zola Budd can come in at such a late juncture, get a British passport at incredibly short notice and take a place in our team," she said. "I intended to run in the British Olympic trials in June but now I'm considering pulling out as a matter of principle."

Jane Furniss, a Sheffield runner who had finished seventh in the world 3000m final in Helsinki the year before, was also annoyed. After giving up her job as a dental nurse to focus on making the Games, Furniss finished a fine fifth in a World Cross Country Championships won by Puică in late March 1984 and saw Zola as a threat. "I feel very strongly that Budd should serve a year qualification period," she explained. "That is the period laid down in the rules if you change clubs in Britain so I think it should be the same if you change countries. Before Budd came here, I thought I had a good chance of going to the Olympics. I will be upset if my plans are wrecked."

Predictably taking Zola's side, the *Daily Mail* issued a harsh verdict, saying: "With the exception of Wendy Sly who, on present form, will be in the Olympic team whether Zola runs or not, Britain is hardly well-endowed with world-class middle-distance girl runners."

Defending the British-born athletes, *Athletics Weekly* editor Watman responded: "What an insult to Jane Furniss, Chris Benning, Chris Boxer, Angela Tooby and the rest! Has it been forgotten that Britain fielded three finalists in the 1983 World Championships 3000m? Our girls, so long maligned, have been making splendid progress lately – particularly in the 3000m – and they need encouragement not disparagement."

Such resentment added to Zola's woes. On first arriving in Britain, she said: "I just hope the other British athletes are friendly. They can't realise what it has been like running on my own for so long." It was wishful thinking, although she did manage to find some friends amid the madness.

Among these was Mel Batty. An effervescent character from Essex, he had won the English National Cross Country title twice and set a world record for ten miles on the track. Now, he was working for the Brooks running shoes and clothing company and his charming, humorous personality helped him pull off one of the sports sponsorship deals of the era when he managed to get the most famous barefoot runner on the planet to wear Brooks footwear.

Later, on the eve of the Olympics, Zola signed a two-year deal with Brooks worth £53,000. Although somewhat bizarrely it included a clause saying the athlete did not have to race in shoes.

Prominent promoters of the period such as Andy Norman from the UK and Svein Arne Hansen from Norway also endeared themselves to Zola. Norman was a controversial character but he was adept at dealing with the challenges thrown up during the period of 'shamateurism', where athletes were paid via brown envelopes handed over in hotel lobbies or through the official system of putting money into trust funds.

Not even an influential figure like Norman could help, though, when plans for Zola's second race in Britain fell through. Hoping to stretch her legs over 1500m in Crawley, at a meeting to celebrate the opening of the town's new £300,000 sports arena, her participation was blocked by the Labour-controlled local council.

"We have consistently refused to become involved in political arguments," said Labuschagne, after Zola withdrew from the event. "Zola is a runner and I am an athletics coach and that's what we want to be allowed to do here."

Instead, Zola found a 1500m race at a Southern Counties Athletics Association open meeting at Crystal Palace on 25 April where she cruised around the famous London track to win in a routine 4:10.82 despite protestations from Peter Pitt, chairman of the Greater London Council's arts and recreation committee. Saying he was "horrified" by the idea, Pitt argued: "Even if she runs in the Olympics, this girl is South African and has been brought over here as part of a publicity stunt."

Worse still, ugly scenes accompanied the Crystal Palace race as it was marred by anti-apartheid demonstrators who carried a sign that read "white trash go home" and hurled comments such as "racist bitch!" at her as she sped around the track. Not surprisingly, a post-race press conference was cancelled as the tearful athlete was ushered away from the south London stadium.

The press did get some quotes on the incident, though, from none other than the Prime Minister Margaret Thatcher the following day in the Commons. "The treatment meted out to a seventeen-year-old girl was utterly appalling and a disgrace to those who gave it to her."

"No British athlete should be unwelcome at any British track," the events promoter Norman angrily blasted back. "Zola is a British citizen and entitled to the full rights and privileges of one."

A Sports Council statement ruled: "Zola Budd is a British citizen with a British passport and as such is entitled to run at the meeting," while Derek Johnson, Britain's 1956 Olympic 800m silver medallist, put out a press release on behalf of the International Athletes' Club urging "the family of athletics to welcome her with open arms. Let us cherish, protect and defend her from attack and provide her with the support she needs to bring an outstanding talent to full flower."

Over in America, Zola received sympathy, too, when the *Los Angeles Times* condemned the people who abused the runner. "Not since the Luftwaffe has any visitor evoked such contortions of hate on the faces of certain Londoners," the newspaper wrote, "as banners were unfurled, lips were curled and teeth were bared."

Off the track, at least Zola's quest for Olympic eligibility was going well when Willi Daume, a prominent West German member of the IOC, said: "To me the position is perfectly clear – Zola Budd is British. Under Olympic rules a competitor changing nationality by naturalisation must serve a three-year qualifying period except in cases where the two national Olympic committees and the international federation agree. In Miss Budd's case there is only one national Olympic committee concerned because we do not recognise that of South Africa, so if the British and IAAF agree, her eligibility will go before the IOC executive board (in late May) and I can only think that their decision will be positive."

One of the quirks of the rulebook also stated Zola was entitled to run in the Olympics for Britain from the moment her father took up British nationality.

Not only had Zola and her coach failed to do their homework on their rivals, but they inexplicably went into the Games with no tactical plan. Naturally, they assumed Mary would lead and apart from that were happy to play it by ear, which was a casual approach for a race of such magnitude.

Unlike the final, the heats would pass without incident. Mary won the first in 8:44.38 from Canadian Lynn Williams. "Effortless," Mary described it, "except for Lynn stepping on my heel four times."

In the second, Kraus of West Germany clocked a slower 8:57.53 to beat Joan Hansen of the United States with Sly third. Such was the excitement in the stadium, Hansen took off on an impromptu lap of honour and the crowd, unaware of the etiquette, cheered her to the rafters.

Once she had finished, heat three got underway with Puică sprinting past Zola to win in 8:43.32 as the youngster, who was racing barefoot despite previously saying she would wear spikes in her heat to help avoid injury, was content to cruise home in third in 8:44.62 just behind runner-up Bremser. "This has to be a tough situation for Zola, running with people who are with her all the way," said Bremser. "Before, she could just get on a track and run a race. She never had a real kick before and I guess she doesn't have much of one now because we went right by her and I really wasn't pushing."

In fourth place, meanwhile, was one of several little-known South African-born athletes who were competing at the Games with nowhere near the same hullabaloo as Zola. Cornelia Bürki had been born in Humansdorp on the Eastern Cape in 1953 but moved to Switzerland in 1973 and was competing in her second Olympics. A close friend of Zola, she was an outsider for a medal in Los Angeles after reaching the 1500m and 3000m finals at the 1983 Worlds in Helsinki.

Further South African-born athletes at the 1984 Games included Johannesburg-born Israeli middle-distance man Mark Handelsman and Soweto-born Botswanan distance runner Matthews Motshwarateu, although the celebrated Cullinan-born miler Sydney Maree missed his chance to compete for the United States due to injury.

By now the predictions were starting to roll in thick and fast. Previewing what he called "the most charismatic clash of the entire Games" in the *Daily Mail*, Wooldridge suggested Mary had looked "edgier" during the build-up than Zola and added presciently: "If they don't watch out, Maricica Puică,

92   COLLISION COURSE

a comparative old lady at thirty-four, could steal their thunder. Stunningly attractive, with a flying mane of blonde hair that will have instant appeal to the directors of TV commercials, she is a major threat to them both.

"Not too much should be read into heats, but Miss Puică looked in devastating form and came past Miss Budd in the home straight like a grown woman overtaking a child. Zola went out in front, like she has in her last 50 races, only to discover that cunning around here is the better part of valour. If she does that again in the final, the old hands will shadow her for almost exactly 2950 of the 3000 metres and then conduct their own shoot-out in front of her."

In *Sports Illustrated*, Kenny Moore wrote: "Once together, the impatient natures of Budd and Decker may create a spectacular race, one that isn't tactical and jostling and infuriating and won with a late sprint the way the men's races will certainly be. Decker loves to lead. Budd has never done anything else but lead. If each is equally uncomfortable in the wake of the other, each will pass, and be passed and repass."

Moore, a fine runner himself who had finished just outside the medals in the 1972 Olympic marathon, continued: "If that happens, it won't be a race decided by late speed, in which Decker would probably prevail, but by the ability to run when totally exhausted. There hasn't been an Olympic distance race like that since Vladimir Kuts of the Soviet Union destroyed Britain's Gordon Pirie in the Melbourne 10,000m in 1956.

"Making the prospects for this race even more intriguing is the presence of Puică, the world cross country champion and women's mile world record-holder (4:17.44). Puică's ability to close fast will influence Decker to run with a little something in reserve."

Mary's coach, Brown, predicted a world record pace. It made little sense to change the front-running strategy that had worked so well for her in Helsinki, but unlike twelve months earlier Brown now advised Mary to allow someone else to take a share of the work at the front during the first six laps if they tried to pass her. And if it was Zola, that would be fine, because privately they did not consider the teenager to be a genuine threat.

Crucially, though, they were determined to be in the lead during the final couple of laps where Mary would ideally wind up the pace, hitting top speed in the last 300m. If this plan was predictable, then so was Puică's. The Bucharest-based athlete had studied videos of her competitors' past races and decided it was best to hover behind the leaders before striking late into the race.

Like Wooldridge and Moore, *Athletics Weekly* did not make the mistake of overlooking Puică either when it said in its Olympic preview special: "The advance publicity is concentrating on the clash between Decker and Budd but with Puică in the field – not forgetting Kraus and Sly – it won't be a two-girl race. All the elements of a classic, world record race are there."

The magazine then delivered some expert medal predictions. Stan Greenberg, the long-time BBC statistician, went for a one-two-three of Decker to win, Budd in second and Puică third; fellow British statistician Ian Hodge predicted Decker, Puică, Budd in that order; Richard Hymans, editor of the *International Athletics Annual* in 1984, plumped for Decker, Puică, Kraus; while Watman went for Decker, Puică, Budd. Most of the *Athletics Weekly* quartet were known to enjoy a flutter in betting shops or casinos, but no one was bold enough to predict a Puică win or a medal for Sly.

To be fair, nobody foresaw the demolition derby that was about to play out. At 5ft 5in in height and 8st 6lb in weight, Mary was four inches taller and two stone heavier than Zola in the tale of the tape, but athletics is a non-contact sport and even on the most testing of cross country courses footraces are not usually decided by who can stay on their feet.

Mary's and Zola's date with destiny was due to take place at 6:40pm local time on the Friday evening. This meant the race would start at 2:40am in the early hours of Saturday morning in the UK and 3:40am in South Africa. In 1984, it was several years before the advent of twenty-four-hour television in the UK and most channels closed down just after midnight. Even breakfast television was in its infancy, but the Olympic Games was an exception and broadcast live through the night for sports fans and night owls.

Heat and smog had been a factor during the Games, with British middle-distance runner Ovett among those to suffer breathing difficulties in the 800m a few days earlier. By early evening, however, the temperature fell to a reasonable 24°C with the stadium half-bathed in sunshine and half-covered in shadow. With the women's high jump already underway, the first track final of the night would be the women's 100m hurdles, followed by the blue riband women's 3000m race and then the men's 3000m steeplechase. A busy session would see 4x400m semi-finals, too, plus men's 1500m semis featuring Coe, Ovett and Cram.

Twelve nervous competitors gathered on the back straight of the track for the first-ever Olympic women's 3000m final. There were two Britons and three Americans, including Bremser and Hansen, Puică of Romania, Bürki of Switzerland, Possamai of Italy, Kraus of West Germany, Lynn Williams of Canada, Aurora Cunha of Portugal and Dianne Rodger of New Zealand.

"Mary, Mary!" chanted the partisan crowd of more than 85,000 as the nerves tightened further and the athletes were introduced over the tannoy. Drawn on the inside, Puică was first to be called to the curved starting line. A few moments later, Mary acknowledged her name on the loudspeaker by raising her right arm, a gesture that was matched by a wave of applause in the Coliseum.

The double world champion looked cool and resplendent in her red, Kappa-sponsored American kit. Across the top of her chest three large white letters – USA – left no one in any doubt as to which country she represented. Underneath, her race number of 373 had been trimmed with scissors to take off a surplus section featuring her surname, the Olympic rings and a large "LA 84" logo, while some superstitious spectators might have noticed it added up to thirteen – an unlucky or lucky number depending on what part of the world you live.

Zola stood tentatively, pacing her feet back and forth on the start line. As expected, she had no shoes on and her race number 151 flapped around loosely over a predominantly white vest that featured a small adidas motif and similar-sized Union flag.

The gun fired and Mary shot straight to the front, immediately shadowed by Puică. Briefly lost for pace, Zola found herself boxed in back in eighth place, but coming into the home straight for the first time after the opening 100m, she swung out into lane two and eased her way into second place on the shoulder of Mary and with Puică tucked inside on the kerb.

After an opening lap of 66.9 and second lap of 68.6, the kilometre mark was reached in 2:50.43. Mary, Zola, Puică and Sly were the leading quartet as little more than 10 metres covered the tightly-knit field of a dozen runners. On schedule to run a final time of 8:30 – which was just outside Mary's best but seven seconds quicker than Zola had ever run – Mary then let the pace slow and she passed 1500m in 4:18.6 and 1600m in 4:35.9, causing the group behind her to become even more squashed and resulting in the first fall of the race when Hansen tripped on Cunha's heel and impeded Rodger in the process.

"Mary went off like a bolt of lightning," Zola later wrote in her autobiography. "Fortunately the pace slowed in the middle of the race and it was the bunching as we all came together that contributed to Mary's fall. The stage was set for disaster when Mary, who was in the lead with me outside her and Puică behind, slowed down. But the most important figure, one who was virtually ignored in the endless post mortems afterwards, was Wendy, looming up on my outside and starting to box me in."

Zola continued: "I could feel her bumping my arm as she raced into contention and I had three choices: take the lead, drop back, or run wide. I couldn't get behind Mary because Puică was there and I couldn't go outside because Wendy was there, coming closer all the time and crowding me, bumping my arm. The only place left was the front, so I started accelerating to get out of trouble."

After exactly a mile had been run, Sly began to put pressure on Mary and Zola, drawing alongside them and almost taking the lead despite running wide in lane two as they hit the bend. This spurred Zola into challenging Mary for the first time and the barefoot runner began to edge ahead of the American. Coming out of the bend and into the home straight with just over three laps to go, Zola was running on the outside of lane one and marginally ahead of Mary on her inside.

Then it happened. A combination of Zola's wide-arm action, hesitation to surge into a firm lead and Mary's reluctance to concede pole position was a recipe for disaster. First, there was a small clash when Mary's knee nudged against Zola's left leg, which should have acted as a warning. Five strides later, at 1730m into the race, there was a far bigger one as the runners collided with more disastrous consequences.

Struggling to keep her balance, Zola's pencil-thin left leg flicked out sideways, tangling with Mary's right leg and the American stumbled as if she had caught her feet on a trip wire, plunging forward violently with a thud onto the grass on the inside of the track. Around the arena, spectators gasped in horror. In the press seats, hundreds of journalists yelled in unison "she's down!" in a dozen different languages.

"Mary didn't respond immediately to my change of pace and when I saw she wasn't coming with me as I picked up the pace I cut inside," recalled Zola. "There was still a bit of bumping – Wendy was moving in – but I didn't see Mary's fall and my conscience is clear."

When the tumble took place, Mary was in Zola's blind spot. Straight after the collision, though, Zola glanced sharply to her left to see what had happened, slowing down in the process as Puică and Sly stormed past her to take the lead.

"As far as I could see, the inside lane was open because I was overtaking Mary and I wouldn't have moved across the track if it hadn't been clear," Zola continued. "I almost fell, but I didn't know if it was Mary, Wendy or Puică who bumped me. With Wendy coming closer it was a case of either going to the front or losing a place and another lap went by before I realised that something was terribly wrong."

Sometimes runners quickly get up from a fall and get back into the race. Most famously, Lasse Virén of Finland tripped badly just before halfway in the 1972 Olympic 10,000m and rose from the track to claw back the deficit and win the first of his four Olympic golds in a world record. In that race, though, Viren had 13 laps to resurrect his chances, whereas Mary only had three.

Unlike Viren, she also injured herself in the fall. Reaching instinctively out with her arms to cushion the blow, Mary's hand caught the race number pinned to Zola's back and ripped it off as she dropped to the ground. Pulling a hip stabiliser muscle, she was physically unable to get up and writhed around in agony, clutching the left side of her body and rolling first onto her back and then onto her right-hand side as she realised her Olympic curse had struck again. "My first thought was, 'I have to get up'," she said. "But when I made the slightest move I felt the tear in my hip and it felt like I was tied to the ground and all I could do was watch them run off."

Immediately, Mary was surrounded by medics who began examining the injured left hip. Not that this mattered now. Mary's pain was probably more mental than physical as it dawned on her that her chance to win gold had disappeared in a flash. Back in the race, Zola quickly regained the lead ahead of Sly and Puică, passing the 2000m mark in 5:44.09 as the three had broken clear from the rest of the field in the melee.

Then the booing started. Zola had grown accustomed to pockets of the crowd shouting anti-apartheid abuse at her, but this was on an entirely different scale. The whole stadium, it seemed, began to direct its fury towards the barefoot Briton as a cascade of whistles and boos rained down from the stands. An Olympic final had descended into a pantomime, where Zola was the villain and the heroine was lying prone on the in-field.

Writing in one of her *Daily Mail* columns a few days later, Zola said: "I couldn't believe it. It was terrible. I wanted to stop. I wanted it all to end. And, in truth, the race for me was really over. Instinctively, I kept on running. When you've trained for thousands of miles, you don't just quit.

"The booing came down like a tidal wave of concentrated hostility," she added. "It was like being punched in the stomach. More than ever I wanted to stop and for the whole thing to end. What I really wanted at that point was to go somewhere and hide, but there was nowhere to go, so I had to keep running."

Now running with a gash on her left leg – a bloody reminder of the incident – and tears in her eyes, Zola intuitively realised someone had fallen but claimed she was not completely certain who until she completed a further lap and approached the point where Mary was lying, at this stage on her back, in floods of tears and surrounded by medics and cameramen. Remarkably, as if the race had not produced enough carnage, Kraus was also now out of contention with a leg injury and sitting dejectedly on the in-field.

"As Zola came past the scene of the accident, she glanced down at her crumpled idol," wrote Wooldridge in the *Daily Mail*. "She seemed mesmerised by it, as we are mesmerised by the mangled wreckage on a motorway hard shoulder. She looked as stunned as someone who had slashed the Mona Lisa in a moment of madness."

Amid the chaos, Sly and Puică kept their cool. The crowd's boos were breaking Zola's spirit, but her British team-mate and the Romanian were focused on winning medals. "I told myself not to be disturbed by the commotion," said Sly, "and to think only of winning the gold medal. After the Decker incident I realised a big gap had opened up and this was the chance."

With a lap-and-a-half to go, Sly again challenged for the lead, in a similar fashion to the way she did before Mary's fall. Only this time she was more decisive and coming into the home straight with just over a lap to go, she surged past Zola into the lead with Puică following in her slipstream. "Out in the lead I felt inspired," said Sly. "I was prepared to die for victory."

Zola instantly began to drop back and within a few seconds was 20m behind as Sly hit the bell in the lead with Puică on her shoulder. Now there were only two athletes capable of winning – Sly and Puică – a scenario no one had predicted.

Sensing victory, Puică drew alongside Sly as the two women charged down the back straight and then cut loose with 250m to go, bursting into the lead and establishing an advantage of four or five metres as they hit the last turn.

With 70m to go, as Puică charged past Mary for the last time, the distraught American was still on the floor and accompanied by a growing number of medical helpers and cameramen. Extending her lead over Sly, Puică ran her last 200m in 31.8 and final lap in 65 seconds to clock 8:35.96 as Sly took a hard-fought silver medal in 8:39.47.

The Canadian, Williams, charged through for a surprise bronze in 8:42.14. Still in third with 200m to go, a disconsolate Zola tailed off to finish a weary seventh in 8:48.80 after virtually jogging her final 400m in 77 seconds. It was almost as if she was postponing the moment when a fresh nightmare of accusation and counter-accusation would begin.

Finally staggering to her feet and helped by medics and officials, Mary began to limp out of the arena, sobbing uncontrollably. Sly stood, resplendent, raising her arms to the crowd as her medal-winning performance sank in. Puică whipped off her yellow spikes and carried them around the track as she enjoyed a lap of honour. Ironically, the race now had a barefoot winner, although not quite the one many had expected.

"I regret what happened," said Puică. "Zola Budd tried to get to the front. Mary Decker tried to run straight ahead and pushed a bit and tried to remain in front of Budd. She put her hand in front and lost control. I had to avoid her not to run over her. It was a tough competition, but I also thought that I could win."

To their credit, the Coliseum crowd applauded Puică as she jogged her victory lap. Romanians were popular competitors at the Games due to their country defying the Eastern bloc boycott and the blonde-haired middle-distance runner was finally tasting track glory after being knocked out of the 1500m heats at the 1976 Olympics, finishing seventh in the 1500m at the 1980 Games and missing Helsinki 1983 due to an injury sustained playing basketball.

"When Mary decided not to run the 1500m in Los Angeles, I knew something was wrong with her," said Puică. "I watched the strain on her face when she qualified for the 3000m and knew she could not beat me. Then in the final she slowed down after the third lap and I had no doubt who would win."

Full of emotion, Mary was in no doubt as to whose fault the fall was. "Zola Budd tried to cut in without being basically ahead," she said. "I think her foot caught me and to avoid pushing her I fell. When I think about it, I should have pushed her. But tomorrow the headlines would have read 'Decker shoves Zola'."

Initially, Zola was disqualified after a track official felt she had broken IAAF Rule 141 which read: "Any competitor jostling, running across or obstructing another competitor so as to impede his or her progress shall be liable to disqualification."

Andy Bakjian, the commissioner of officials at the Games, issued a formal DQ, but on reviewing the video evidence from six different angles the jury of appeal voted unanimously by a score of 8-0 to reinstate the Briton and made reference to Mary's "aggressive tactics".

Memorably, Mary was carried off the track and into a brief post-race press conference by her fiancé Slaney. As the huge discus thrower picked her up, the diminutive athlete looked like a broken doll in his powerful arms. "There is one great thing that can happen in an Olympic final but there are 5000 bad things that can happen," he would later reflect.

The British strongman stood at her side as she continued to vent her frustration to the media: "There wasn't anything I could do," she said. "And when I did fall, I tried to react and tried to get up, but when I tried to twist that's when I felt the muscle problem in my hip.

"I don't think there was any question that Zola was in the wrong . . . she was not in front," added Mary, who had trained with tightly-packed groups of men in order to get used to scenarios like this. "You have to be a full stride in front and she was cutting in around the turn and she wasn't anywhere near passing. And I DO hold her responsible for what happened, because I don't feel I did anything wrong."

Just as upset was Zola. Her own race ended in failure and she had suffered the pain of being booed in the closing stages by a huge crowd who blamed her for tripping up an athlete she had always held on a pedestal.

So when she saw Mary after the race in the tunnel that led away from the track, the shy teenager offered her apologies and said, "Sorry". Unimpressed, Mary snapped back: "Don't bother!"

CHAPTER SIX

DEATH THREATS AND FALLOUT

"Our greatest glory is not in never falling, but in rising every time we fall."
Confucius

BEFORE THE SWEAT had dried on the foreheads of the athletes, the blame game began. Just whose fault was it? Zola's, Mary's or both? Absurdly, some felt Zola tripped Mary on purpose. There were even calls for the race to be re-run.

Soon the debate took a more sinister turn when Zola received death threats. The runner was used to having a police escort at races, but when people were vowing to kill her it led to a considerably elevated level of security and a police helicopter kept an eye on her from the skies as she left the Coliseum.

For most of the summer, Zola had been a reluctant runner. She yearned for a return to the sunny and quieter climes of South Africa and she increasingly viewed the Los Angeles Olympics as her exit route.

In August 1984, the collision in the Coliseum was truly global news – on a par with the death of actor Richard Burton and even President Reagan's infamous gaffe when he was unwittingly caught on tape joking about outlawing and bombing Russia. Pat Butcher, athletics correspondent for *The Times* during the 1980s, described Mary's fall from grace as "just as famous in athletics history as the assassination of the Archduke Ferdinand on a broader stage ... and the biggest collision outside the *Titanic*".

Sports Illustrated writer Moore called it "darkly historic", which given the death threats is not an exaggeration. John Rodda, the long-time *Guardian* athletics writer and Olympics historian, wrote: "A large part of America seems to have had a mental breakdown on the sight of Decker crashing to the track."

Arguments raged on either side of the Atlantic. Adding to the confusion, Puică's quotes were interpreted in the United States as being sympathetic to Mary, whereas in Britain and the rest of the world the Romanian was billed as a critic of the American, saying the fall had been her fault.

The fact she barely spoke any English did not help, although it turned out the Puică camp felt both Mary and Zola were to blame. "The victory was a magnificent experience," said Puică, who had neatly hurdled Mary at the critical moment of the race. "Of course, the accident was very unfortunate. But if an athlete is well-trained for an event and certain of her race plan, accidents like this should not happen."

Unlike Mary and Zola, the Romanian had doubled up at the Games. The day after the 3000m she took to the Coliseum track again and, running on tired legs, took bronze in the 1500m behind team-mate Melinte and the winner, Dorio of Italy.

With an interesting theory, she continued: "I realise the shock and pain that Mary felt. To be honest, I think I would have tried to get up and fight back. It would have been so beautiful, so exciting, if she had tried to finish. She owed it to her home crowd."

Eight years later, British sprinter Derek Redmond would produce one of the greatest Olympic moments when he tore his hamstring halfway through his 400m semi-final at the Barcelona Olympics but limped to the finish in tears helped by his father, who had leapt onto the track from the stands and brushed officials aside to help his son. Redmond "only" had 250m to limp home, though, whereas Mary would have faced a further three laps and physically just could not get up.

Ion Puică, husband and coach of the winner, felt both Mary and Zola were responsible for the fall. He said: "I believe the lack of international experience of both runners contributed to the accident. However, I truly believe that even if the accident had not happened the result would have been the same."

Sly's verdict was more clear-cut when she told the London Evening Standard: "I'm convinced the fall was Mary's fault. In the previous lap she just wasn't concentrating and I deliberately ran wide of her and Zola because I was sure there was going to be some bumping.

"I spoke to Zola in the Olympic village beforehand and told her I was sorry she had suffered from so much publicity. But I will not accept she was badly affected when Decker went over. After all, she and I and Puică covered the next lap in 66 seconds. I've never been so determined to do well and I was certain I could finish with some kind of medal."

Sly also had the satisfaction of having the last laugh after being treated as little more than a medal outsider in the run-up to the Games. At one stage, for example, she was on a gentle training run in London and trying to overcome her injury problems when some children jeered: "Who do you think you are? Zola Budd?"

"In spite of the medal, I expect that could still happen again!" she reflected, after becoming the first British middle-distance woman for twenty years to stand on an Olympic podium.

Nick Whitehead, a GB team manager who successfully appealed against Zola's disqualification, argued: "I don't see how a young lady leading a race can be disqualified when an experienced athlete tried to go past on the inside. Zola was emotionally drained and upset that a great athlete went down on the track. But when another driver rams his car into the back of another, he's at fault.

"It was not wilful obstruction on Zola's part and she had the lane. She has scratches on the back of her left leg. Her performance was superb for a young person in her first international competition."

John Holt, general secretary of the IAAF, agreed: "Decker was her own victim. A video showed Budd did not do wrong. In fact Decker tried to get at her three or four times."

Mary Peters, women's team manager of the Great Britain and Northern Ireland team at the 1984 Games, used a similar car analogy to Whitehead when she argued: "If you're driving down a motorway and a car cuts in too sharply, then you slow down. Mary didn't do that but kept running at the same pace."

Predictably, Bürki also sprang to her friend's defence. The Swiss runner had stuck up for Zola during the brief post-race confrontation with Mary and insisted: "It was definitely Mary's fault. She tried to push her way through and she sprawled over Zola's legs."

Similarly, Zola's family rallied behind her. Back in Johannesburg, Zola's sister Estelle said: "It was not Zola's fault at all. She would not harm a fly and, knowing her, she will be suffering as much, if not more, than the Decker girl."

Coach Brown hit back, saying: "Mary has voiced concern over a consensus opinion that she was trying to go up the inside and pass Zola. That was not the case. She was trying to maintain pace. Nobody associated with all this feels that anything was done intentionally. It was just very unfortunate," he added.

Far from being aggressive, though, Brown tried to act as peacemaker. First, he showed considerable goodwill by calling the British team management to express his regret that Zola had received such fierce criticism. The coach also went to Zola's room to attempt to smooth things out and after the Games rumours persisted that a plan to get Mary and Zola to march together in a show of friendship at the closing ceremony of the Games almost came off.

Zola's camp was not going to be appeased that easily, though. "Zola is not too happy with Mary's reaction," said GB head coach Frank Dick, the day after the race. "It wasn't her fault. She knows that."

As support for Zola gradually grew, Rodda wrote in the *Guardian* three days after the race: "Miss Decker was at fault. She is a vastly experienced runner who ought to have spotted, if she did not really know beforehand, that Miss Budd, for all her lack of height, has a long, awkward stride and big elbows. Decker should not have been running so close to trouble, unless, as the Secretary of the International Athletic Federation, John Holt has hinted, she was trying to harass the British girl."

Rodda added: "The Olympic athletics arena has its sprinkling of raw inexperienced runners, and the Americans, of all people, should know and remember it. Jim Ryun, a solid gold medal hope for the 1500m in 1972, went tumbling out on a misplaced African leg. Miss Decker had plenty of opportunity to find space for herself, but she chose not to, and disaster overtook her."

If anyone was going to have sympathy with Mary, though, it was Ryun. "Basically, Mary had the right of way," the former world mile record-holder said. "When a runner is trying to overtake, they should be a stride's length in front but Zola simply didn't have the lead."

Another heavyweight of the British sports-writing world, David Miller, wrote in *The Times*: "Millions of people had been claiming on the blurred evidence of television that Budd broke the rules – that she had not allowed Decker enough room. Yet all that the rules say is that one runner must not impede another.

Sixteen-year-old Mary Decker sets a world indoor senior record for 1000 yards with 2:26.7 at the Sunkist Invitational Track Meet in LA in 1974. *Getty Images*

A delighted Mary is interviewed after winning the women's 880-yard run at the Amateur Athletic Union Indoor Championships in New York, aged only fifteen. *Getty Images*

Zola Budd on a training run near her home in Bloemfontein, 1983. *Mark Shearman*

Zola at home in Bloemfontein, 1983. *Mark Shearman*

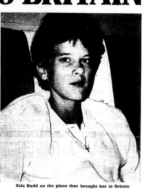

The *Daily Mail* presents Zola to the British public with their front page splash.

Zola runs (in shoes) at Dartford in April 1984, in her first race on British soil and outside South Africa. *Mark Shearman*

Mary wins the women's 1500m at the 1983 World Championships in Helsinki as the falling Zamira Zaytseva of the Soviet Union finishes second. *Mark Shearman*

INCORPORATING WOMEN'S ATHLETICS, MODERN ATHLETICS & WORLD ATHLETICS

athletics
weekly

SEPTEMBER 17th 1983 40p

World Champion
Mary Decker

Mary adorns the cover of *Athletics Weekly* in September 1983.

The 'Decker Double'. Mary atop the podium with one of the two gold medals she won at the 1983 World Championships in Helsinki. *Getty Images*

Mary posing with her husband, British discus thrower Richard Slaney, during photo shoot for *Sports Illustrated* in 1983. *Getty Images*

INCORPORATING WOMEN'S ATHLETICS, MODERN ATHLETICS & WORLD ATHLETICS

athletics
weekly

APRIL 28th 1984   40p

Inside: Zola Budd's Career . . . Daley Thompson Interview

Zola takes the cover spot on *Athletics Weekly* in April 1984, as her life and career is profiled.

Mary leads Zola, Wendy Sly and Maricica Puică early the final of the Olympic 3000 metres.
Mark Shearman

Neck and neck in the Olympic final, Mary and Zola come together at the head of the pack.
Getty Images

A moment that has seared itself into Olympic history as Mary crashes off the track. *Getty Images*

Mary is a forlorn figure at the side of the track as an official rushes to her aid. *Getty Images*

Devastated that her Olympic dream is over, Mary is helped from the track. *Getty Images*

Right: Back competing: Mary and Zola go head-to-head once again in the 3000m at the 1985 Rome Grand Prix. Olympic champion Maricica Puică is just behind them. *Mark Shearman*

Left: Ahead of Norwegian legend Ingrid Kristiansen, Zola is on her way to winning the World Cross Country Championships in Lisbon, Portugal, 1985. *Mark Shearman*

Athletics Weekly

MARCH 29th 1986 50p

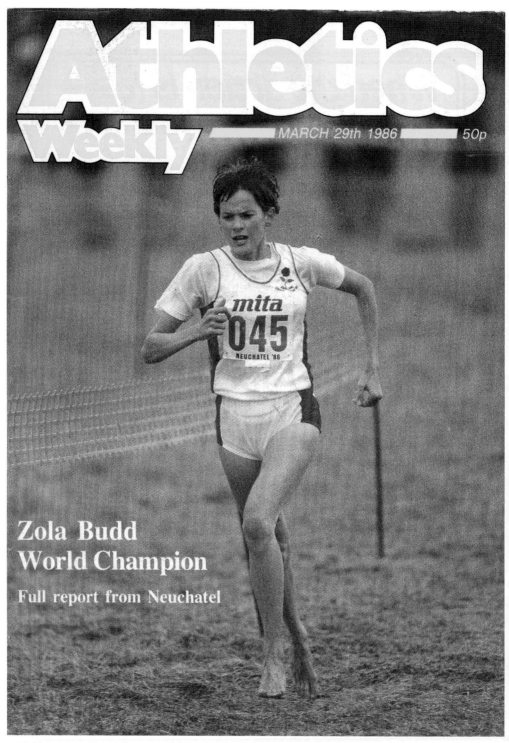

Zola Budd
World Champion

Full report from Neuchatel

Athletics Weekly celebrates Zola's triumph at the 1986 World Cross Country Championships.

South African running legend Bruce Fordyce kisses Zola during the
2012 Comrades Marathon in Durban, South Africa. *Getty Images*

Mary runs again . . . almost. Here she climbs a mountain road during the
2015 Elliptical Cycling World Championships in California.

"It was always clear to me that Decker and Budd had been running in established positions within the same inside lane for some 30 to 40 yards; and with Budd in the lead on the outside of the lane, ahead by some two or three feet – half a stride – as they came off the bend into the straight. In such a position it was Decker's responsibility to adjust, not Budd's."

Miller, an ultra-experienced journalist who had, among other things, written Coe's biography, added: "What was needed was for Decker merely to touch Budd's shoulder in order to let her know of their proximity."

Notably, even ABC TV in the United States began to shift the blame towards its own runner. In a rare moment of neutrality during its coverage, ABC altered its initial view that Zola was at fault when an apologetic Marty Liquori, a former leading US miler who had turned his hand to TV commentary, conceded that after studying a slow-motion video he felt Zola was marginally in the lead when the impact occurred.

In an article headlined "Don't persecute Zola for Decker's downfall", Mike Lupica of America's biggest-selling newspaper at the time, the *New York Daily News*, compared the jeering Coliseum crowd with the mobs of the original Colosseum in Rome. "Was Zola guilty?" asked Lupica. "Not a chance. Mary must take the rap. She did it to herself."

David Wallechinsky, in his definitive *Complete Book of the Summer Olympics*, wrote: "The truth is that neither Budd nor Decker was actually at fault, although both made mistakes. Budd should not have cut in so sharply. However, such moves are not uncommon and never cause for disqualification. Decker, for her part, should have known better than to bull forward like a tailgating commuter rushing home on a Friday evening.

"She could have given Budd a slight push. Decker's other alternative was to do what she had done in Helsinki when she was cut off by Zaytseva in the last lap of the 1500m: slow down and pass on the outside."

Irishman Eamonn Coghlan, the 1983 world 5000m champion, offered his view: "You're supposed to be one stride ahead before you can cut in. But this happens all the time. You have to protect yourself out there. Perhaps it was inexperience on Zola's part. Perhaps it was being too ladylike on Mary's part. You can't blame either one."

Steve Scott, America's No.1 miler at the time, was especially critical of his team-mate. Usually polite and diplomatic, Scott called Mary a "baby" and "spoiled" and told the *Los Angeles Times*: "Mary blamed Zola for the fall, but that's ridiculous. It was one of those things that happens in racing. Mary wanted Zola to apologise, but if anything, Mary should apologise to Zola. We saw the real Mary Decker after that." The respected 1500m runner, who had won world silver behind Cram in Helsinki in 1983 and finished a disappointing tenth in the LA Olympics, added: "Her attitude is horrible."

Wysocki, who finished sixth and eighth in the Olympic 800m and 1500m after earlier beating Mary at the US trials, was especially cutting when she said: "Some of us are relieved the public knows the Decker we all know."

A few pundits drew comparisons with Mary's ill-tempered baton-throwing episode from 1974, not to mention the Millrose Games in 1983 where she had pushed a lapped runner in the back. If history is anything to go by, they argued, Mary's tantrum at the LA Games was no surprise.

Reminiscing on the 1974 incident in *Track & Field News* in 1980, for example, Mary had commented: "I got elbowed by a Russian and I threw a relay baton at her. I was a little girl having an emotional reaction and I would never do that now."

With words that were now coming back to haunt her, Mary had continued: "I learned what real hardcore competition is like. Before that, I couldn't conceive that people would elbow you or cut you off or things like that. But I learned the hard way that it happens."

The fifteen-year-old Mary could be forgiven for throwing a baton in a huff at a rival, but people expected a twenty-six-year-old to show more maturity. The crying and complaining aside, though, it was something that Mary did not do that counted against her most in the battle to regain the love of the sporting community. She failed to apologise.

As the criticisms piled in from all directions, Mary was named 'the year's sorest loser' in *Esquire* magazine and 'whiner of the year' in *USA Today* newspaper. Yet a simple 'sorry' might have avoided most of this. Even when she eventually returned to competition early in 1985, she was adamant: "I don't feel that I have any reason to apologise. I was wronged, like anyone else in that situation."

With everyone weighing in with their view and after Mary had given Zola such short shrift straight after the race, a considerable amount of ill will was threatening to snowball out of control. In the United States, a sizeable section of the public was turning against the golden girl of American athletics after what they viewed as unseemly histrionics and an ungracious attitude. In the UK, a British public that had started 1984 by applauding the beautiful chemistry of ice skaters Torvill and Dean at the Winter Olympics in Sarajevo now found themselves watching an altogether nastier relationship between two sportspeople whose names would be forever linked to the Summer Games of the same year.

GB team manager Peters, who as an athlete won the 1972 Olympic pentathlon title in Munich, had a specific role of looking after Zola at the Games and in an interview for the British Library oral archives in 1997 described her as "such a little misfit". Her comment was more affectionate than it sounds, though, as Peters added: "She was only a child and was thrown into this cauldron of pressure and stress before she even stepped onto the track, whereas Mary had been built up as the queen of the track by the American public."

Peters helped get Zola back to the Athletes' Village and fielded a barrage of calls from journalists and abusive messages from either Americans angry that Mary had tripped or anti-apartheid demonstrators. "Zola sat in a room reading a book while all these calls were coming in," Peters remembered. "A BBC radio chap called me and said, 'How does Zola feel about being reinstated?' I said, 'Actually she didn't know she'd been disqualified'. So I said, 'Excuse me,' and I covered the mouthpiece and I said, 'Zola, the good news is you've been reinstated. The bad news was you were disqualified'. And she just said, 'Thanks,' and went back to reading her book!

"I would have loved if she'd shown some emotion and screamed or cried or sobbed or laughed or shown some expression of her torture and hurt that she must have felt so strongly. But she just sat reading her book until the phone call came to say that her coach was at the gates of the Village."

Peters continued: "Meanwhile the team doctor John Fox had arrived – he was a lovely man – and between us we made her laugh and we accompanied her to the gates of the Village where she was able to meet, I suppose, the people who understood her better than we did. I often reflect on that particular minding job and wonder if I could have done more, but I never really got to know Zola. She was just a little lamb who got lost along the way, I'm afraid."

Zola went back to her mother's hotel, found a blanket, curled up in an exhausted ball on the couch and went to sleep. On awakening, she could not wait to pack her belongings and get out of LA. She felt battered and bruised by the experience and as a gesture that symbolised her misery she threw her shoes in a bin. "I felt like I'd been thrown to the lions in the Colosseum," she later recalled.

Around her, friends and family offered mixed levels of support. After leaving his teaching job in South Africa to help Zola fulfil her potential on the world stage, Labuschagne felt let down and his relationship with the runner was crumbling. So Zola sought solace in the arms of her mother, who like Zola spoke little English and had been staying in a hotel in downtown Los Angeles, and the pair shared the intense desire to return to South Africa.

When she was finally able to flee Los Angeles, Zola was given an escort by police armed with submachine guns right up to the doors of the jumbo jet that would take them home and she was subsequently met by armed security in London. "Zola was taken out of the airport under a police guard because of death threats we believe came from the United States," a spokesman for London Heathrow said. "Police took the matter very seriously."

On returning to the British capital for a two-day stopover before continuing to Johannesburg, Zola attempted to patch things up with her father, whom she had fallen out with on the eve of the Games and who had consequently not been in LA with her. But her olive branch was rejected and she carried on to South Africa with her mother while Frank stayed in England.

A couple of months later, Frank returned to Bloemfontein, but his relationship with Tossie and Zola seemed permanently damaged. Transforming the garage into a bedroom, he lived and slept there for a while before a divorce eventually went through in November 1986. With hindsight, it was clear the stressful run-up to the LA Games proved the catalyst for the marriage to break up.

On returning to South Africa, there was no respite from the media for Zola. Local journalists were camped out at Jan Smuts Airport and desperate for interviews and photographs. South Africa still treated Zola as one of its own and had hoped she would deliver them an Olympic gold medal by proxy in Los Angeles. Given this, the race attracted much attention in her native country with newspapers producing special breakfast-time extra editions with headlines such as "Zola's disaster".

Despite the continuing press attention, the runner felt relieved and reinvigorated to be back on African soil. Reunited with her animals Fraaier and Stompie, plus Johnny the cat, her mood began to brighten. Arriving home, there was another symbolic act as well when she took down the photo of Mary in her bedroom.

Over in America, Mary's spirits began to rise as she tried to put the events of 10 August behind her. In philosophical mood, she joked with friends, "Here's to Zürich!" as she made a toast to the prospect of getting back to winning ways at the big end-of-season Weltklasse meeting in Switzerland. It was wishful thinking, though. There would be no further races for her in 1984, as the injury from the fall took longer to heal than she feared.

Coach Brown put on a brave face, saying: "People think Mary was emotionally very down after the Games, but that just wasn't the case. She realised that the controversy with Zola will never be settled, so she put it behind her. She's going to run for eight more years, so she figured why dwell on it?"

When it came to running after the Games, Zola was different as she had emerged relatively unscathed with just a few nasty cuts on her left leg. In the immediate aftermath of Los Angeles, her appetite for athletics predictably waned, but it did not take long for it to return and she began to plot a return to racing.

The biggest dilemma related to where she would live and who would she race for? Would Great Britain be happy with her spending most of her time in South Africa and racing occasionally in Europe? It was a delicate issue, but ultimately Zola was driven by the desire to live and train in the warm and familiar veldt as opposed to the cold, grey and damp environment in England.

During the months after the LA Games, BAAB secretary Cooper flew out to South Africa to woo the athlete back to Britain but was told she wanted to stay because her mother was in poor health and there was talk of a boyfriend in Bloemfontein. Zola needed to be careful, though, because if she raced in South Africa she would break IAAF rules and create a new set of problems. For a while she appeared to be prevaricating as well and showed interest in running a race in Stellenbosch in November. Consequently, her future as an international athlete was on a knife edge.

"For a few reasons I have decided to stay in South Africa and it is mainly because I enjoy my athletics here more and more," she told the Afrikaans-language newspaper *Die Volksblad*. "It was always for me important to enjoy my athletics and I hope in the coming years to mean something for South

African athletics. The experience in Britain was instructive but I choose rather to stay in South Africa."

Backing up the comments on South African television, she added: "I feel so much happier running in the country where I have my family, friends and pets around me. I feel very sorry for all the people who worked so hard to help me establish an international running career but I have to make my own mind up."

Predictably, such an about-turn led to complaints from Britons who felt she had abused a passport of convenience to run at the Olympics. "Probably the most discreditable part of this story is the way this immature young lady has herself been used and manipulated," said former Labour sports minister Howell. "The large financial rewards she has received may prove no compensation for the ordeals to which she has been subjected."

The Anti-Apartheid Movement weighed in with a told-you-so style letter to Home Secretary Brittan, saying: "We trust the Government and sports minister will have the humility to apologise for the abusive remarks they made against those who criticised the exceptional arrangements that were made for her to compete in the British team in the Olympics."

With the *Daily Mail's* contract with Zola having expired after the Games, she was free to do as she pleased. Cooper was doing his best to persuade her to continue to run for Britain, though. "Her talent ought to be on the world stage not hidden away on a small track in Bloemfontein," he argued, while Zola's father added: "It's tragic and a slap in the face to a country and people that took her to their hearts."

Before long, Zola began building a team around her and a delicate compromise was agreed whereby she would spend most of her time in South Africa but continue racing for Britain internationally. Jannie Momberg, a prominent member of the South African Amateur Athletics Union and a successful wine farmer, together with another wine farmer, Graham Boonzaaier, started helping her ahead of her post-Olympics comeback. Among other things, Zola's finances needed attention.

With the sport still struggling to embrace professionalism, prize money for athletes continued to be stored in trust funds. Zola's British earnings were safely held in a trust fund organised by the BAAB, but athletics officials in Zola's original country had frozen her South African trust fund during 1984 due to displeasure over her overseas move. In addition, Zola's father frittered most of the money the *Daily Mail* had given him in order to lure the Budd family over to England. So to partly remedy this, a Zola Budd Sports Trust was set-up – with Momberg, Boonzaaier and Labuschagne acting as her representatives – as the young runner tried to get back on track and capitalise on her talent.

Increasingly, Zola began to spend more time in Stellenbosch. Her first race back, though, would be in Zürich, Switzerland, although not in the famed Weltklasse but an 8km road race on December 30 which she won in 26:27. By the time of this race, it seemed an agreement had been reached for Zola to live in South Africa and race for Britain on the international stage. "At least we now have a very strong chance of saving the career of this great athlete," said Momberg.

"Zola cannot have her cake and eat it," an angry Professor Charles Nieuwoudt, president of the South African Amateur Athletics Union said. "The whole situation has become an embarrassment to South Africa, not only to athletics but to the sport as a whole. If she wants to compete internationally, she must go back to Britain, live in Britain, become part and parcel of the community. Otherwise she will have to let her British citizenship go."

British athletics officials were so keen for Zola to run for their country, they helped set up the Zürich road race. It brought to an end a turbulent year for the youngster, although her place in the sport was put somewhat in perspective when the British Athletics Writers' Association named double Olympic 1500m champion Coe and javelin star Sanderson as its senior athletes of 1984, while Zola merely took one of the junior athlete of the year awards alongside Ade Mafe, who reached the Olympic 200m final in LA aged only seventeen. Soon after, statistician Peter Matthews, in his UK merit rankings, placed Zola only third behind Boxer and Benning in the 1500m and second behind Sly in the 3000m.

With the dust settling on the Coliseum collision, Zola and Mary had time to take stock and plan their future. Mary would only be twenty-six years old going into the 1985 season – an optimal age for a middle-distance runner – while Zola would turn nineteen in May 1985 with everyone wondering when her steep year-on-year improvement would plateau out.

Speculating on their future, Wooldridge wrote in the *Daily Mail*: "Mary may find it difficult to recover; whereas Budd, whose attempted apology to her childhood heroine was discourteously rebuffed in the tunnel after the race, has a whole promising career ahead of her in more mature years. She may become an outstanding runner for the 10,000m when that event is introduced in 1988 or the marathon. With or without the collision, she was never going to win a medal. What she needs now is a good dose of anonymity."

It was sound advice, but there was probably little chance of Zola disappearing entirely. Race organisers were already clamouring for a "Decker v Budd rematch" and there was some lucrative money to be made from such an event. Mary had left the Coliseum a limping, tearful wreck, but still earned an estimated $355,000 during the year and ironically her typical fee for a race rose from about $3,000 before the Games to $11-13,000 afterwards.

One South African businessman offered to put up $65,000 to hold a head-to-head over 3000m. "I feel particularly sympathetic to Zola," said Joe Berardo, director of the Bank of Lisbon in Johannesburg, "because this could break her confidence badly. I think another race now would be very good for Mary and Zola."

New York City Marathon race director Fred Lebow, meanwhile, said he had been approached by "two US TV networks, some foreign TV people, two major corporations and a sports promotion firm" offering "six figures" to bring Mary and Zola together in a road race.

A big money rematch was indeed around the corner, but would not happen until midway through the 1985 season. For now, the athletes were forced to lick their wounds and reflect on the tumultuous tumble in Los Angeles. An amazing year ended on a good note, too, when Mary finally said 'sorry' in a letter to Zola.

It read: "Dear Zola, I've been wanting to write this letter to you for a long time. The reason I haven't sent this letter before is because I was sure that you would not receive it personally.

"I simply want to apologise to you for hurting your feelings at the Olympics. There are many reasons that people react the way they do at certain times in their lives and I'm sure you understand that that was a very difficult time for me. I'm sorry I turned you away after the race, it was a very hard moment for me emotionally and I reacted in an emotional manner.

"I know that we do not know each other personally, but the next time we meet I would like to shake your hand and let everything that has happened be put behind us. Who knows; sometimes even the fiercest competitors become friends. Yours in sport, Mary Decker."

PART THREE

LIFE AFTER LA

CHAPTER SEVEN

WEDDED BLISS AND A BIG-MONEY RE-MATCH

"This is the rematch the world has been waiting for."
Andy Norman, promoter of the 1985 Peugeot Talbot Games

FOLLOWING HER DISASTROUS Olympic year, 1985 started happily for Mary when she got married to her discus-throwing British fiancé. The wedding took place on New Year's Day in Eugene and proved to be the prelude to a vintage season.

Undefeated all year, Mary broke the world record for the mile and set American records at 800m, 1000m, the mile, 3000m and 5000m. During this phenomenal run of form, she defeated Zola and Puică in convincing fashion several times. It was a powerful statement that suggested she would have won Olympic gold if she had managed to stay on her feet in Los Angeles the previous August.

What made Mary's victories sweeter was that she beat her main rivals when they were in great form. In 1985, Puică ran the fastest times of her life for the mile and 3000m. Still only 19, Zola similarly clocked times for 1500m, the mile, 3000m and 5000m that remain her best-ever marks to this day. Looking back, the athletes undoubtedly benefited from each other's presence, thrived on the rivalry and spurred each other on as they battled through a series of post-Olympic rematch races.

One runner who was missing, though, was Mary's fearsome foe Kazankina.

While 1985 saw Mary and Zola at the height of their powers as they raced against the in-form Puică across the athletics circuit, the Russian runner was missing from the circuit after having suffered a gigantic fall from grace towards the end of 1984.

The multiple Olympic gold medallist had been one of Mary's closest rivals in Helsinki in 1983 and was expected to be one of the key contenders for gold in Los Angeles. Forced to sit out the Games due to the Soviet-led boycott, in late August of 1984 she smashed Ulmasova's world 3000m record by four seconds with 8:22.62 in Leningrad. Sending a fierce message to the West, Kazankina's team-mate Nadezhda Ralldugina also ran the fastest 1500m in 1984 with 3:56.63 as Russian runners dominated the rankings for the season.

But the year ended miserably for Kazankina when she was given a doping ban. Racing over 5000m in Paris in September, the veteran Soviet runner refused to take a drugs test at the meeting because there was no doping official from her own country to accompany her. Violating the rules, she was given a 'lifetime' ban by the IAAF. The Russian would later return to competition, but never again ran with the same speed and ferocity that she showed during her 1976-84 heyday.

The Soviet-led boycott of the LA Games had hit the women's middle-distances more than most events. The phenomenal performances from Kazankina and her kin during 1984 haunted the competitors in Los Angeles and served as an ugly reminder that many of the best athletes in the world were missing from the greatest show on earth. But after their self-imposed exile during Olympic year, the Soviet Union's star runner Kazankina would now miss the 1985 season and beyond as she fought to have her drugs ban overturned.

The news helped lift Mary's post-Olympic gloom. The American always had her doubts about how clean the athletes from behind the Iron Curtain were and now her suspicions were vindicated with Kazankina receiving a ban.

For Mary, 1985 signified a fresh start in more ways than one. Her hip injury sustained in the Olympic final caused her to miss two months of training but in the early part of the winter she steadily got back into shape and was rounding into fine form.

Her wedding was a short, twenty-minute ceremony at a small Methodist church in front of about 250 guests, including a number of well-known athletes, Mary's sisters, coach Brown and a thirty-five-part choir who sang

'Amazing Grace' and 'The First Noel'. Sadly, Mary's father was not there to walk her down the aisle, having dropped out of her life when she was a child, so instead Slaney accompanied his bride to the altar as Salazar acted as groomsman. Three months later, the pair enjoyed a second ceremony for British relatives and friends in Crawley, although Fleet Street photographers did their best to ruin the day by accidentally pushing Richard's sister over in their frenzy to get some pictures. With a rich twist of irony, it meant Mary was, like Zola, eligible to run for Great Britain in theory.

While Mary's first marriage to Tabb was destined to break down soon after it started, her second to Slaney was built to last. The couple have remained together for more than thirty years with the strongman acting as a protective, good-humoured foil to a wife whose emotional and explosive personality belies her petite and sometimes fragile appearance.

Writing in *Sports Illustrated* in the mid-1980s, Moore described their home life, saying: "Mary's hillside house, which is not sumptuous, speaks of a love of order, a congenial domesticity. A visitor is likely to find her sewing pillowcases or mending one of Slaney's shirts. There is a warm fire, cushiony furniture and friendly animals – cats Tigger and Jezebel, and a Rottweiler named Samantha. On a shelf, among a glittering welter of the trophies Mary has won, rests a silver tray awarded to Slaney by the British meat industry for being Britain's Strongest Man."

Mary's therapy during the post-Olympic period included helping her new husband set up a local tanning salon, which he had taken part ownership of. Improving her mood further, she was inundated with messages of goodwill from fans. Thousands of letters arrived, almost all of them supportive and many from children wishing her well. Some sent her their own medals to replace the Olympic gold they felt she deserved. Remarkably, a former soldier sent her his Purple Heart, the oldest award given to US military members.

While they were nice gestures, the best way for Mary to pick herself up from the disappointment of 1984 was to get back to winning ways on the track. It is common for Olympic champions to endure a dip in form the year after victory in the Games. Winning a gold medal often sates an athlete's appetite and combined with new-found demands from sponsors and the media it means the post-Olympic year often sees the emergence of athletes with greater hunger and fewer distractions.

Minus a medal from LA, Mary fell into this latter category. She went into 1985 determined to re-establish herself as the world No.1 and her mission began with the Sunkist indoor meeting in Los Angeles on 18 January.

There, racing on a tight, 160-yard wooden oval in front of a crowd of nearly 14,000, she smashed Podkopayeva's world indoor best for 2000m with 5:34.52 and in the process left her main rival at the event, Wysocki, half a lap behind. The woman who had beaten Mary in the US trials 1500m the previous year gamely tried to stay with the leader as the newly-married Mrs Slaney led through 1000m in 2:46 and one mile in 4:31. But looking smooth and confident, Mary pulled ahead to win by 11 seconds.

"Richard requested a wedding present from me tonight," she said, before settling down for a marathon autograph-signing session. "He asked me to run well, feel good and set a world record. Not because he wanted it, but because he knew I wanted it."

Ironically, the race took place in the Los Angeles Sports Arena, which was right next to the Coliseum. Not surprisingly, the events of 10 August 1984, were still a little raw and far from forgotten, too, as Mary told the *Chicago Tribune*: "On the way over here, I said, 'I might as well go in and reminisce'. I'm at the point where I have to take it lightly, as a joke."

Some simmering frustration also still existed, as she added: "I think it's time the press started telling the truth and not make up stories about me. What really bothers me is that they portray me as being bitter. I'm not bitter at all. I know what Zola did was unintentional. You can tell. We tried to set up breakfast, lunch or dinner with her the next day—and nobody wrote about this—but they never responded."

Mary's husband added: "We hold no bitterness towards Zola. Actually, I feel sorry for her. She was used and she was in a no-win situation unless she actually won the Olympics. There is no way she is in the same class as Mary."

Expanding on his wife's personality, Slaney once answered a journalist: "Is Mary a bitch, do you mean? She happens to be one of the most honest and genuine people I've ever met. Too honest, sometimes. I think she deserves all the acclaim she gets – and more. She's been through a lot of savage injuries and emotional problems but always comes back better and better."

Mary was due to race in New York's Millrose Games the following weekend but it almost did not happen after she was mugged during a training run at home in Eugene. Approaching Mary on a bicycle, the attacker threatened Mary with a knife and tried to steal her jewellery, but he got more than he bargained for as the athlete fought him off, suffering bruises on her thigh in the process.

In order to avoid a lot of fuss before Millrose, Mary kept the incident to herself in the days leading up to the meeting. She then said in New York that a man in his mid-twenties to thirties knocked her to the ground and put his hand over her face. "The incident took an emotional toll on me that was worse than anything physical that happened," she explained. "It was one of the most frightening things that ever happened to me. I felt that I didn't have the emotional spark here (in New York). I felt that I was just plodding along. I felt lucky to get away unharmed."

It did not seem to affect Mary's form at the Millrose Games. She breezed to a 4:22.01 victory in the Wanamaker Mile, finishing 1.51 seconds outside her own world record and nine seconds ahead of Sly, who was a relative novice indoors and struggled on the tight bends. Similar to the Sunkist event the previous weekend, the Millrose meeting saw Mary attract a few boos when she was introduced to the crowd but there were generally more cheers than jeers, especially at the end of each race when her win was given a warm applause.

A tremendous runner during the winter season on the boards, Mary had not been beaten indoors since 1976. Her next race in East Rutherford, New Jersey, on 9 February began brilliantly as well as she was on course to become the first woman to break four minutes for 1500m indoors. Then disaster struck as her right calf muscle suddenly cramped and she pulled up sharply to drop out of the race. "I've never had a tear or a pull like this," she said, although she was back in training by the following month.

Likewise, Zola began 1985 in good form but with the odd, unexpected and controversial blip. First, she enjoyed some solid season openers before being forced to drop out of a big cross country race near Liverpool when anti-apartheid campaigners ran onto the course.

Back in the 1980s, the premier indoor track in the UK was housed inside a large Royal Air Force hangar in Cosford near Wolverhampton. Zola had never even seen an indoor track before 1985, but at the Pearl Assurance AAA Championships at Cosford on 26 January she beat a battling Yvonne Murray by five seconds in a UK all-comers' record of 4:11.2.

A few days later she braved the cold winter weather to win the South of England cross country title in Ipswich on 2 February. Again, she did so without any shoes, which must have had Brooks questioning its decision to sponsor her.

Zola won easily in Ipswich but somewhat bizarrely was unable to represent her English club at the event because she had not been resident in the region for the stipulated nine months. This was despite her having raced for Great Britain at the Olympics the previous year. So the title instead went to the runner-up, Rachel Disley, a Borough of Hounslow runner who finished 88 seconds adrift.

Moving back indoors to Cosford, Zola broke Paula Fudge's UK and Commonwealth indoor 3000m record as she clocked 8:56.13 to win at the GB versus West Germany match on 9 February, although she fell short of Mary's world best of 8:47.3. Following this, she headed to Birkenhead on Merseyside for the Provincial Insurance Women's English National Cross Country Championships where she would face icy, snow-covered ground and the additional hazard of mid-race intruders who were determined to destroy her attempts to finish.

Previously, Zola had been easily protected at track races, but cross country events were a different, open environment and at Arrowe Park in Birkenhead it was easy for demonstrators to invade the course. The course was well marshalled and had a police presence, but three-quarters of the way through the first lap a couple of people jumped out in front of the runners in a blatant attempt to obstruct them.

At this point, Zola was not leading. Setting the pace at the front was Angela Tooby – one of two talented twin sisters who were making an impact on the domestic distance running scene – and the no nonsense twenty-four-year-old brushed the demonstrators out of the way.

Twenty metres behind, though, Zola was not so adept at evading the intruders and instead veered into a bush and stopped running. "I saw the runner in front being knocked and suddenly everyone was standing in front of me," said Zola, who was wearing spikes for once to combat the frozen ground. "There was a policeman with a truncheon and all these people on the course. I was frightened and realised if I tried to run on and get past I might get hurt and almost certainly disrupt the race, so I ran off the course. I was not touched physically," she added.

Shaken up by the incident, Zola had to go to hospital for a tetanus jab after scratching herself on the bushes and later described the intruders as "rabid" and "like something from a bad dream", comparing them to the infamous English football hooligans of the era. Tooby, who went on to win the race, said: "Two lads jumped out in front of me but I just pushed them out the way. It was a tragedy for Zola and for me, as I wanted to beat her," while her coach, Ann Hill, added: "I think I'll have to get heavyweight boxing champ Henry Cooper to give some lessons to protect my athletes."

Three demonstrators were arrested, including two women, and the incident was all over the next day's newspapers. Never before had the women's national cross country championships received such media coverage, although the winner was unimpressed. "My glory was overseen in all the press by the fact that Zola, 'the true winner', was removed from the race," said Tooby. "It was frustrating because up until then Zola hadn't even been in the frame and I was in really good shape. In the press the next day there was not one photograph of me!"

"The boorish and shameful behaviour was quite inexcusable, though predictable," wrote Jimmy Green, the founder of *Athletics Weekly*, in his magazine. "Unfortunately cross country running lends itself to disruption and it is impossible to police or steward a whole lap of anything from one to two miles. Zola was, unfortunately, used and manipulated when she first came to this country and though this was no fault of hers it did cause resentment. But this shy slip of a girl has shown, with dignity, that all she wants to do is run and become integrated into our athletics scene as 'one of the girls' – if they will let her."

Green continued: "The younger athletes idolise her and the older ones admire her for her magnificent running. At Cosford and Ipswich she showed us all just what she can do and it was a great shame that an epic race was ruined by one-track mind hoodlums."

Escaping the icy fields and angry anti-apartheid campaigners of England, Zola's next racing stop was a 10km in Phoenix, Arizona, on 2 March, but she suffered another setback when she was beaten easily by Olympic silver medallist Sly in the Continental Homes road race. Taking her head-to-head score against the South African-born athlete to 2-0, Sly broke away at the halfway point to win by 100 metres in 32:03 as Zola clocked 32:20 in second and Priscilla Welch, a forty-year-old Briton twice Zola's age, was a further five seconds back in third.

Curiously, Mary had also been due to take part in the race but withdrew from the event despite having a five-year contract with the organisers. "Mary did not leave the Phoenix race because Budd is in it," insisted coach Brown. "Mary pulled out of that race well before it was known that Zola was running," he added, blaming an error in Mary's contract with the organisers.

Certainly, the American did not seem motivated by money during her career. "I could make a fortune in one year of road racing," she once said. "But my concern is I don't know what shape my body would be in when the year was over."

Due to the invasion in Birkenhead a few days earlier and death threats in Los Angeles the previous year, Zola was escorted through the road race by two policemen on motorbikes and then whisked away by plain clothes police straight after the race. Such was the concern for her safety, it took two divisions of Phoenix police to look after her. There was consolation for her, though, in the shape of a handsome $20,000 appearance fee which Boonzaaier had negotiated for her, while Sly took the winner's prize of $5,000.

The result was deceptive because Zola was on the verge of the most pleasing performance of her career. Her next race on March 24 was the World Cross Country Championships in Portugal and saw her win gold in what she described at the time as "the greatest moment of my life".

Everything was ideally set up for Zola. Racing barefoot, she relished the rich, green turf of the Hipódromo do Jamor course in Lisbon and the warm, Portuguese weather. There were no demonstrators to ruin the race – although organisers took no chances by dispatching 200 police to guard the course – and Zola benefited from the absence of Waitz and Puică, who between them had enjoyed a seven-year stranglehold on the event.

That is not to devalue Zola's performance. She destroyed the challenge of Kristiansen, a Norwegian who was poised to retain her London Marathon title in a world record of 2:21:06 the following month. "Zola proved what many believed," wrote athletics writer Butcher, "that cross country is her forte, when she won the world title by 23 seconds."

It was a huge margin of victory over a largely flat course of barely 5km in distance. She did it in the white vest of England as well due to the British home countries entering separate teams for the championships.

After losing to Sly in Arizona, Zola had returned to South Africa to prepare for the championships. Back there she trained with her friend and fellow Olympic finalist, Bürki, and completed sessions such as 5x1km in 2min 52sec and with the last effort in 2:49 with two minutes' jogging between each repetition. It told her she was ready and in Lisbon she not only won by almost half a minute but at eighteen years and 302 days old became the youngest winner of a senior world cross country title. "An astonishing run," said BBC commentator Ron Pickering. "She hasn't shown any signs of fatigue or faltering at all."

Avoiding the controversy that dogged her in both Los Angeles and seemingly every race in the UK, Zola thoroughly enjoyed the experience in Portugal. Her critics, though, were never far away and some were unimpressed with her spending just two days in England after the victory before flying to South Africa to train until mid-June.

While winning the world cross country title in Lisbon was immensely satisfying for Zola, the rest of the world yearned for a rematch of the Olympic 3000m race. After plans to get the two runners together at the Continental Homes 10km fell through, the summer track and field season was now approaching and a showdown became inevitable.

Back in South Africa, Zola's training went from strength to strength as her mileage nudged 100 miles per week. Her first outdoor track race of 1985 was a baptism of fire, though, as she was outsprinted by Darlene Beckford of America over 3000m at the Dale Farm Ulster Games in Belfast on 24 June. Racing barefoot again and struggling to get to grips with a wet track that had been drenched by a rain shower, Zola finished three seconds behind Beckford in 9:01.71. "I had a bad day and would have preferred a smaller race to start my season," she said.

Five days later things improved for Zola with a 3000m win in 8:44.54 in a UK v France v Czechoslovakia match in Gateshead. But on 4 July she finished well down the field in a 5000m in Helsinki. The race had been billed as an attempt on Kristiansen's 14:58.89 world record, but Zola faded from first place with a lap to go to sixth as Olympic champion Puică roared home to win in 15:06.04. Still, Zola's 15:13.07 was an official UK record despite being 12 seconds slower than her South African best.

"We came within minutes of catching a flight back to Britain," said Labuschagne, complaining that he did not know about Puică's presence in the race. "Zola had prepared for a time trial of even pace and our tactics were geared to that. Puică was never mentioned to us and we found out she was running in the newspapers. We would not have minded if we had known a few days earlier out of courtesy."

Puică said: "I wanted to beat Zola very much and I was surprised she did nothing to take command of the race after going to the front. You must accelerate every now and again to hurt those who follow but she always had the same tempo."

Finishing seven seconds behind the Romanian, the heavy defeat gave fuel to the critics who argued Zola was a one-paced runner lacking the change of pace necessary to win last-lap burn-ups. In an article entitled "Some Budding Beliefs" in *Athletics Weekly*, Jerome Gardner noted Zola's "clumsy and energy-wasting outward arm action, which threatens to get her tripped and bumped whenever she competes in a large-ish field."

On a clash with Mary, Gardner continued: "I'd stake my life on one thing: Zola hasn't a hope in hell of ever beating her one-time idol as long as her arms are failing to give forward drive. Lately she does seem to have learned to shorten her stride and increase cadence to the finish, but there is still no real feeling of a 'gear change' in her finishing speed."

In comparison, Mary's season started smoothly. She kicked off her outdoor campaign with a 5000m American record of 15:06.53 at the Pre Classic in Eugene on 1 June as she beat Cindy Bremser by 13 seconds. Always wanting more, she said: "I wanted to run between 14:30 and 14:35 but I went out too fast."

A world record attempt at the mile followed in Vancouver but Mary had to be content with a routine win in 4:22.3. Into July, she set a US record for 1000m of 2:34.08 in Eugene before travelling over to Europe where she won an 800m in Cork, Ireland, in a fast 1:57.68 and then a 3:59.84 victory over 1500m in Paris.

As the 1985 season unfolded, Decker also split from Brown to be coached by Luiz Alberto de Oliveira, a thirty-five-year-old Brazilian who guided Joaquim Cruz to the Olympic 800m title ahead of Coe in Los Angeles. "It was a mutual decision," said Mary. "It was nothing personal but at this point I have to do what I believe will help my running career the most. Dick (Brown) was great and I needed someone who could keep me healthy. But he was too protective and to improve I have to do better training."

As Moore once wrote in *Sports Illustrated*: "More than any other runner, Mary blooms in partnership with others, with coaches, with close friends, with lovers."

Zola's questionable form did not lessen the public's appetite for a "Decker v Budd rematch". Nor did it prevent meeting organisers trying to pull it together. Huge interest surrounded a possible clash and a date and venue was finally arranged. The Peugeot Talbot Games at Crystal Palace in London on 20 July would be the scene of a head-to-head over 3000m and the media immediately began to bill it as a "grudge match". It is, meeting promoter Andy Norman announced: "The rematch the world has been waiting for," while fellow British promoter Alan Pascoe called it "one of the big personality races of the century".

Privately, Zola winced at the way it was portrayed in the build-up. She described it as "the equivalent of a boxing prize fight" and too artificial to take seriously and she did not want to take part. Ultimately, though, she was seduced by the chance to earn £90,000 (the equivalent of almost £260,000 today) which was an unprecedented amount for an appearance fee and a figure that also became public knowledge, which only made things worse for her because she was viewed by some as a money-grabbing mercenary.

Ironically, Zola's advisors believed their £90,000 demand was so outrageous that it would not be taken seriously. But to their amazement, they paid every penny. "It is ridiculous that a teenager can earn that kind of money," said Derek Johnson from the International Athletes' Club of Zola's fee. "It is an insult to everyone from the greatest athlete down to the lowest."

In comparison, Mary was paid £36,000 as the two runners swept up the bulk of the meeting's budget in appearance fees. In more recent years, Usain Bolt has commanded between $200,000-350,000 per race, but the Jamaican sprinter is in a league of his own when it comes to money-earning ability in today's world of track and field.

The mid-1980s was an era when greed was good and mobile phones were as big as bricks. But Zola's £90,000 appearance fee left a bad taste in the mouth of many, especially as it came only seven days after a Live Aid concert was held elsewhere in London to raise money for the Ethiopian famine appeal.

Such was the outrage over the payment, Channel 4 produced a television documentary entitled "Take the money and run" about the staging and management of the Peugeot Talbot Games head-to-head. Adding to the ridiculousness, Zola's huge cheque – the equivalent of virtually £10,000 per lap – was not deemed to break any rules, whereas the following month in Scotland a ten-year-old boy who finished runner-up in a 60 yards race at the Montrose Highland Games was briefly banned by the Scottish Amateur Athletics Association for accepting the prize of a ten pence packet of sweets.

Notably, the Olympic medallists Puică, Sly and Williams were not in the big Crystal Palace race. After terrific form earlier in the year where she had beaten Zola and Waitz in separate road races, Sly's summer track season was ruined by a knee injury. Puică, however, was in top form despite officially entering the 'veteran' category by turning thirty-five in July 1985, but the Romanian Athletics Federation was seemingly unimpressed with a $2,000 fee to run and the race went ahead minus the presence of the Olympic champion. Privately, one British official described the offer to Puică as "peanuts" and claimed it was due to the desire of British and US television executives not to dilute the drama of a Mary versus Zola "rematch".

Mary and Zola did their best before the race to dampen the hype. "I frankly don't think I can win," said Zola, speaking at a press conference at the Waldorf Hotel in London on the eve of the event. "If you look at the statistics there is an eight-second difference between her best time and mine," she added, while Mary described the race as "more of a personal battle between myself and the clock" and that Zola was "a good athlete with a lot of potential."

To the morbid delight of the media and meeting organisers, some ill-feeling remained in the air, though, when Mary said she still blamed Zola for the fall in Los Angeles. "I may forgive, but I don't forget," she told the media at the Waldorf.

Originally due to be held on a Friday night, ABC TV in the United States asked for the women's 3000m to be delayed until Saturday. So the meeting quickly morphed into a two-day affair with most events in their original Friday slot and the clash between Zola and Mary part of a thin Saturday schedule. Jim Rosenthal, commentating live on the British ITV television channel, said: "An estimated audience of 100 million are watching this race around the world." But plenty of empty seats on the back straight stands showed that perhaps television was more interested in this manufactured showdown than the ticket-paying public and the race proved to be a mild anticlimax.

As the runners warmed up in chilly and breezy conditions, Mary and Zola exchanged a brief, friendly 'hello' and a handshake. As with all Zola's races, a police presence was needed but the anti-apartheid demonstrations were limited to a few leaflets handed out near the railway station outside Crystal Palace stadium.

Puică and Sly were missing but the field was strong and it was far from a two-horse race. Kristiansen was on the start list along with Bürki and the Britons Boxer and Murray. From the gun, though, Mary stamped her authority on proceedings with a 66.5-second lap followed by a series of 69s as Zola, Kristiansen and Bürki fell in behind her.

Unlike Los Angeles, Zola did not seriously challenge for the lead, later saying: "Mary was running a fast pace so it was unnecessary for me to go to the front." The teenager was also feeling the pace and with just over two laps to go Mary effortlessly began to open a gap.

Clad in her red and blue Athletics West attire and looking smooth and confident, Mary drew away as the barefoot Zola faded. Ironically, another South African-born athlete, Bürki, surged into second place as Mary cruised home in 8:32.91 to win with ease.

Making sure everyone knew who was number one, Mary ran a UK all-comers' record and a time that was three seconds quicker than Puică ran to win the Olympic title. Six seconds behind, Bürki set a Swiss record, while Kristiansen was third and Zola fourth in 8:45.43.

Going through the motions in the final stages in similar style to Los Angeles the previous year, Zola wound up a weary-looking 13 seconds behind Mary and looked relieved to simply get the race over with.

"I'm surprised they all dropped back with two laps to go when I pushed the pace. I think Zola ran a good race," said Mary, who received a magnum of champagne from triple jump legend Willie Banks for achieving the performance of the day, not to mention a further £18,000 prize to go with her £36,000 appearance fee. With wishful thinking, she added: "I hope the Mary-Zola thing is over. This doesn't prove anything – the Olympic champion is still Puică."

Summing up the result, Brasher wrote in the *Observer*: "Mrs Slaney showed at Crystal Palace what she might have done in last year's Olympics if she hadn't tripped over Zola Budd's leg. She won the 'revenge match' with all the majesty of a world champion and it is clear Zola is a one-paced runner and Mary is the complete athlete."

In the *Mail on Sunday*, Patrick Collins wrote: "Zola was sacrificed to the talent of Mary Slaney upon an altar of American television money and, as ever, the little girl was the willing victim. At the finish, Budd was broken and bewildered. If this was revenge for the Los Angeles collision, it was a hollow kind of revenge."

Slowly but surely Zola's form improved as she began to resurrect what had been, up until here, a pretty dire season. Off the track, she continued to be dogged by anti-apartheid demonstrations and her next race – the Dairy Crest Games in Edinburgh on 23 July – was disrupted when a hooligan ran onto the track and sat on the inside lane, forcing Zola and her rivals in a mile race to run around him. With protest banners around the Meadowbank Stadium as well, it caused television broadcasters Channel 4 to pull its coverage and the station showed a documentary about supermiler Cram in its place. At the meeting, though, Zola won the mile in 4:23.14 in the kind of cold, rainy conditions she despised.

Three days later, Zola's form continued to improve as she won the 3000m at the TSB Women's AAA Championships in Birmingham in 8:50.5 before going to Gateshead for the Kodak Games where she improved her mile mark to 4:22.96 with another victory. Frustratingly, Zola had wanted to race in a higher-profile Oslo meeting but was persuaded to compete in England instead to appease her critics. She reluctantly agreed and this left Mary free to enjoy a 4:19.18 mile victory in the Norwegian city over a young Kirsty Wade on a night where the highlights were a world mile record of 3:46.32 by Cram and a world 10,000m record of 30:59.42 by Kristiansen.

With the so-called grudge match now well out of the way, it released Mary and Zola to engage in a series of superb end-of-season races. These clashes were minus the same hype that accompanied the Peugeot Talbot Games two months earlier and the two runners, plus Puică, set the tracks of Zürich, Brussels and Rome alight with superlative performances.

As a taster, Zola went to Moscow to represent Britain in the Europa Cup and scored the greatest track victory of her career over 3000m. Around 100,000 fans crowded into the Lenin Stadium to watch the two-day meeting and were thrilled to see Zola lead all the way before streaking away from her two pursuers, Zaytseva from the host nation and Ulrike Bruns of East Germany, in the home straight. Zaytseva was the Soviet athlete who dramatically lunged at the line in a desperate effort to beat Mary in the world 1500m final in 1983 and she challenged Zola in similar fashion here but the youngster lengthened her stride and found another gear in the final 60 metres.

Relishing the hot weather, Zola produced a 64.3 final lap and 31-second last 200m to come home in 8:35.32. The time beat Sly's Commonwealth record by two seconds and it was the first time since leaving South Africa that she had beaten one of the performances she set as a seventeen-year-old in one of the standard metric events.

"After all the bad races this season, I'm glad to have done my best time," said Zola, who was finally finding her form. "I knew it was fast but I concentrated just on running hard. I decided to run my own race and with 200m to go I knew I was going to win."

To make things better, the British athletics fraternity was becoming more welcoming. In 1984 she faced opposition from athletes frustrated at the idea of her taking a place in the Olympic team. Now, in Moscow in 1985 she found the GB team management telling the Russian organisers they would refuse to compete following a suggestion that they might not honour her British passport.

Celebrating her twenty-seventh birthday at the start of August, Mary's great form continued too. Racing again at Crystal Palace and over the mile in an IAC Grand Prix, she clocked 4:19.59 in poor conditions. "The weather was kind of awful," she said. "I didn't think it could be worse than a few weeks ago (when racing Zola) but it was!"

A few days later, in better conditions and after a short spell of training in the mountains of Switzerland, Mary smashed her US 800m record in Bern with 1:56.90. It was a superb demonstration of speed and set the scene for the epic end-of-season encounters against Zola and Puică.

First was Zürich on 21 August. Along with Brussels and Oslo, the Weltklasse in the Swiss city was one of the biggest grand prix meetings of the season and Mary and Zola were set to clash with Puică over the classic distance of one mile.

The race did not disappoint. Once again, Mary took her usual position at the front, pushing the pace and almost daring her rivals to take her on. Zola settled in behind with Puică in third before the Romanian moved threateningly up into second and onto Mary's shoulder halfway through the final lap.

Quickening her pace, Mary strode away to a world record of 4:16.71 as Puică finished second in 4:17.44 with Zola close behind in a Commonwealth record of 4:17.57. Elsewhere on the night, Cram beat Olympic 800m champion Cruz over the Brazilian's specialist distance, Saïd Aouita of Morocco ran a sparkling 3:46.92 mile and Coe suffered a shock defeat by local runner Pierre Délèze over 1500m, but the female runners were no longer bit-part players and the women's mile was one of the highlights of the evening.

Four days later the athletics caravan rumbled into Cologne and in the German city Mary handed Puică another defeat. This time it came over the LA Olympics distance of 3000m as the American sped through the last lap in 61.2 to clock 8:29.69 ahead of Puică's 8:30.32.

Temporarily going her separate way, Zola raced at Crystal Palace the following day and smashed the world 5000m record with a fantastic new mark of 14:48.07. Joining her in the race was Kristiansen, the world record-holder for 5000m, 10,000m and the marathon, but Zola destroyed the Norwegian, breaking the world record by ten seconds, beating the Norwegian by nine seconds and clocking a time that was 18 seconds quicker than both Mary's and Puică's best. Symbolically, the performance also consigned the 15:01.83 unofficial world record she set in South Africa in January 1984 to the history books. The only blow was that Zola missed out on a £50,000 prize offered by Mumm Champagne for the first British athlete to break a world record on British soil because the 5000m was not yet an Olympic discipline.

In contrast to the head-to-head against Mary at the same venue earlier in the season, organisers made a deliberate decision to avoid publicising Zola's participation until the last moment. Such a tactic did not give time for anti-apartheid demonstrators to mount a protest and Zola went into the race in relaxed mood and agreeing with Kristiansen to share the pace two laps at a time.

Such was Zola's form, she passed 3000m in 8:50.5 – a time she had struggled to achieve earlier in the season – as she broke away from Kristiansen to claim her first official world record. Four days after the race and in great spirits she travelled to Brussels to take on Mary and Puică again, this time over 1500m.

At the Ivo Van Damme Memorial meeting in the Belgian city the trio of middle-distance marvels took part in another classic race. Once again Mary took first place in 3:57.24 – narrowly missing her US record – as Puică clocked 3:57.73 in second and Zola ran a Commonwealth record of 3:59.96 in third. By now the races were unfolding in a familiar pattern with Mary leading and then surging away at the end. Brussels was no different either as she clocked 62.0 for the final lap compared to Zola's 64.3.

It was Mary's twelfth consecutive win of the season but she was not finished. Rome was the next stop on 7 September and another clash with Puică and Zola over 3000m on a warm, sultry night. For the American, things just kept getting better as well as she broke her US record with 8:25.83, while Puică clocked a Romanian record of 8:27.83 and Zola another Commonwealth record of 8:28.83.

As Mary's rich vein of form continued, she scorched through the first lap in 64.4 (8:03 pace for 3000m) before settling into a rhythm that would see her smash her best by four seconds with a national record that still stands today. Behind, it was the first time Zola and Puică had broken the 8:30 barrier for the distance.

Securing the IAAF Mobil Grand Prix overall title in front of a 58,000 crowd in the Italian capital, Mary earned $35,000 prize money. The only blot on the landscape was the fact the now discredited Kazankina still held the world record with 8:22.62.

"Isn't it great?" said Mary after the race as she took Zola's hand. "We all broke records."

A summer that had started with a rather artificial 'rematch' featuring Mary and Zola at Crystal Palace ended with a series of amazing clashes at 1500m, 3000m and the mile. Mary proved she was the undisputed No.1, while the now veteran Puică showed she was a worthy rival and Olympic champion. After an indifferent year, Zola proved she could produce great form when it mattered – firstly at the World Cross Country Championships in March and then during the business end of the European track season.

"What happened in Los Angeles is now history and remains pure conjecture as to what might have happened if Mary had stayed on her feet," wrote Watman in *Athletics Weekly*. "What the Rome race underlined is that Mary is back to her World Championships form of 1983 and simply unbeatable. The race also demonstrated that Puică, at thirty-five, is running faster than ever in her long career, but still not fast enough, strong enough or resolute enough to

CHAPTER EIGHT

THE TWILIGHT ZONE

"The teeth of the piranhas, and her own self-inflicted wounds,
have reduced Zola to a skeleton."
Chris Brasher, *Observer*

NEVER AGAIN WOULD Mary and Zola run as quickly as they did during their vintage 1985 season. The duo raced head to head one final time, in a low-key road mile race in Sydney in 1992 which was won easily by Mary. Yet the final decade of their international running careers would not be without incident.

For such a quiet soul, Zola has an unfortunate knack of attracting attention and controversy. After already achieving infamy as a political pawn on the global sporting scene, the twilight years of her career would subsequently be soured by an international ban from competing, divorce, suicide and even murder.

As for Mary, she was destined never to climb the same heights that she scaled during 1982-1985. A declining force, she increasingly struggled to compete with the world's best and her track career ended in ignominy when she was involved in a bitter dispute over a positive drugs test.

On the good side, both women enjoyed the taste of Olympic competition as they attempted to bury the ghosts of Los Angeles. Zola raced at the 1992 Games, notably donning the colours of South Africa as opposed to Great Britain, while Mary ran at the 1988 and 1996 Games, albeit finishing adrift of the medals. Outside athletics, the two women would become proud mothers. There would even be one final moment of global glory for Zola when she successfully defended her world cross country title.

Following the routine that had ultimately led to a world 5000m record, world cross country title, Europa Cup victory and multiple Commonwealth records the previous year, Zola opened her 1986 campaign with a couple of indoor events at RAF Cosford and some cross country racing. Flying into England from South Africa, she firstly won the British 1500m title in a Commonwealth indoor record of 4:06.87 on 25 January. Moving outdoors, she then easily won the South of England cross country title on a cold and wet day in Peterborough on 1 February before returning to Cosford on 8 February to set a world indoor 3000m record of 8:39.79 in the Peugeot Talbot Games.

Still only nineteen, Zola took more than two seconds off Olga Bondarenko's world best and ran seven seconds faster than Mary's former world indoor mark. Notably, she also ran 16 seconds quicker than in her corresponding run over the same distance twelve months earlier as she sped around the Cosford track barefoot with only her toes taped up for protection. "The crowd helped a lot and if it wasn't for them I doubt I would have broken the record," she said. "I have done more speedwork than usual and it has helped make me sharper indoors."

Proving her form in these races earned Zola preselection to run for England in the World Cross Country Championships in Neuchâtel, Switzerland, on 23 March. All of which was probably a relief because it meant she did not have to do the English National Championships – the event that demonstrators had forced her out of, mid-race, twelve months earlier.

Arriving in Neuchâtel, Zola was met by beautiful weather, but it soon changed as her worst fears of cold weather materialised. On race day, temperatures dipped as icy rain and blustery winds whipped down from the nearby Jura Mountains. To make things worse, Zola gambled on running barefoot on a course that became increasingly greasy as the day wore on.

It was a decision Zola would regret, but such was her superiority she was able to prevail as she slipped and slid her way over the undulating terrain to gold. Her margin of victory was not quite as big as twelve months earlier, but she nevertheless finished with an 18-second buffer over runner-up Lynn Jennings of the United States and Annette Sergent of France in third. Such was the strength of the field, Jennings and Sergent would go on to win five world cross country titles between them from 1987-1992, while in fifth place and almost half a minute behind Zola was Portuguese marathoner Rosa Mota, a runner famed for winning Olympic, world and three European titles at 26.2 miles.

Describing the conditions as treacherous, Zola said: "It was dreadful and my feet were frozen. Barefoot on firm ground is one thing, running without shoes in mud quite another and it was a big mistake. While naturally pleased, I didn't experience the elation of Lisbon the previous year, rather a sense of relief."

If she had worn spikes, the result would surely have been more emphatic. But Zola not only retained her individual title but won team gold after her team-mates Carole Bradford, Ruth Partridge and Jane Shields placed well to earn England the title in front of a live audience on both BBC and ITV television in the UK.

Getting hold of the medals proved trickier than expected, though, when Lamine Diack, a vice-president of the IAAF, refused to present Zola with her prize. "As far as I am concerned, she is a South African," snapped Diack. "I have nothing against Miss Budd, but I cannot give a prize which will be seen as propaganda for South Africa."

Twenty years later, as president of the IAAF, Diack made amends by inviting Zola to the global governing body's annual gala in 2006 in Monte Carlo, where he made his peace with her by inviting her on stage for an impromptu presentation. Still, Diack's Swiss snub spoiled Zola's moment of glory in 1986 and the Senegalese sports official was destined to suffer a humiliating fall from grace when he was embroiled in a corruption scandal shortly after leaving his post as IAAF president in 2015.

Diack's frosty treatment of Zola mirrored a wider pan-African antipathy towards the athlete. Across the continent there was wholescale disgruntlement that a South African-born athlete, who was still largely living in South Africa, was running on the international scene and the disgruntlement from various African nations would ultimately force her out of the major event of the year, the Commonwealth Games, which were due to be held in Edinburgh in July and August.

The controversy surrounding her desire to run in the Commonwealth Games would soon consume her and her form began to slide. Straight after the world cross country win, Zola won a televised road mile race in Newcastle but was then beaten by Jennings in the Cinque Mulini – an historic cross country race in Italy with a unique course that sees runners pass through a series of water mills.

Returning to training, Zola hurt her hamstring during a circuit training session in May. It seemed an innocuous injury at the time but ruined her season and she would later look back on it as a turning point in her career as it created a domino effect of physical problems.

The injury combined with scrutiny over her "Englishness" and pressure to spend more time living in Surrey instead of South Africa ultimately led to her being forced out of the Commonwealth Games. Still only nineteen, she naturally wanted to be with her friends and family in South Africa. To make matters worse, 1986 saw Zola visiting England for races for the first time without Labuschagne, which added to her difficulties because despite their increasingly strained relationship she did miss his company.

Earlier in the year Marea Hartman from the Women's Amateur Athletic Association of England had sent Zola a letter about her eligibility for the big Edinburgh event and warned her that she needed to have spent at least six months living in England during the twelve-month run-up to the Games. As the debate swirled, Zola was not the only sportswoman drawn into the crossfire, with Annette Cowley, a South African-born swimmer with British parents but who was living and studying in the United States, finding herself in a similar position.

Initially, Zola did not think the residency issue would be a big issue but the Commonwealth Games Federation was displeased with the scenario and not happy with the idea of a South African-born athlete being at the Games. Anti-apartheid groups were also angry and Sam Ramsamy of the South African Non-Racial Olympic Committee led the complaints when he said: "Zola's record is abysmal. She comes to England only for athletics events. Banning Zola Budd means putting another nail in the coffin of apartheid."

In her 1989 autobiography, Zola wrote that she was "bewildered by the controversy my trips to South Africa had stirred up, hurt by the antagonism of the African countries, indignant at the attitude of the Commonwealth Games Federation, at a low ebb emotionally from my clashes with Pieter and literally hamstrung, I reached the point where I was simply fed up with the whole thing."

In the end, Zola and Cowley were ruled ineligible for the Games. Despite this, British sporting links with South Africa still led to the event suffering a massive boycott and only twenty-seven of the fifty-nine eligible nations took part as African, Asian and Caribbean countries voiced their protest by not turning up.

Doing her best to try to shrug off the problems, Zola's outdoor track campaign started well with an impressive 4:01.93 win at the TSB Women's AAA championships in Birmingham. It was an exceptional time in windy conditions as Zola blew apart a field that included Sly – the Olympic silver medallist having beaten Zola in their only two previous clashes – and observers such as former UK 1500m record-holder Boxer felt it was worth 3:58 in stiller conditions.

But in such poor spirits mentally and struggling with an injury, Zola's season soon went downhill. After nursing her sore hamstring through a low-key 3000m in 8:34.43 in Belfast, she headed into a 2000m race against Puică in the Peugeot Talbot Games at Crystal Palace and suffered a painful defeat at the hands of the Romanian. The Olympic champion had been a notable absentee at the same meeting twelve months earlier when Mary and Zola clashed over 3000m, but this time she stormed home in a world record of 5:28.69 ahead of Yvonne Murray while Zola, who was unwisely racing barefoot on a wet track, wound up third in 5:30.19 and could barely walk afterwards due to the pain in her thigh.

Murray, who would later go on to win European and Commonwealth titles and Olympic bronze, became only the second British athlete to beat Zola after Sly and she said: "I'd always dreamed of beating Zola although I never thought it'd come true."

To make things worse, Zola was quizzed after the race about the Commonwealth Games and said: "I am not the real reason for the boycott. They are using me as a pawn and it makes me angry. I have my personal political opinions but I don't see the necessity to make them public. It is against my principles to make my political opinions public."

Zola's wretched season continued with an 800m in Barcelona where she clocked only 2:07.04, the kind of time she had run aged 15. Then, after watching the Commonwealth Games from the sidelines, she finished only fourth over 2000m in 5:44.48 in a UK versus Commonwealth match at

Gateshead. Running a sluggish 72 seconds for the final lap compared to 66 seconds by the winner, Debbie Bowker of Canada, Zola was also beaten by Benning and Liz Lynch – the latter, like Murray, a rising Scottish star who had just won Commonwealth 10,000m gold and would go on to win the world title five years later as Liz McColgan.

Zürich's Weltklasse followed on 13 August with another heavy defeat for Zola. Still struggling with her hamstring tightness, she finished 11 seconds behind Kristiansen over 3000m as the Norwegian beat Puică with 8:34.10. Back on British soil a few days later, though, she defied her grumbling hamstring by beating Kirsty Wade, a Welshwoman who had won an impressive Commonwealth 800m and 1500m double in Edinburgh, over 1500m in 4:05.56 in an international match at the Copthall Stadium in north London.

It was a much-needed confidence boost prior to the European Championships in Stuttgart. After being thwarted in her attempt to race at the Commonwealth Games, the continental clash in Germany became Zola's sole championship focus for 1986, but it was to end in failure.

Relying on anti-inflammatories to numb the pain of her hamstring injury, Zola boldly tackled the 1500m and 3000m in Stuttgart. The longer distance came first and, wearing spikes on a wet track, she was overtaken by Puică and the Russian Olga Bondarenko halfway through the last lap before Murray also stormed past in the home straight to earn the bronze as Zola finished out of the medals. Bondarenko, who would go on to win Olympic 10,000m gold in 1988, ran 8:33.99 to beat Puică by two seconds, while Zola was more than four seconds behind the winner in 8:38.20.

The omens were not good for the 1500m and Zola predictably struggled. After a spell at the front, she was thrashed by a field that was so strong that even Puică could manage only fifth as Zola finished back in ninth in 4:05.32. In a time just outside four minutes but with a sizzling last lap of 58.9 seconds, Ravilya Agletdinova and Tatyana Samolenko scored a Soviet one-two and to add insult to injury Zola was only the second Briton home again after Wade passed her to finish seventh.

Stuttgart '86 was a glorious championship for British athletes with victories from Coe, Cram, Thompson, Whitbread, 5000m runner Jack Buckner and sprinters such as Linford Christie and Roger Black, but Zola's performances epitomised the lack of success on the track for British women.

A season that started so promisingly with a world cross country title defence ended miserably on a damp track in Stuttgart. The year did, however, see Zola gain a new-found independence and she remained keen to pursue her international running career. So much so that she finally split with Labuschagne at the end of 1986 and on the advice of British promoter Norman she began to train under the guidance of Harry Wilson, a coach who had guided Ovett to world records and Olympic 800m glory in Moscow. What's more, she decided to flip her life around by living in England and spending holidays in Bloemfontein and looked into joining a university course at Surrey University or Kingston Polytechnic.

For American athletes, 1986 did not feature any major championships. Some got stuck into the grand prix circuit and others treated it as an off season, while Mary saw it as an ideal chance to become a mother.

The 1985 season had not only been a fantastic year for Mary, but husband Richard built on his fourteenth place in the 1984 Olympics by throwing a lifetime best of 65.16m in the discus to rank twenty-seventh in the world. When it came to the end-of-year awards, the honour of being named top woman athlete of the year was close between Mary and East German sprinter Marita Koch. But Koch's late-season 47.60 400m at the World Cup in Canberra, a time which still stands as a world record today, edged it for many, with *Track & Field News* naming the East German as its number one ahead of Mary, although Koch's achievements have since been discredited due to the discovery that GDR athletes were part of a state-sponsored doping programme.

Settling into a family routine, Mary soon fell pregnant. "I plan to stay fit through the whole pregnancy," she said. "I will run and train pretty hard but I'll just be a little more cautious with the way I feel."

Unable to race, she watched as rival runners took some of her titles and records. During the indoor season, for example, Jennings broke Mary's world two miles best. But it was a happy period for the American as she basked in the glory of her 1985 triumphs and on 30 May 1986, she gave birth to a 7lb 5oz girl, Ashley Lynn Slaney. "Motherhood hasn't changed my perspective on running at all or slowed me down. I think I can compete for another seven years at the highest level," said Mary, who started running again just six days after the birth.

According to sports science theory, female endurance athletes often return from childbirth stronger than before. But Mary's first race back – fourteen weeks after giving birth – ended in defeat as she was beaten by Puică in the Fifth Avenue Mile on the roads at the end of the 1986 season. With 4:19.48, Puică broke Sly's course record by three seconds as Mary wound up sixth in 4:32.01, more than 12 seconds behind the Romanian.

The following week Mary won a low-key mile race in São Paulo in 4:42.64. But it would prove her last track race for eighteen months as a new wave of injuries turned her comeback into one long series of setbacks, starting with a tailbone fracture sustained during childbirth and an Achilles operation in November 1986.

Increasingly, Mary and Zola were spending more time on the physiotherapist's couch than the training track. After a couple of road races in Japan and Phoenix in February 1987, the year turned into a write-off for Mary due to injuries with further Achilles surgery in June. Zola fared little better either, missing the 1987 track season due to a stress fracture in her right hip and then racing only a handful of times on the roads during the English autumn period.

It meant both athletes missed the 1987 World Championships in Rome – an event that saw Tatyana Samolenko of the Soviet Union win the 1500m and 3000m, while Kristiansen took 10,000m gold. Instead, Mary spent the period enduring several operations on her right Achilles tendon, undertook work as a television analyst and remained driven to get fit for 1988. "The Olympics are extremely important," she said. "Everything I do between now and then is with the Olympics in mind. If it means risking injury, I am not going to do it. The Olympics mean too much to me."

As well as Rome, Zola missed the chance to seal a hat-trick of world cross country titles in Warsaw in March 1987. In an attempt to stay in shape, she began swimming a lot but it was only when she was introduced to a Johannesburg-based kinesiology expert that she began to solve her injury nightmare.

Dr Ron Holder met Zola on the eve of her twenty-first birthday in May 1987 and would become a key figure in the latter part of her career. Originally, Holder had trained as a chiropractor but was enjoying success as a sports injuries guru who specialised in creating running shoe inserts – or orthotics – to solve biomechanical problems. Such was his ability, one of his clients, an arthritis sufferer, left him a Van Gogh painting in her will. For Zola, the doctor's techniques soon unlocked the mystery of her hamstring problems and the duo became friends.

Meanwhile, Fanie van Zijl, one of South Africa's top middle-distance runners, was developing from a friend and advisor into Zola's unofficial coach. A South African champion from 800m to 5000m in the late 1960s and early 1970s, van Zijl possessed the knowledge and background to help Zola re-establish herself on the world scene now that Labuschagne was no longer guiding her.

So began a strange period where van Zijl operated secretly as Zola's coach while, back in England, Wilson was an unwitting 'front man' – a ruse designed to avoid annoying the critics who were agitated by her South African links. British athletics officials even supported Zola's lifestyle by using money from her trust fund to fly her back to South Africa three times a year so she could train in warmth and see Holder and van Zijl as much as possible. Clearly disgruntled by the arrangement, Wilson voiced his disapproval in July 1987 when he heard Zola was trying to get back running by using Holder's orthotics. "I am very concerned about her," he complained. "If she continues running on the hip, it may affect her walking in the future."

A coaching relationship that had been manufactured by Norman was inevitably doomed and Zola soon officially split with him. Bryant, her old friend from the *Daily Mail* who was now working at the *Independent* newspaper, was appointed as the new coaching 'front man', while van Zijl carried on advising her behind the scenes. It was a bizarre set-up and one that would end in disaster.

Older, wiser and slightly heavier – especially around her shoulders due to all of her swimming and cross-training – Zola was making big changes in her life and the next men to be dispatched were Boonzaaier and Momberg as her business advisors. With this, she extricated herself from the Zola Budd Sports Trust and attempted to start a fresh chapter with a new team behind her.

On returning to racing in September 1987 after her spell on the sidelines, Zola made the dubious decision to race under a false name in a minor cross country race in Horsham. Ironically, she had used an alias during her original arrival into England in 1984 and now she was using another bogus identity – this time Miss T Davies – so the press would not realise she was back racing.

Predictably the move backfired and the media had a field day with the story. Not that Zola was too concerned. By now she was becoming more bulletproof to their coverage, partly by refusing to read articles written about her, and was mainly concerned with improving her fitness now her injury had been solved. "It's not magic but science. Just biomechanics," said Zola, when asked about Holder's treatment. "He found my hamstring was not the problem, only a symptom of it."

Building momentum, in late September Zola ran a pleasing 32:17 over 10km in Bangor, Northern Ireland, and then beat Elly van Hulst, the world indoor 1500m champion, over 3km on the roads in Biella, Italy. The success would be short-lived, though, as Zola's career was about to come tumbling to a halt. More injury problems were poised to emerge, but the real damage was done by African members of the IAAF who were determined to stop her racing at the 1988 Olympics.

The seeds of Zola's problems in the run-up to the 1988 Games were sowed in June 1987 and on New Year's Eve in '87 when she attended a couple of South African athletics events. At the first, in Brakpan, she was merely watching the action but made the mistake of doing a training run while the races were taking place, innocently overtaking a few veteran competitors in the process. "One of the high points of the day was when Zola Budd came and ran a couple of laps," reported the *Brakpan Herald*. "She really made people's heads turn and soon had the crowd in a buzz."

Then, at a New Year's Eve 10km race in Randfontein, she cycled around the course before being unexpectedly coerced into giving out a few flowers to athletes. It was all very innocent but when the news found its way to the IAAF it infuriated some members who felt she had breached IAAF rule 53 (1) which said an athlete should be suspended if they have "taken part in any athletics meeting or event in which any of the competitors were, to his or her knowledge, ineligible to compete under IAAF rules".

With South Africa still banned by the IAAF, Zola was judged to have "taken part" in the event. It was all hugely debatable because she certainly did not race and neither did she officially hand out prizes. The athlete later described it as a "witch hunt" and broke down with nervous exhaustion as IAAF council members tried to drive her out of the sport in Olympic year.

Desperate to race again in the World Cross Country Championships – held in Auckland in March 1988 – Zola ran in the McVitie's British cross country trials in Gateshead on 30 January. But struggling with more injury niggles and with pressure beginning to mount from the IAAF following her South African athletics 'appearances', she finished fourth in a race won by Angela Tooby. Although it did not affect the result, the race also suffered from another course invasion when a trio of demonstrators burst onto the course carrying an anti-apartheid banner before being hustled away by officials.

Looking a shell of the athlete who had won world cross country titles in 1985 and 1986, Zola finished half a minute behind Tooby over a distance of little more than 5km, but it was good enough to qualify for Auckland. The problem, though, was that African nations were now threatening to boycott the event if she ran. So Zola reluctantly made an honourable decision and ten days before the championships she pulled out in order to avoid jeopardising the chances of her GB team-mates.

It was just as well because the situation quickly escalated, making the race in Auckland seem the least of her problems. By March the IAAF went through with its threat to suspend her from all international competition for breaking its rules by attending the South African races the previous year. Basing its decision on newspaper articles and without taking the trouble to actually hear from the athlete herself, the twenty-three-man council found Zola guilty and in April recommended to the BAAB that she should be given a twelve-month ban.

The get-together at the Park Lane Hotel in London of the IAAF council, which included Diack, left Zola waiting nine hours for the verdict, which conveniently meant they ran out of time to discuss the men's long jump scandal from the 1987 World Championships in Rome where host nation officials tampered with one of Italian Giovanni Evangelisti's marks in order to get their man onto the podium. Added to this, IAAF president Primo Nebiolo was under pressure to help IOC president Juan Antonio Samaranch avoid the kind of boycott that had blighted the 1980 and 1984 Olympics, not to mention the 1986 Commonwealth Games.

"Whatever the BAAB decides, it cannot win," wrote Martin Bailey in the *Observer*. "If the Board supports Budd and refuses to suspend her, it risks being expelled and British athletes could be excluded from world events, including the Seoul Olympics. If the Board bows to international pressure and bans Budd, she could go to the courts, the suspension could be overturned and the legal costs could bankrupt the body that runs British athletics."

Bailey continued: "It is a sign of Budd's naivety that it apparently never occurred to her that the brief appearance (in Brakpan) would provide the ammunition which her critics were looking for to try to end her Olympic hopes."

Unimpressed with the IAAF's treatment of Zola, Prime Minister Thatcher described the suspension as "repugnant". Around 100 Conservative MPs signed a paper urging the BAAB to reject the IAAF's demand for Zola to be suspended and Thatcher said: "A number of us find it repugnant that so much effort is being expended in stopping a young woman from competing in international athletics."

By now, though, the situation was beyond repair. After having tried to make things work in her new country, Zola decided all her efforts were in vain. Whatever the BAAB ultimately decided, in the eyes of the global governing body of the sport she was now officially an athletics outcast and she saw no point remaining in England and had no stomach for an expensive and prolonged legal battle. The BAAB was due to stage its hearing on 21 May to consider her case, but she realised the writing was on the wall and on 9 May she packed her bags for South Africa.

"Despite having reassurances that I have broken no rules," she said. "I am not well enough to continue the fight to prove my innocence. I am, therefore, on medical advice, withdrawing from international competition during this period of recovery. I sincerely thank the many people in Great Britain who are supporting me during this crisis and I hope that in future I will be able to represent them internationally once more."

Beneath the polite statement, though, Zola was crumbling and a British doctor who examined her during the period described her as "a pitiful sight, prone to bouts of crying and deep depressions".

"The IAAF is altering the rules to suit a political stance," blasted Bryant, as he appeared with Zola on ITV television to talk about the suspension. Rules are rules and must be kept to, but on this occasion no rules have been broken."

Showing little mercy and justifying the pressure on her, IAAF member Hassan Agabani of the Sudan argued: "She has a South African coach, a South African doctor, a trust fund in South Africa and a sponsor with South African interests. Zola was granted British citizenship at seventeen and we hoped she would cut her ties with South Africa. But now she has turned twenty-one there is no excuse for her behaviour."

Tony Ward, the BAAB spokesman during the mid to late 1980s and early 1990s, said: "There's no doubt Les Jones and Andy Norman warned Zola about her repeated trips to South Africa but she seemed quite insensitive to their advice and suffered from being too single-minded, not uncommon among athletes. Another problem was that everyone involved with her became overprotective and there was no one capable of forcing her to stand up for herself."

Rumours in the press that Zola was contemplating suicide were over the top. But Zola was without doubt emotionally exhausted and Brasher summed it up in the *Observer* when he wrote: "The teeth of the piranhas, and her own self-inflicted wounds, have reduced her to a skeleton."

With Zola forced into exile, her old adversary began to recover her fitness during 1988. The Seoul Games in South Korea were fast approaching and Mary was increasingly poised to race in only her second Olympics.

The Oregon Twilight Meet in Eugene on 7 May 1988, was Mary's first track race since becoming a mother and her first on the track for almost two years. Showing little sign of rust, she coasted to an easy 1500m win in 4:09.14 and was in an optimistic mood as she looked ahead to the rest of the season, saying: "I've never experienced pain like I did during labour. Now I can push myself so much harder. I don't think women have pushed themselves as far as they can physically, which is why I believe women are going to run a four-minute mile one day."

Tuning up for the US Olympic trials with an 8:49.43 3000m in San Jose and a 4:21.25 mile in Eugene, Mary appeared to be easing back into her best form. Then, racing over 1500m and 3000m in Indianapolis in July, she qualified for the Seoul Games in style, although Florence Griffith Joyner soaked up most of the plaudits by setting a phenomenal world 100m record of 10.49 in a glamorous one-legged sprint suit.

Competing first in the 3000m at the US trials, Mary clocked 8:42.53 for an easy win. She then faced tougher competition from Regina Jacobs in the 1500m but scorched to the third fastest American time in history with 3:58.92. After such a commanding display, Mary looked on course to challenge for gold at the Seoul Games, but her Olympic curse was set to continue.

Travelling over to Europe for a couple of races on the eve of the Games, Mary suffered a surprising defeat over 3000m at Zürich's Weltklasse when she was out-sprinted by the Dutch runner Elly van Hulst – 8:33.97 to 8:34.69. Disastrously, Mary had come down with a viral infection which led to her returning home to Oregon where she took a course of antibiotics before beginning her second Olympic campaign feeling not at her best. Then in her first race in Seoul – a 3000m heat – she hurt her calf muscle after becoming tangled with other runners. "I don't run well in traffic, obviously," she said.

Mary's races in Seoul took place in the shadow of the Ben Johnson drugs scandal, which unfolded when the Canadian sprinter tested positive after running a world 100m record to beat Carl Lewis. If Moscow 1980 is remembered for Coe versus Ovett and LA 1984 for Mary's clash with Zola, then Johnson's sprint performance would be the dominant story of the 1988 Olympics and would later be described as 'the dirtiest race in history'.

The day after this infamous 100m final, Mary forged to the front in typical style in the women's 3000m final and ran the first kilometre at world record pace. Still in the lead at halfway, she had not managed to break the field and with the pace slowing and with two-and-a-half laps to go, her US team-mate Vicki Huber, British runner Murray, Paula Ivan of Romania and 1987 world champion Samolenko swept past, causing Mary to almost trip in the process.

There were shades of LA four years earlier, but Mary stayed on her feet this time to finish, although she faded woefully to wind up tenth in 8:47.13 and 21 seconds behind the winner, Samolenko, who with a sub-60 last lap clocked 8:26.53 to beat Ivan, with Murray third and the Olympic silver and bronze medallists from Los Angeles, Sly and Williams, finishing seventh and eighth.

"It was a textbook case of what happens when you go out too fast," she told reporters at the Games, shrugging her shoulders. "I ran a good race, for the first half, but I played into other people's hands. I went out too fast and was a little too ambitious. I just thought I was going to do my best and see what happens. This being the Olympics, I just didn't want to get caught, get trapped."

Gallantly, Mary went on to contest the 1500m as well, but was again found wanting and finished eighth in 4:02.49 as the 3000m runner-up Ivan led from start to finish to clock an Olympic record of 3:53.96. In the early stages, Mary tried to go with Ivan, but the Romanian was determined to run the sting out of the finish of Samolenko and eventually broke away to win by a massive seven seconds clear of runner-up Laimutė Baikauskaitė of the Soviet Union and later Lithuania as Samolenko took bronze.

For the second Games in a row, Mary saw gold go to a Romanian rival. Unlike Los Angeles, though, there were no histrionics or tears. Instead she said philosophically: "All in all, considering past Olympics to now, this one was pretty good. I made it through the Olympics without being devastated. I've been trying so long and so hard to be successful at the Olympics, it's almost like it's not meant for me. I've been obsessed about it but not anymore. My life has become so much more rounded now with my family. Before it was always just my running. Now I have things that mean more."

Mary and Zola are renowned for their controversial clash in 1984, but their lives were arguably embroiled in just as much scandal from 1989 to 1997 as their careers entered the home straight. Most of it happened off the track, too, especially for Zola, who was afflicted by personal problems, including divorce and the death of her father.

Following the IAAF's decision to suspend her, Zola spent 1988 on the sidelines and skipped Seoul. The next year, though, proved just as eventful, though, when she got married, dealt with the news that her father had been murdered and brought out an autobiography that saw her denounce apartheid publicly for the first time ever.

"You only have to study the Bible to recognise the injustice of apartheid," she wrote in a life story simply entitled *Zola*. "The Bible tells me all men are born equal and that we will all be equal before God. I can't reconcile segregation along racial lines with the teaching of the Bible and as a Christian I find apartheid intolerable."

Justifying her long-time silence on the topic, she explained: "As a sportswoman, I should have the right to pursue my chosen discipline in peace. Wendy Sly isn't asked if she voted Labour or Conservative. Seb Coe does not get asked to denounce Soviet expansionism; and Carl Lewis is not required to express his view on the Contra arms scandal. But I was not afforded that courtesy and it became a matter of principle for me not to give those who were intent on discrediting me the satisfaction of hearing me say what they most wanted to hear. But that was not the only reason why I remained silent," continued Zola, who also went on the BBC with her belated denouncement of apartheid. "Only a fool speaks publicly on a subject they know very little about and in my late teens I was certainly no expert on political systems."

There is no doubt Zola would have saved herself a lot of heartache if she had mentioned these views earlier. Years later, it emerged Momberg had tried – and failed – to get her to sign the following: "I, Zola Budd, hereby declare my total objection to any form of discrimination, be it race, religion or language." It was a short, simple statement but her fiercest critics later admitted they would have left her in peace if she had put her name to that solitary sentence. Yet instead she waited until she had been pushed out of the sport before saying something.

The seventeen-year-old girl who had been cast into a whirlwind of pre-Olympic hype and expectation at the start of 1984 was now a young woman in her early twenties. Older, wiser and more mature, it was time to make public the views she had always held privately. It was also time to get married and on 15 April 1989, she wed Mike Pieterse, the son of a wealthy Bloemfontein businessman whom she had first met in 1986.

"At a time when I was feeling very unsure of myself after being sacrificed by the IAAF as they pandered to their Third World members," Zola wrote in her autobiography. "I suddenly found this lovely man – my big cuddly teddy bear is how one press report described him – and it was virtually love at first sight. He was the sort of man a girl dreams about – solid, dependable, loving and a lot of fun."

Zola was so besotted, she took the unusual step of proposing to him and the wedding was a happy day in many ways bar one. Zola was still at odds with her father and despite putting him on the guest list she wanted her brother, Quintus, to give her away.

Not surprisingly disgruntled by the news, Frank threatened to take Quintus out of his will. In the end, Frank was uninvited from the wedding and Zola's father-in-law walked her down the aisle.

Afterwards Frank told a reporter: "I no longer have a daughter called Zola." He also angrily forbade her from attending his funeral or being buried in the Budd family plot, although no one could predict he would die later the same year.

Secretly, Frank had been undergoing chemotherapy for cancer of the liver, but it would not be the disease that would kill him. Instead, he was murdered on 22 September by a twenty-four-year-old Afrikaner, Christian Johannes Botha Barnard, who claimed Frank had made homosexual advances towards him.

Frank's blood-soaked body was discovered lying sprawled across his bed. The fifty-six-year-old's cheque book and pick-up van were both missing and he had been shot twice with his own gun. An occasional worker on Frank's farm, The Hope, in Bloemfontein, Barnard was arrested the following day and convicted of murder and theft but was sentenced to only twelve years in prison because of 'extenuating circumstances'.

Barnard had at least seven previous theft and fraud offences to his name and was described in court as a dishonest witness. But the judge decided there was reasonable possibility that Barnard had been provoked into the killing following the sexual advances.

Looking back, Zola said of her father: "We had no contact before his death. I would have liked to have a reconciliation. I would have liked to remind him that I had once loved him. There was no chance and it is a terrible thing not to have said, 'I love you'."

On her father being a closet gay, she added: "If he had been born twenty years later, his life too would have been different and he might never have got married. But society didn't accept homosexuals back then and it all took a terrible toll on him."

Zola's friend Bryant once maintained that Frank had two ambitions – to shake the hand of the Queen of England and be worth a million pounds. "He nearly achieved both," Bryant added.

Looking back, Frank's behaviour was more of a hindrance than a help to Zola during the traumatic 1984 period. Greedily squandering most of the fortune the *Daily Mail* had bestowed on the Budds, he spent lots of his time in posh hotels, did not travel to Los Angeles in 1984 after a spat with his family and then after the Olympics sold his story to the British tabloid *Sunday People* newspaper. A cantankerous character, in addition to spoiling Zola's wedding he stayed outside the church when Zola's sister Estelle got married because he had lost an argument with the minister over what music should be played.

At this stage in their careers, Zola and Mary were not as intense about their athletics results. Compared to her meltdown in 1984, Mary treated her 1988 defeats with a relative shrug of the shoulders and seemed to have come to terms with her career being defined by performances outside the Olympic arena, whereas Zola was happily settling into what would become a temporary retirement. "I've seen it all and been through it all," Zola told Julie Cart of the *Los Angeles Times* in early 1990. "Running is very artificial and when I look back on three years of running, I don't really feel I have achieved a lot, especially as a person."

Midway through 1989, soon after her wedding, Zola also cut her ties with Britain irreparably when she released a statement saying she had "decided not to return to the United Kingdom to pursue my running career".

Then there were the ravages of injury, which were the bane of Mary's life and had also affected Zola from 1986 onwards. The middle of 1989 also saw Zola suffer from tick-bite fever and encephalitis, the latter being a debilitating illness with flu-like symptoms and a swelling of the brain.

Neither Zola nor Mary could stop running, though. The simple act of putting one foot in front of another had brought them lots of heartache, yet it remained their passion and their cathartic escape from the stress of everyday life. They were born to run and getting their daily fix of endorphins from a simple training spin around the local roads or trails was as much of a habit as brushing their teeth.

When asked about her addiction to running by *Running Times*, Mary said: "It's a feeling that's difficult to put into words. It's like being a junkie. I love to run. I crave it. I get my fix and I just want more. Running isn't hard for me. I don't equate running with pain. For me, the only time running hurts is when I'm injured."

Inevitably, though, they began to slow down as the rare talent they had been blessed with began to evaporate with age. Mary's air of invincibility was vanishing fast, while Zola stretched her legs on the South African scene in low-key events.

Given Mary's catalogue of injuries, it is a miracle that she would enjoy one final Olympic appearance in 1996. These included Achilles surgery in June 1989 and more Achilles problems in 1990, while in 1992 the combination of recovering from surgery on a tendon in her foot for plantar fasciitis and an iron deficiency led to her finishing a disappointing sixth in the US Olympic trials 3000m in New Orleans behind winner PattiSue Plumer. "I felt fine for the first few laps, when I led. But then, I just didn't feel all that good," said Mary, who clocked a slow 9:02.60 – more than 20 seconds behind Plumer.

In the 1500m at the 1992 US Trials, Mary fared a little better as she finished fourth – missing a place in the team by one tenth of a second. Ahead of her, Jacobs won the race from Plumer with third-placed Suzy Favor Hamilton denying Mary the chance to go to Barcelona as she passed her in the home straight. It would be the first of three Olympics for Favor Hamilton, who a couple of decades later gained notoriety after admitting to leading a double life as an escort.

More surgery in May 1993 and September 1994 almost broke Mary and she finally considered quitting. "The pain was like toothache, throbbing whether I was standing, sitting or lying down," she told the Eugene *Register-Guard* newspaper, describing her Achilles problems.

The 1995 season was no kinder as she suffered three stress fractures in her feet. Yet somehow she ploughed on, now coached in the post-Seoul era by Bill Dellinger, the 1964 Olympic 5000m bronze medallist and former assistant coach in Oregon to Bowerman, together with increasing input from Salazar as the distance legend's competitive career drew to a close.

"I knew she was a good runner and she was talented but it has kind of caught me by surprise just how talented she really is," said Dellinger. "It's hard to compare women runners to men, but she is probably the most talented person I've ever worked with."

As she tentatively returned to running after her eventful 1988-89 period, Zola found a new coach as well in August 1989. Enjoying life as a newly-wed back in South Africa, she got into a routine of running every morning at dawn followed by a session with a group of nearby college runners who trained under the wing of Van Zyl Naude.

At the Pieterse household on the outskirts of Bloemfontein, Zola typically surrounded herself with a menagerie of animals – five dogs, three cats, turkeys, chicken and geese. In such a happy environment she soon began to regain her old fitness and in the early months of 1991 began to enjoy a series of clashes with rising South African star Elana Meyer.

Born only a few months after Zola in 1966, Meyer had lost many times to her rival during her youth. But while Zola bloomed at an early age, Meyer had developed more steadily and was now, aged twenty-three, reaching her peak. Establishing herself as the new South African number one, Meyer broke Zola's national 5000m record and then, after the pair had swapped victories during the season, Meyer won a big 3000m showdown in late April in Durban.

Racing in the city's Kings Park Stadium in front of an 11,000-strong audience at the Nedbank Prestige meeting, Meyer ran 8:32.00 to beat Zola's 8:35.72 – both times being the fastest the world had seen for two-and-a-half years.

Then the unthinkable happened. South Africa had not competed in the Olympic Games since 1960, but moves to let the country take part in the 1992 Olympics in Barcelona began to gather momentum.

Zola originally moved to England partly because she could never foresee South Africa being allowed to take part in international sport during her lifetime. Yet now it was looking increasingly likely to happen following the efforts of the nation's state president, FW de Klerk, to push through reforms that would see the end of apartheid. Allied to this, IOC president Samaranch was keen that his home city in Spain would host not only the historic reintegration of South Africa into the Olympics but would witness a unified German team for the first time since 1936.

"This time I will wait until there is some final word that we are truly welcomed back," said Zola cautiously. "I shan't go near an aeroplane leaving South Africa until the official stamp is on the invitation. But, oh, when the time comes, it will be wonderful – especially when we are allowed into the Olympics. There we will be, a true South African Olympic team, and many of us will be black, of course, and we will be marching into the stadium in Barcelona, all together. There will be lots of tears and very full throats on that day. I look forward to it very much."

The political will to end the boycotts that blighted sport in the 1980s was obvious and the Barcelona Games ushered in a new era where major sporting events once again featured a truly global line-up of competitors. Not only did South Africa and a unified Germany take part in the 1992 Games, but Cuba and Ethiopia returned to the Olympics for the first time since 1980, a dismembered Soviet Union competed under the title 'Unified Team', while the Baltic states of Latvia, Estonia and Lithuania arrived in Spain as individual nations.

The scene was set for an emotional, indelible moment that would capture the mood of the occasion. It came in the women's 10,000m and involved a white South African runner, but it was not Zola but instead her fellow countrywoman Meyer, who was involved in a memorable duel with Derartu Tulu of Ethiopia.

Despite her fame and the hoo-ha surrounding her participation in Los Angeles in 1984, Zola was destined never to win an Olympic medal. South Africa had been excluded from the Games since 1960 and before that the only female athletes to win medals for South Africa were high jumper Esther Brand, with gold, and 100m sprinter Daphne Robb-Hasenjäger, with silver, at the 1952 Helsinki Olympics. As South Africa re-entered the Olympic arena in 1992, Zola seemed the most likely South African to break the medal drought. Yet the honour ironically fell to an old teenage rival whom she had regularly beaten during the early part of her career.

With a typically gritty mid-race surge, Meyer overtook reigning world champion McColgan and broke away part way through the 25-lap race, drawing Tulu with her. The pair then became locked in battle for the final two miles until Tulu finally sprinted clear to become the first black African woman to win an Olympic medal, while Meyer earned South Africa's first medal since 1960.

Joining hands, Tulu and Meyer enjoyed an emotional lap of honour that instantly became a classic Olympic moment. At the time, the athletes barely realised the significance of their post-race embrace, but it created an iconic image, reminding the world that the friendships forged at the Games can transcend political and racial differences.

As for Zola, she was not at her best and finished ninth in her 3000m heat in Barcelona. Racing in the green and yellow colours of South Africa, she ran only 9:07.10 to finish 20 seconds behind her heat winner, before seeing a final won by Russian Yelena Romanova in a slow 8:46.04. Drained by the tick-bite fever she had contracted a couple of years earlier, Zola suffered relapses from the infection for a further decade before it eventually left her system. "Tick-bite fever is like Lyme disease," she told *Sports Illustrated*. "It never leaves your system."

Post-Barcelona, Zola's form failed to improve as she was easily beaten by Mary in a road mile race in Sydney in October. Naturally, Australian journalists billed it as a 'rematch of the LA 3000m', but it was now eight years after the 1984 Games and both athletes were past their best, so it not surprisingly ended up as an anti-climax as Mary led from start to finish to win in 4:22.68 to Zola's 4:32.60 as Krishna Stanton of Australia finished third in 4:35.20. With the city keen to impress as it bid to stage the 2000 Olympics, an estimated crowd of 250,000 lined up to watch the runners charge down the city's George Street, but they were merely experiencing the end of an era.

Later, Australian television successfully got Mary and Zola into the same studio for a joint interview. But like the road race itself, there were no fireworks as both athletes politely insisted they bore no grudge over what happened in LA, although there was still a little tension in the studio during an awkward few minutes of questions.

If Zola's career had a last hurrah then it came five months later at the 1993 World Cross Country Championships in Spain. Again running in South African colours on a flat course in Amorebieta in the Basque Country, Zola managed to beat the Barcelona one-two of Tulu and Meyer, not to mention McColgan and a young Paula Radcliffe, but was still outside the medals.

Meyer led in the early stages, but faded out of contention to finish sixth, while Olympic champion Tulu failed to finish due to a knee injury, McColgan was fifth and Radcliffe 18th on her senior World Cross Country Championship debut. Up ahead, Zola wound up in fourth place, ten seconds behind winner Albertina Dias of Portugal with Catherina McKiernan of Ireland second and Jennings third.

Zola would make three further appearances at the World Cross Country Championships but she was unable to recapture her winning form of 1985-86. Twelve months later, in Budapest in 1994, for example, she finished in seventh and was one place behind Meyer in a race won by Hellen Chepngeno of Kenya. On home soil in Cape Town in 1996 she was fifty-ninth and in Turin in 1997 the demise was complete as the two-time champion wound up eighty-sixth, a full two minutes – or almost half a mile – behind the winner, Tulu.

Despite her declining form and the fact she now represented South Africa, Zola remained a big draw in England. In January 1994, for instance, she was paid £10,000 to take part in her first cross country race on British soil since leaving the UK in 1988. Racing in Durham, Zola finished eight seconds behind Radcliffe, although the winner received only £2,000. "I was surprised to learn what she was paid," said Radcliffe, "but then Zola has achieved so much more than me and I don't run for money."

Approaching thirty, Zola felt it was time to start a family. Her daughter, Lisa, was born on 24 October 1995 and on 20 April 1998, she gave birth to twins, Azelle and Michael. Thereafter, not surprisingly, Zola's elite racing career fizzled out, although she has never completely stopped running or racing.

The swansong of Mary's career would come in 1996-97 when she raced in the Atlanta Olympics and then won silver, aged thirty-eight, at the World

Indoor Championships before later being stripped of the medal by the IAAF for an anti-doping offence. What should have been a glorious end to a mammoth career was instead clouded with controversy and a drugs positive test that still causes confusion to this day.

First was the US Trials in Atlanta in June 1996 where Mary attempted to earn selection for the 5000m, an event that was making its Olympic debut that year. Aged thirty-seven, Mary clocked 15:29.39 to finish runner-up close behind Jennings. Qualification for the Games was not without a fright, though, as she was tripped slightly from behind by Amy Rudolph with 200m to go.

As she stumbled and nearly fell, was there a flashback to LA '84? "Yes, briefly," she told reporters, before being asked how the achievement of making the 1996 Games rated in her career. "It's right up there," she replied, "simply because it was a long shot to be here."

Mary was not so fortunate in the 1500m at the trials as she failed to make the final. But the real disaster happened off the track at the event as she failed a drugs test that would not become public for a considerable time after.

The following month at the Olympics, Mary failed to make the 5000m final as she ran only 15:41.30 for seventh in her heat. In her absence, gold was won by Wang Junxia, a controversial Chinese runner who had smashed world records in unbelievable style three years earlier fuelled by, among other things, a diet of turtle blood and caterpillar fungus.

Licking her wounds after the Games, it seemed as if Mary was now too old and injury prone to make an impact on the global scene. "How can I be in this stadium and not run well? I tried, but it just wasn't there," said Mary, who soon after the Atlanta Games was diagnosed with exercise-induced asthma.

She had done well to merely make her third Olympics and could not expect much more. Or could she? Because seven months later she almost snatched victory in the world indoor 1500m final in a close battle with a fellow veteran runner.

Rolling back the years, Mary found herself challenging one of her old Russian foes, Podkopayeva, for the title in Paris as the two athletes gave runners half their age a lesson in middle-distance running. Amazingly, Podkopayeva was forty-four years old and had won a bronze medal in the outdoor world 1500m final behind Mary fourteen years earlier in Helsinki, but she held on to win by three hundredths of a second from the thirty-eight-year-old American in 4:05.19.

It was a tremendous way to conclude a phenomenal career. There was just one problem. Mary's drugs test positive from the 1996 Olympic Trials would soon rear its ugly head and cast an unshakeable shadow over her career.

CHAPTER NINE

DISAPPEARANCE

"Dwelling too much on what's already happened
– good or bad – will drain you."
Mary Decker Slaney

THE IRONY OF Mary's drugs positive test at the 1996 US Olympic Trials is that throughout her career she had always been a fierce anti-doping campaigner. She did not hesitate to pour scorn on Eastern bloc runners who produced suspiciously strong performances and was an outspoken critic in numerous interviews.

"I'm proud I've got to where I have got to without drugs," she told *Women's Own* magazine in 1985. "When you look at some of the unfeminine women on the circuit, it's enough to make you think twice about considering them."

Later, in 1990, she claimed that ninety per cent of the world's top twenty athletes in each track and field event took drugs. "I've walked into restrooms in Europe and seen the backs of athletes and thought I was in the wrong restroom," she said.

In comparison with muscular Eastern bloc athletes, Mary always gave the impression of being a natural runner. Like Usain Bolt and Haile Gebrselassie in more recent years, her smooth, graceful style and slim physique meant she did not arouse suspicion among fans. This did not make her immune to allegations from cynical observers, though.

These began as early as her teenage years, as she told *Track & Field News* in 1980: "It (my success) isn't something my local pharmacist has given to me to make me great – which has been insinuated. That is depressing and irritating."

Keen to emphasise she was drug-free, for a while she wore a T-shirt given to her by a friend that carried the slogan: "100% Natural – No Chemical Additives". She explained: "It's appropriate because the first questions people have asked me are 'How?' or 'Why?' and the second is, 'What are you taking?' Don't they realise I have had enough already that I don't need things like that?"

So when she failed a drugs test late aged thirty-seven, it came as a shock to many. Lots of fans in the sport had fond memories of 'little Mary Decker'. As a teenager in the 1970s, she oozed raw talent as she whizzed around the track with her pigtails flapping in the wind. She then went on to be a standard bearer for women's distance running through the 1980s. Given this, the news was met with disappointment and disbelief.

Here are the facts of the case. Mary's urine sample at the US Olympic Trials in June 1996 had tested positive for the male sex hormone testosterone. She received a letter after the event to tell her the news but was allowed to continue racing at the Atlanta Olympics and the following year's IAAF World Indoor Championships, where she won silver.

Belatedly, the news of the positive test eventually broke in May 1997, two months after her world indoor medal-winning run. Although even then the revelations came not from her national or international athletics governing bodies but via her lawyer, Doriane Lambelet Coleman, a professor of law at Duke University and former 800m runner, who told the *New York Times*: "There is no question Mary is innocent. She's been tested probably more than any other athlete. She's never tested positive. She's never taken testosterone or any other steroid. We feel the evidence is clear and will be proven."

At this stage Mary had not been suspended and was free to compete and was targeting the IAAF World Championships in Athens in August 1997. Not surprisingly, though, once the news of the drugs failure became public it was difficult for Mary to train and race.

Within days, the IAAF suspended her from competition without due process. The governing body had grown frustrated with the fact the case had taken more than a year to be sorted out. "The IAAF has rules and when a federation does not follow them we have to do something," said IAAF president Nebiolo. "I've become numb," said Mary, who was forced to sit out her national championships in July 1997. "For months I've been jumping through bureaucratic hoops."

Three months later, though, she was cleared and reinstated by her own national governing body. Two lawyers, a pharmacologist, a statistician and an endocrinologist – all paid for by Nike – presented her case to the USA Track and Field doping hearing board, while Don Catlin, head of the IOC accredited laboratory in Los Angeles, spoke on Mary's behalf. "Mary Slaney committed no doping violation last year," the hearing concluded.

After being cleared by USATF, she furiously demanded compensation, saying: "I'll go to litigation. I'll take no prisoners. I'm angry. Why would I have taken drugs? What kind of compensation would I have in a good result if it wasn't natural or legal?"

Yet Mary's nightmare was far from over. After the USATF decision, the IAAF cleared her to compete but took the case to arbitration where, in April 1999, a panel ruled against her. This led to a retroactive ban, which meant she was stripped of the world indoor 1500m silver she won behind Podkopayeva in 1997. Refusing to concede defeat, Mary filed a law suit against the IAAF and the US Olympic Committee – the latter being the body in charge of the original test – but the court ruled it had no jurisdiction on the matter.

"It is a sham," said Mary's lawyer, Coleman. "It is sad that the worldwide governing body of track and field should choose to prop up this sham doping test programme at the expense of one of its greatest athletes. That they have chosen this course merely reveals the corrupt nature of that organisation and the fact it has no interest whatever in a scientifically sound programme."

The drugs positive test outraged Mary and the details of the case created widespread confusion. To fail a drugs test, the ratio of testosterone to epi-testosterone had to be greater than 6/1. The normal ratio is 1/1 and Mary's was 9/1. But Mary claimed she was menstruating at the time of the US Olympic Trials, taking birth control pills for the first time in her late 30s and had enjoyed a couple of glasses of red wine the night before her race and subsequent drugs test – all factors which could have caused fluctuations in the ratio of testosterone and epi-testosterone.

This was supported at the time by studies conducted by Manfred Donike, a former Tour de France cyclist and chemist who was an expert in the area of drug testing. In his experiments, Donike showed that on the twenty-first day of a menstrual cycle, one woman's ratio of testosterone to epi-testosterone varied from 1.72/1 to 12.6/1 and another woman's from 1.4/1 to 8.2/1 – both on a single day – with alcohol seemingly helping to act as a catalyst.

Then there was the case of Diane Modahl, a British 800m runner who won Commonwealth Games gold in 1990 but failed a drugs test for testosterone in 1994. Initially, she was branded a cheat but she always maintained her innocence, despite a testosterone to epi-testosterone ratio of 42/1, and was eventually exonerated after proving that the laboratory in Lisbon, Portugal, that analysed her sample had seriously flawed test procedures. This included storing her urine at 35°C for several days, causing bacterial degradation of the sample.

After a lengthy, bitter and expensive legal battle, Modahl was cleared and the costs of the case helped bring the British Athletic Federation to its knees as it went bankrupt in 1998. "We can no longer trust the laboratories to get it right," said IAAF general secretary István Gyulai. "We have to test the testers more often."

The Modahl case was playing out when Mary tested positive, so there were logical comparisons between the two cases. As part of her defence, Mary also claimed her ratio of testosterone to epi-testosterone had been 3/1 at the Pre Classic in late May, a fortnight before her positive test, all of which created doubt over a case that was far from straightforward.

The law of strict liability in drugs testing says that athletes are responsible for what is in their body. Yet the Modahl case showed doping tests can be flawed and the testosterone to epi-testosterone ratio test has since seen its standards tightened from 6/1 to 4/1, while testers also run a carbon isotope test on unusually high readings.

"Cases today are prosecuted only on the basis of valid and reliable evidence," Coleman later wrote. "That was Mary's goal in suing the IAAF. Despite press reports suggesting otherwise, Mary did nothing wrong."

Speaking to the *Register-Guard* in 2001, Mary said: "The most positive thing that came out of it is that USA Track & Field recognises that it's a flawed test. And as an American, this is where I live and people know and understand I'm not a cheater. And that's important to me, all by itself. Some people still start stories with 'she had a positive test'. Well, it wasn't a positive test. It never was . . . and yet you get this little demerit next to your name. Well, it's a big demerit from where I sit."

Twenty years later, Mary is still fuming about the case and her husband told Kerry Eggers of the *Portland Tribune* in 2015: "The test was total BS. The problem is, somebody leaked it to the press. The initial statement was, 'Mary tested positive,' which was not true. Had they not leaked it to the press, no one would have ever heard of it, because the test was clearly wrong."

He added: "The fight stopped being about Mary. The fight became about the test. It was just ridiculous. I spent a year of my life learning something that was totally useless in anything else I ever did. All it did was make me angry, because they knew that they were doing it wrong."

Details behind doping bans vary hugely. Lance Armstrong infamously took a cocktail of drugs for years and was protected by the omerta – or code of silence – in the Tour de France peloton until finally admitting he had cheated in an Oprah Winfrey interview. Ben Johnson took steroids to break the world 100m record in Seoul in 1988. At the opposite end of the spectrum there are cases that divide opinion, such as Maria Sharapova's positive in 2016 for meldonium, a substance which had only just appeared on the list of banned substances and which the tennis player claimed she was given by a family doctor. Or how about Christine Ohuruogu, the world and Olympic 400m champion, who was given a one-year ban and castigated in the media after missing – as opposed to failing – three drugs tests.

Whatever the circumstances of the drugs ban, though, the athlete's reputation is damaged irreparably in the eyes of many. So despite the confusion surrounding Mary's test in 1996 and the fact she was cleared by her own athletics governing body, her image took a serious hit and it undoubtedly contributed to her withdrawing from the athletics scene.

Mary raced just a handful of other occasions. In late August 1997, while suspended by the IAAF and USATF, she ran for a Nike elite team in the Hood to Coast Relay in Oregon. This was followed in spring and early summer 1998 by three wins in Eugene, including a 5000m victory at the Pre Classic in 15:23.72. Then, on the eve of her fortieth birthday, she tackled the 5000m at her national championships in New Orleans in June and dropped out with two laps to go with a sore right foot as a competitive running career that had started in 1971 finally drew to a close.

Banned from competing and with age and injuries taking their toll, Mary drifted away from the sport. After years in the spotlight, she retreated into a quieter, family life in Oregon. Similarly, Zola became less visible on the sporting scene as she busied herself by bringing up her three children and took part in fewer top-flight competitions.

The intrusive media attention that had plagued Zola since 1984 had also made her weary. She was still viewed as the 'villain' in some quarters as well. Her long-time refusal to denounce apartheid had not impressed many people, while a few continued to blame her for tangling with Mary in Los Angeles.

At one stage, Zola even compared herself to Osama bin Laden to illustrate the ill-feeling some Americans felt towards her. Summing up the misfortune that dogged her during her life, William Oscar Johnson described her in *Sports Illustrated* as having "the legs of an antelope, the face of an angel and the luck of a leper".

Despite increasingly keeping a low profile, Zola was born to run and could not resist testing herself in road and cross country events especially. Granted, her best days were behind her, but she continued to race regularly in South Africa and even occasionally on the international scene.

At times, it was a humbling experience. At the 11.5km Corrida de São João road race in Portugal in June 1999, for example, she was twenty-third and three minutes behind the winner, Julia Vaquero of Spain, while at the South African 10km championships in November 1999 she finished eleventh in 35:35, well behind runners she would have easily beaten in her heyday and three minutes behind Meyer, who won in 32:01.

Into the new millennium, Zola even returned to England a few times to race on the roads in London. "After everything that happened, I suppose some might be surprised that I have the audacity to run again," she said.

Again, her results were a far cry from her peak period in the early to mid-1980s. But she was enjoying her running and building up to tackle one of her biggest, unfulfilled ambitions – the marathon.

Her debut over 26.2 miles came in London in 2003 and naturally spawned a flurry of articles, especially in the British press. Most notably, the *Daily Mail* covered Zola's comeback in London with one of the key writers when the paper brought her to England in 1984, Wooldridge, penning an almost apologetic column to welcome her back. "It is a relief to see her with a ravishing smile on her face," Wooldridge wrote, sounding more than a little guilty as he compared Mrs Pieterse's happy demeanour to the miserable Miss Budd who had endured a British baptism of fire in 1984.

Wooldridge added that he regretted mentioning Zola's British grandfather when he first started writing about her in early 1984 and admitted that he later tried to dissuade his editor from going ahead with the plan to bring the athlete to Britain. "I cited the fact that, fast though the seventeen-year-old may be against the clock, the shoving, elbowing, hurly-burly of the Olympic track would be too much for her slender frame and inexperience," he explained, before concluding: "We wish Zola a much happier stay in London over the coming weekend. I guess it's the least we can do."

The mood of the British media was very different to 1984 as they sheepishly set the scene for Zola's marathon appearance on the roads of the British capital. They were not the only ones who had changed, though. Zola's looks and personality had altered considerably. It was a topic Wooldridge touched upon, but Rory Carroll in the *Observer* went into more detail.

"She does not resemble the Zola Budd that Britain remembers," Carroll stated. "The hair is longer, the legs tanned and muscular for so small a frame, the feet bare, the face of a pixie, with lines around the eyes indicating this is no longer a teenager. The biggest difference is the expression. Photographs from the 1980s show a jaw-clenched grimness as if she is angry, or about to cry, but today she seems genial and relaxed. Red-painted toenails make even the famous feet look cheery. Budd, thirty-six years old and a married mother of three is vaulting out of obscurity and back into the public eye to run in the London Marathon."

On the eve of the race, she suggested she would be keen to run for South Africa in the Athens Olympic marathon in 2004, although it came with a disclaimer. "I do not want to become a professional athlete again, not with three kids," she said, "but I believe I can run a sub-2:30 marathon."

Unfortunately, the race did not go well. Zola's pre-race goal on her London debut was 2hr 40min, which was the kind of time that would have placed her about fifteenth and put her within striking range of the 2:32 Olympic marathon standard. But she dropped out with six miles to go with low blood sugar levels.

Before the race, Zola had joked: "Paula Radcliffe will be showered and changed and on her way home by the time I cross the finishing line." It did not turn out to be much of an exaggeration either as Radcliffe set one of the most incredible world records of all-time with 2:15:25 – a time so fast that it proved beyond any British male runner in 2003.

A rough debut marathon did not put Zola off the event. Runners typically say 'never again' after tackling 26.2 miles, but ultimately cannot resist doing it again at some stage in future. Once bitten by the marathon bug, the distance has a powerful pull and Zola went on to run several more as she entered her forties.

She even won a few – in Bloemfontein in 2007 in 3:10:30, in Charleston, South Carolina, in 2014 in cold, windy conditions in 2:59:42 at the age of forty-seven and also in Columbia, South Carolina, in 2015 in 3:05:27. The most high-profile marathon appearance, though, came in New York City in 2008 when she broke the three-hour barrier by a few seconds on a course not renowned for being fast. Later, in 2012, Zola ran a little quicker, too, when she clocked 2:55:39 in Jacksonville, Florida.

The 2003 London Marathon illustrated that Zola could savour her running without the fierce expectation and criticism that ruined the enjoyment of her sport in 1984. "My life is happier and more stable than ever," she said. "I'm a survivor."

Zola was enjoying being a mother and in 2002 finished a psychology degree. Unlike most of the previous men in her life, her husband also stayed out of her running and left her alone to enjoy it. She had seemingly engineered a near-perfect lifestyle, although the married bliss would soon end in dramatic style.

In March 2006 Zola filed for divorce due to her husband having an affair with a South African socialite and beauty queen contestant called Agatha 'Pinkie' Pelser. Back in the 1990s, Zola had forgiven Mike Pieterse for a fling with a student and the pair had undergone marriage guidance to help cement their relationship, but the Pelser affair was the last straw.

"I suspect they are still having an affair," said Zola. "He is getting a house ready for her in Waverley (a Bloemfontein suburb). She has played a role in our divorce. I have no idea how long it's been going on for, but I guess about a year."

As well as the longevity of the affair, Zola held suspicions that Pelser tried to poison her dog. Given this, she was also worried about the safety of her three children and frustrated by her husband's attitude, as she explained: "Why do all husbands deny it? I have no idea. But I have more than enough evidence that he is having an affair. More than enough."

In July 2006, Zola won a legal order preventing Pelser from coming anywhere near her. During the court hearing, Zola claimed Pelser had called her at 2.00 a.m. one night, saying "this is a fight to the death". It also emerged that police had been involved in a lengthy stand-off with Pelser after being told she had a gun in a house she was renting from Zola's husband and was planning to shoot herself, or anyone who entered the building. Finally, after seven hours of negotiations, police talked Pelser out of the house and she was charged with a firearms offence and also breaking into the property of Zola's now estranged husband.

Once again Zola's life had been thrown into turmoil and was attracting negative headlines from the press. Eventually, she was reconciled with her husband. "Marriage is like cycling," Zola later told Steve Friedman in a *Runner's World* feature. "There are only two types of cyclists – those who have fallen and those who are going to fall. It's the same with marriage – those who have had problems and those who are going to have problems."

The whole Pinkie Pelser episode ended in tragedy, though, when she committed suicide four years later. Aged just thirty-eight, the twice divorced mother of two was found dead in a car behind a petrol station near Bloemfontein. A pipe was connected from the exhaust to the inside of the vehicle and there were pills and alcohol in the car too.

During the stressful separation from her husband, there was a happier moment for Zola towards the end of 2006 when she was given a special, surprise award at the IAAF Annual Awards gala. Twenty years earlier, IAAF official Diack refused to present Zola with her medal at the World Cross Country Championships due to her South African links. But now, after rising to become IAAF president, Diack made amends by inviting Zola to the governing body's grand gathering and then inviting her on stage.

"I had a lot of admiration for her as a runner because, even barefoot, she proved that Africans could win major competitions," said Diack. "But I refused to present her medal in Neuchâtel because for a lot of years I was fighting apartheid and she was a symbol of it."

He added: "This wasn't an apology for what happened in 1986. That was made in 1992 when South Africa returned to the sporting community. Zola was a young girl and not responsible for what was happening but we were not prepared to make any sort of compromise. I tried to find a way of getting her to Monaco for our gala and fortunately this year she accepted my invitation."

A surprised Zola responded: "I didn't think that after all these years something like this would happen. It shows how the world can change. I knew at the time that he had refused to present me with my gold medal but I saw it as part of all the hassles that were happening around me."

In 2008, Zola's life entered a new chapter when she moved from Bloemfontein to the United States. In spring of that year, she made her peace, albeit posthumously, with her father by visiting his grave for the first time since he died nine years earlier. Then, during the summer, she moved to Myrtle Beach in South Carolina with her husband and children.

Travelling on a temporary visa, Zola's arrival in the United States coincided with the eve of the New York City Marathon, which she completed in 2:59:53. "Somehow," wrote Bryant in 2009, "the years, the troubles, the traumas, the protests and the injuries have never robbed Zola of her passion for running."

At her new home, situated on the eastern coast of America and renowned for its year-round sunshine, Zola was able to enjoy daily runs on the long stretches of sand and grass, while husband Mike, a keen golfer, was excited by the excellent courses on their doorstep. It was a pleasant place to raise a family and the move fitted in with Zola's ambition to race on the US masters scene for veteran runners.

With the use of the internet and emails now widespread, Zola was also able to keep track of news in South Africa and it was impossible not to notice the rise of a teenage running phenomenon called Caster Semenya. In 2009 Semenya burst onto the international scene by breaking Zola's South African junior 800m record with an impressive 1:55.45 to win the world title in Berlin and it is a measure of Zola's continuing interest in the sport that she emailed one of her old *Daily Mail* minders, Neil Wilson, to alert him to the doubts over Semenya's gender about a month before stories and speculation appeared in the media concerning the athlete's sex.

The controversy over Semenya and the dramatic rise and fall of Paralympic sprinter Oscar Pistorius ensured that South African athletics stayed in the spotlight. Yet even at the height of their infamy they struggled to generate as many headlines as Zola was capable of. It was now many years since she had tangled with Mary in Los Angeles, but she just could not shake off her celebrity status.

The name 'Zola Budd', for example, became embedded in South African culture as a slang term for a taxi. "Only a Zola Budd will get me to work on time now," locals would say. It was a topic that Brenda Fassie, an anti-apartheid pop star who was nicknamed 'the black Madonna', found herself singing about the runner with the lyrics: "Zola . . . taxi, runner, you decide," while there was a similar ditty by British band Chumbawamba on their Sportchestra album.

Perhaps making up for missing a normal student life in her late teens, Zola completed a masters in pastoral counselling in 2010 and signed up to become a volunteer track coach at Coastal Carolina University. "We value her ability to relate to the athletes and share the wisdom of her experience," Alan Connie, long-time coach at Coastal Carolina University told *Grand Strand* magazine. "They have a great respect for what she's accomplished in her life. She is one of the most famous track-and-field distance runners that has ever lived."

Keen to keep strong links with South Africa, Zola's family spoke Afrikaans at their home in Myrtle Beach. Mike Pieterse maintained business links in Bloemfontein, too, while Zola took on the job of marketing the Newton Running shoe brand in South Africa.

A relatively young company in the running market, Newton bills its products as 'natural running shoes' and has ridden the wave of interest in minimalist footwear in recent years as it has grown rapidly out of its Colorado base. Due to her background and notoriety as a barefoot runner, Zola seemed the perfect ambassador to promote such shoes and was employed to boost the brand, especially in her homeland. Linked to this, Zola also wrote the foreword in a book by Ashish Mukharji called *Run Barefoot Run Healthy*, where she pointed out running without shoes was normal in South Africa and her national record-holder for the women's 100m and 200m and the first South African to run a sub-four-minute mile were barefoot runners.

Around this time, Zola's children were beginning to show some talent. Following in her mother's barefoot strides, daughter Lisa began to show particularly good ability when she was sophomore at Carolina Forest High School in early 2013. This included winning a state title and an 18:35 clocking for 5km where she shattered the former high school course record of 20:07 before soon after improving to 17:47; although there was a dash of irony at one big race when she tripped and fell shortly after the start of the South Carolina Cross Country Championships, finishing fifth.

"She made me run when I was younger, but just to stay healthy and active," Lisa said of her mother in an interview with *My Horry News*. "I won a local meet in my age group and that influenced me, it clicked that maybe I have talent."

Lisa's siblings, Mikey and Azelle, are also talented. After her own athletics excellence led to such a traumatic period in her late teenage years, though, Zola is cautious and is keen to play down their ambition. "Running should not be too goal-focused at that age," she said, adding: "There is more to life than being a full-time runner."

Children often copy their parents, though, and Zola was leading by example with her marathon victories, while in 2011 she appeared at the World Masters Athletics Championships in Sacramento, California, where she won silver in the 8km cross country race. Racing in the over-35 category for South Africa, the forty-five-year-old finished runner-up to Soledad Castro Soliño of Spain and told the *Sacramento Bee*: "I probably started out a little too fast, but it was good healthy competition and I really enjoyed it. We were having fun and it's more low-key than other international competitions."

Being the child of a famous athlete is never easy. They will often inherit their parent's talent, but along with this there is an unfair pressure from onlookers for them to perform in the same style. Zola refused to put this burden of expectation on her children and Mary adopted the same attitude. Her daughter, Ashley, grew up without any great interest in athletics, despite going to lots of track meetings as a child when Mary was still racing competitively. The young Miss Slaney was more into dancing and learning languages than running, although she did enjoy a one-year stint as an editorial assistant at *Triathlete* magazine as she began to forge a career in journalism.

After initially studying romance languages for four years at the University of California, San Diego, Ashley went on to do a master's degree in journalism and digital media at Arizona State University before settling down to work in Chicago. "We have a beautiful, smart, talented daughter," said Mary in the *San Diego Tribune* in 2009. "And I'm very proud of Richard. His business (buying and selling aircraft) is doing well. We live in a beautiful part of the country."

Increasingly at one with herself, Mary had just two problems. The first – and worst – was that she could no longer run freely due to all the injuries she had sustained during her career. Then there was the non-stop, repetitive questioning about her fall at the 1984 Games. Such hassle has no doubt partly led to her dropping out of the spotlight, although her thoughts on the 1984 incident never bore fans fascinated by it.

"I want to look at what comes next," Mary once told John Brant in *Runner's World*. "Dwelling too much on what's already happened – good or bad – will drain you." Her husband agrees it is not healthy to live in the past, saying: "There is no axe to grind. I'm sure there is some feeling inside but if you look inside, it eats you away. It's not like the Olympics owe you something."

Of course requests for comments would usually peak when one of her long-standing records fell. The most notable of these was probably in 2015 when Shannon Rowbury finally broke Mary's thirty-two-year-old US 1500m mark. "To break an American record that's stood for almost thirty-two years and was held by a woman who was really accomplished in our sport, I'm really proud of that," said Rowbury, in praise of her predecessor. Actually getting hold of Mary for reaction, though, is not simple.

Compared to Mary, Zola was maintaining a higher profile as the two women settled into middle age. Acting against type, Zola even embraced the opportunity to take part in a reality television programme when she joined fellow ex-athletes Fatima Whitbread, Kriss Akabusi and Dalton Grant in 2011 in the cooking contest Come Dine with Me. Appearing on Channel 4 in the UK, Zola prepared a cucumber zucchini salad, Malay beef curry and malva pudding but finished fourth and last. "She didn't stretch herself or do anything extraordinary," said Akabusi with a harsh verdict on her culinary skills, although Zola was still smiling as she described the experience as "definitely one of the strangest weeks of my life, but one of the most memorable as well."

When it comes to odd experiences, Zola had notched up more than most people. There was more to come, too. Since 1984 the runner's life had been a rollercoaster ride of controversies and another one was just around the corner when she was disqualified from South Africa's biggest running race.

The Comrades Marathon was first staged in 1921 and is not only a national institution in South Africa but the world's oldest and best known ultra-marathon. Taking place between Durban and Pietermaritzburg, it is a gruelling fifty-six-mile race and regarded as a rite of passage for any South African distance runner worth their salt.

After tackling a few marathons, moving up to the ultra-marathon and tackling Comrades was a logical step for Zola. Her debut came in 2012 when she clocked 8hr 6min 9sec – finishing thirty-seventh woman home – and then intended to have another crack in 2013 but withdrew with flu.

It did not take long before she was lured back by the challenge of Comrades. On 1 June 2014, Zola again took on the distance and ran superbly, aged forty-eight, to clock 6:55:55. Racing for the Umhlanga-based Hooters Running Club and as a tribute to Pierre Korkie, a running friend who was being held hostage by al-Qaeda in Yemen, Zola finished as the first South African woman home, seventh female overall and leading runner in the women's 40-49 age group. "When she came into the stadium at the finish, the entire stadium chanted 'Zola, Zola'. It was wonderful for her," said her manager, Ray de Vries.

Unfortunately, the celebrations did not last long. Word reached the KwaZulu-Natal Athletics, the association governing the sport in the area, that Zola's race number did not include the obligatory tag to state her age category. Pouncing on this technicality, Zola was stripped of her age-group prize. She still received her 25,000 Rand (about $16,000) overall prize money and medal for a sub-seven-hour finish, but she was denied the 12,000 Rand for finishing top woman in her age group.

Not surprisingly, the decision drew widespread criticism. Nine-time Comrades winner Bruce Fordyce said Zola earned her prize "fair and square". Another ex-winner, Tilda Tearle, added: "What a load of rubbish from the officials. Give Zola what she deserves or punish everyone who did not wear an age tag."

An exasperated Zola said: "My whole athletics career has been plagued by politics and interference from administrators who are selective and do not apply the rules consistently. I feel they are targeting me specifically. Why does this rule apply to me and not others?"

But KwaZulu-Natal Athletics president, Sello Mokoena, hit back, insisting the rule was not just a regional requirement but an IAAF rule. "The reason for the rule is so that every runner competing in a race can identify their competitor by their tag," he explained. "The rule is there to be fair to other runners. When one veteran passes another veteran on the road they can see 'here is my competition' and react to that. If you are not wearing that tag, the other runners are unlikely to know you are their competition and they may let you go and not try to run harder. Zola Budd knows that rule very well."

For a while, Zola threatened court action, mainly on a matter of principle. But eventually the matter was dropped as Zola returned to the United States to enjoy her running and family life in relative anonymity.

PART FOUR

WHERE ARE THEY NOW?

CHAPTER TEN

LIFE'S A BEACH FOR ZOLA

"Even now, running is my Prozac."
Zola Budd Pieterse

THE FIRST TIME I saw the barefoot bullet from Bloemfontein in the flesh, I was sitting on a giant rubbish bin. Two months after arriving in England from South Africa during the ill-fated summer of 1984, Zola was racing 1500m at the UK Championships and the venue, Cwmbran Stadium in South Wales, was packed with spectators. So much so that I improvised by viewing the action from the top of a wheelie bin between the main stand and the home straight.

It was a cold and blustery weekend in late May but everyone was gripped with Olympic fever in what was a golden summer for British athletics. A couple of years earlier the same stadium had witnessed judo star Brian Jacks defeating Daley Thompson, rugby player JJ Williams and World Cup-winning footballer Geoff Hurst in the BBC Superstars competition, but now it featured some of Britain's best track and field athletes vying for selection for Los Angeles.

During a busy two days the winners included Peter Elliott in the 800m and Kriss Akabusi in the 400m, while Nick Rose won an Olympic trial 10,000m race ahead of Steve Jones in controversial circumstances after Mike McLeod lost his shoe mid-race after tangling with Julian Goater. Losing almost 100m on the leaders, McLeod finished fifth but would later win Olympic silver in

LA, whereas the runner-up Jones went on to break the world marathon record five months later in Chicago.

As Zola lined up behind the curved start line at the start the back straight, spectators crowded around the grass verge on the outside of the track to get a closer look at the running phenomenon who was dominating that summer's newspaper front pages. Despite McLeod's mishap in the 10,000m the previous day, Zola chose not to wear shoes and she looked diminutive and vulnerable as she took her place in the ten-strong field.

The fears were almost justified, too, as Zola clashed with a rival approaching the end of the first lap, stumbled and nearly fell. But after passing through 800m in 2:12 she cut loose, effortlessly passing the leader Gillian Dainty, leaning into the wind and surging with such intensity that her rival abruptly slowed to a halt and dropped out, seemingly stunned by Zola's acceleration.

A seasoned international, Dainty was the Commonwealth 1500m silver medallist and eight years older than Zola. But the young British newcomer, who had turned eighteen two days earlier, demonstrated the reserves of stamina and speed that lay within her frail-looking body as she drew away from the remaining field to win by six seconds in a world junior record of 4:04.39.

More than thirty years later, Zola is still running. Or at least trying to. To mark her fiftieth birthday in May 2016 she intended to tackle the Comrades Marathon again in her native country. She has unfinished business in the famous ultra-distance race, planned to run in the colours of a company called Water from Air and even went on SABC television in South Africa in 2015 to proclaim her participation, but she later quietly withdrew after her preparations did not go well. "Lekker hardloop!" Zola posted on her Facebook page from her home in the United States on the eve of the race. Or 'have a good run!' in Afrikaans.

Running is still important to her. It defines her as a person and she will forever be a runner. Races like Comrades, though, are nice but not necessary these days. No longer is she a professional athlete but a busy mother who runs for fun and fitness, not to mention health and peace of mind. "Even now running is my Prozac," she told *Marathon Talk* in a podcast interview in 2012.

The shy, nervous waif who was overwhelmed by the events of 1984 is now a worldly-wise woman armed with the kind of confidence that her younger alter-ego would have loved to have possessed thirty years ago. Her child-like features, boyish hair-cut and porcelain skin have also been replaced by a thick mop of wavy hair and the kind of weather-beaten features typical of someone who has lived an outdoor lifestyle. Her pencil-thin legs are a little meatier these days but her running style is still the same, with elbows and heels that kick out slightly as she covers the ground.

More than anything, Zola smiles these days. In the 1980s, she did not do much smiling. Back then she was a forlorn emblem of the acrimony that bedeviled sport during that period. But more than thirty years later, she is a much cheerier character. The former "circus animal" – as she once described herself – has matured into a strong woman in charge of her own destiny.

Part of the reason for her happier demeanor is due to where she lives. Myrtle Beach in South Carolina is on the hub of the Grand Strand on the eastern coast of the United States and is one of the world's most idyllic cities. It boasts the kind of warm climate that Zola relishes and has sixty miles of beautiful sandy beaches – an appropriate landscape for the world's most famous barefoot runner.

The city has been described as the golf capital of the world and Zola's husband, Mike, is able to pursue his hobby on some of its 120 courses. The beach life and climate not surprisingly also makes it a popular tourist attraction.

Ironically, the country that brought her such misery in 1984 has now become her home. After the LA Games she was rushed to the airport under police escort amid death threats, but that turbulent summer of yesteryear is now a distant memory and she is happily bringing up her children – Mikey, Azelle and Lisa – in the same nation.

After initially serving as a volunteer athletics coach at Coastal Carolina University, Zola took on the more formal role of assistant coach in September 2015. So far the university's modest athletics achievements include producing Amber Campbell, an American Olympian in the hammer in recent years, but no doubt Zola will hope to help nurture more middle and long distance runners. Certainly, given her incredible background, she seems ideally suited to advising and inspiring young athletes. You could even argue that her wisdom, knowledge and experience is a little wasted in a modest college role like this.

Due to this, Zola's results as a veteran runner or news of her burgeoning career as a coach are more likely to pop up in *The Sun News* in South Carolina these days than the *Sunday Times* of South Africa or *Daily Mail* in Great

Britain. In 2016, however, Sky Atlantic broadcast *The Fall*, which relived, as this book does, that extraordinary summer of 1984 and both she and Mary featured at length throughout.

Not surprisingly, this is not the first time Zola has been the subject of a documentary. In 1989 the Welsh actor and documentary filmmaker Kenneth Griffith produced a BBC2 programme called *Zola Budd: The Girl Who Didn't Run*. During the programme Griffith, who was also a keen Boer War historian, claimed Zola's career had been undone by liberal hypocrisy.

A further BBC documentary in 2014 was scrapped after they had already conducted interviews with some of the personalities involved in the Budd-Decker story.

"Her life story is intriguing in so many ways," said her manager, Ray de Vries. "From being kicked around like a political football to betrayal both in her personal life and in sport."

Unofficial biographies, it is often said, are more interesting than carefully edited autobiographies. Just as well, because this book profits from the fact it has not been influenced by the demands of the athletes, agents or public relations people, as so many publications are these days.

In some ways, Zola's general lack of co-operation over the years to openly talk about her life speaks volumes too. She has always been something of an anti-celebrity and there are generally not many published interviews with her in recent years.

It is easy to dismiss Zola as anti-social and difficult to deal with, but friends and former athletes speak highly of her, and my own dealings with her have been extremely pleasant – when I was at last able to track her down. Even the fellow athletes who failed to get to know her well speak with sympathy about an enigmatic athlete who was treated like a circus animal by the athletics ringmasters of the 1980s. Others talk about a warm, loyal and kind-hearted personality that remained buried to the majority behind her taciturn and reticent public face.

One of her admirers is Liz McColgan. The 1991 world 10,000m champion and marathon legend is just two years older than Zola and says, "I knew Zola really well as I shared a room on a few trips and spent bit of time with her at some after-events parties. To me she was hugely misguided by the British athletics managers.

"She was very shy but very pleasant and funny. They tried to protect her by pretty much keeping her separate from everyone else, but I was pleased she came over to Britain as she lifted the standard of the girls running 1500m and 3km. I always found her chatty and good to spend time with but the general public never got the chance to know her."

Kirsty Wade, another of Zola's former room-mates and three-time Commonwealth gold medallist during the 1980s, agreed: "It felt like the situation was handled badly and Zola was just caught up in it all. She was probably pretty miserable."

Others were simply in awe, such as the world marathon record-holder Paula Radcliffe, who remembers, "Hers were inspirational performances that made tough targets as British records and I loved watching her run free in her best races."

Radcliffe, who was only ten years old when the Los Angeles Olympics took place, later raced as an up-and-coming athlete against a Zola who was in the twilight of her career. "One abiding memory," Radcliffe recalls, "is of Zola stopping to removing her spikes while she running for South Africa in the World Cross Country Championships in Spain in 1993 – and then coming flying past me barefoot! She was ahead of me early in the race, then stopped at the end of the first lap or the beginning of the second, untied and removed her shoes and then flew past me to finish fourth."

A number of British athletes agree with McColgan that Zola helped inspire a generation of runners. Jill Boltz (née Hunter) won silver behind McColgan in the 1990 Commonwealth Games 10,000m and set a world best for 10 miles on the roads. Now based in Australia, she still exchanges occasional messages with Zola on Facebook and says: "I had a photo of Zola on my fridge door for motivation. I thought she was amazing – running so fast so young and often in no shoes! Then one year I got to race and meet her so of course was absolutely in awe. Although there was no need for me to be as she was so down to earth and encouraging."

Journalists do not manage to get so close, which is understandable after the way they helped made her life a nightmare in 1984. Steve Friedman met her for a *Runner's World* feature in 2009, however, and described her as being "pleasant without being effusive, charming without being gushy". Amusingly, he added, she was not wearing shoes when she answered the door.

Few athletes have attracted as much controversy as much as Zola. From her athletics breakthrough in 1984 to the details surrounding the death of her father to her husband's dalliance with Pinkie Pelser and the society belle's subsequent suicide, there are more than enough awkward incidents in Zola's past to make her wary of prying journalists. It could explain why she has become a slightly distant figure, detached from the core athletics fraternity. Psychologists might suggest she is still trying to run away from her infamous clash with Mary in 1984.

Zola is not totally averse to being interviewed, though. In a two-part interview with Tom Williams from *Marathon Talk* just after the London Olympics, she spoke about why she rarely watches television, struggles with hypoglycemia and ran fast due to her passion and not talent, as Williams tackled the major areas of her life in skilful fashion.

In a similar way to Mary, Zola revealed she first discovered her running ability at school when she found she could out-run older boys in the playground. "When I grew up we were still close to nature, living unspoiled with no technology," she said. "I grew up without any television so most of our time was spent outdoors.

"The first time we got televisions in South Africa was 1976 and I think we got ours later than that, so I wasn't really that aware of what was going on in the rest of the world regarding sanctions and politics, or even what was going on in my own country. I had a really sheltered, protected childhood."

Zola is definitely not a couch potato and the habit of not watching television has carried on into later life. Even today she only switches on the TV to watch channels such as Animal Planet and claims she does not watch the Olympics when it is on.

On running barefoot, she told *Marathon Talk*: "When I was growing up I had two pairs of shoes – one for school and one for church – and that was it. We were barefoot most of the time. Even now the general rule in South Africa is keep your kids barefoot for as long as possible and don't put them in shoes and that's the way to promote healthy development."

On the benefits of sans shoes, she explained: "You don't use your big muscles such as your quads as much. Instead you use your Achilles and your tendons and they don't tire as much. So for me it was more efficient to run barefoot. My cadence would be a lot faster and my push-off much better.

COLLISION COURSE

"It's all about timing, too. When you run with a big cushioned shoe, you don't know exactly when your foot hits the ground. When you are barefoot you know exactly where your body is in space at that moment in time. Also, when you're running barefoot you never put your foot down exactly the same way so your muscles are continuously having to react and respond and strengthen and relax. I felt lighter without shoes but it's not the weight of the shoes but the way you run."

Zola remembers almost stumbling into running as well. "I was really useless at netball and I couldn't swim very well. Tennis was out and I didn't like field hockey. So I was pretty much forced to do running as it was the only thing I could do. When I changed school in grade nine I started training with my then coach and within three years I started running South African records. It's just something that happened in a very short period of time."

Interestingly, when asked about talent versus upbringing, Zola said her performances were more due to the "passion" she brought to the sport. "There are other people who have much more talent than me," she said, explaining what makes her tick as a runner. "I think it's more about the passion for it. It's like Nietzsche said, 'if you know why you do something, you can do anything'.

"When I changed schools our family was struck by a very big tragedy when my sister passed away and she was everything in my life," Zola continued, "and running was more or less my saviour. Instead of turning to something like drugs, I turned to running. I was in a small training group where I felt accepted. I was really shy and it was the only place I really felt safe in a way.

"I put all the anger, resentment and hate that I had into running and it was a nice escape for me. And after training I was tired and I didn't have to talk and I didn't have to socialise. I could just be by myself. So it was definitely more about passion than talent because I ran with a lot of anger."

On being offered British citizenship in 1984 to run in the Olympics, she remembered: "I was racing in Stellenbosch and there were these strange people running around talking to my dad. Next think I knew my dad said, 'You can actually get a British passport and run internationally and in the Olympics this year.' That was like giving a child a free pass in a candy store because I thought, 'Wow, I can actually go and run internationally.'

"I remember asking them if there were going to be any repercussions or problems because of the political situation in South Africa and they just said, 'No'. They thought there might be a few upset people but that was about it!

"Our first international television broadcast in South Africa was a CNN news broadcast in 1989. So I had no idea what was happening in the rest of the world and most South Africans didn't even know what was happening in their own country. People don't believe me when I say that I didn't even know about the existence of Nelson Mandela, but he was born in 1962 and I was born in 1966 and his name or photograph were never published in any (South African) newspapers. Ignorance is not an excuse but if you don't know about something then you don't know about it.

"Going over to Britain was quite an eye opener for me, to suddenly see how my country was perceived and how I was perceived as a South African, as something quite horrendous, was a shock for me. It was both frightening and revealing."

Zola told *Marathon Talk* she did not want to race in Los Angeles due to a mixture of factors. The pressure and hype aside, her parents split up on the eve of the Games, she was struggling with an injury and she was physically and emotionally exhausted after raced on the track without a proper break from the start of the South African season in September 1983 until the LA Games eleven months later.

"So for me the Olympic Games was something I had to get over with so I could start the rest of my life," she said. "I knew once the Games was over the *Daily Mail* wouldn't be involved anymore and I could get on with my own life, start studying and do what I always wanted to do."

Amazingly, Zola still feels she is regarded as a racist by some people as well. "I was an easy target for the politicians at the time," she said. "And because I was Afrikaans and white and came from Bloemfontein, a small town in the middle of the Free State, people just labelled me as a racist and that I was representing the apartheid government. I found it very unfair and that's the way some people still perceive me even today."

As time passes, though, Zola is more philosophical about the experience. "I learned so much," she said. "There are only so many athletes at the Olympics who are able to win and if you don't win then it's not the end of the world. Your life still carries on. The Olympics is about competing and I was there competing. Sometimes I think, 'I could have had an Olympic medal,' but then I look at my life and look at my kids and, you know, it's fine."

Zola was in similar contemplative mood when she spoke to Eddie Wooten of the Greensboro *News and Record* in 2014, saying, "Life is as good as you make it. With age, there's a lot of stability, and I'm fine with that. I think my life is at a point where I couldn't ask for anything more."

In a 2010 interview with Michael Sandrock for *Runner's World*, she said her children have helped put the events of 1984 in perspective. "It was just another life event. It was important, but not as important as having kids."

On her home life, she revealed: "I never talk about my running," adding that 2010 was the first year she put a picture of herself running on the wall in her house.

Zola touched upon her hypoglycemia problem in the *Marathon Talk* interview in 2012 and she mentioned it again in an interview in 2014 with veteran runner and writer Gary Cohen. "I've always been shy about running a marathon because I have low blood sugar, or hypoglycemia," said Zola, when quizzed about stepping up to marathons. "So it's been scary doing the long runs and long races. But now I am getting used to it and for me it is a new challenge. I like to be challenged and that is why I do it – because it's really tough for my body. To start running marathons at my age is difficult but I enjoy the challenge."

This is why she finds ultra-marathon so satisfying, as she told Cohen, "With the Comrades Marathon it doesn't matter if you are first or the last person to finish. There is this elation and a feeling that you've done it. It's so special and all the years I was running, including winning the World Cross Countr Championships, didn't come close to the feeling I had of finishing the Comrades."

During most interviews the road inevitably returns to Los Angeles 1984, though. Speaking on SABC News in South Africa in mid-2015, she remembered, "If you run barefoot, there are three places to be – at the back, out in front, or way out on the outside. Mary was running at the front for the first three and a half laps in LA but then the pace started to slow down and I began to get boxed in.

"I could feel I was getting spiked because when you run barefoot you get spiked really badly – and I remember after the Olympic Games my feet underneath were spiked through. So I was getting bumped around and the only place for me to go was to go in front. This started the chain of events over the next lap that led to her falling.

"There are so many people going to the Olympics with so many high hopes and there are only a few gold medal winners so there are a lot of people – and fans – who come back from the Olympics very disappointed because not everyone can win a gold medal.

"You have to learn to live with what's good enough for you and that's something I was taught at a very young age."

CHAPTER ELEVEN

MARY RUNS AGAIN, ALMOST

"I have arthritis. I've had sinusitis.
I've had all the itises you can imagine."
Mary Decker Slaney

TRACKING DOWN MARY is not straightforward. She is elusive; maybe even slightly reclusive. After being in the sporting spotlight for so many years, she does not seek attention or publicity these days and I am told several times by her friends that she does not like to dwell in the past and prefers to look forward. It is fair to say she does not go out of her way to do interviews.

There is one place you are sure to find her, though. The Elliptical Cycling World Championships takes place just outside San Diego every October and has turned into Mary's main sporting target of the year. Well into her fifties and struggling with both arthritis and the after-effects of more than thirty surgical operations for injuries, she is unable to run freely or without pain nowadays. But riding an elliptical bicycle allows her to enjoy a similar feeling and movement to running, only minus the pounding. "It has," says her husband Richard, "been a godsend to her."

As dawn prepares to break over California on the day of the 2015 Elliptical Cycling World Championships, Mary and about forty other endurance athletes quietly assemble in a deserted car park. As the sun rises, she finishes her warm-up routine with some standing toe touches and makes last-minute adjustments to her racing bike, which differs from a traditional bicycle by being heavier, with smaller wheels and no seat. If she looks slightly nervous then it is because ahead of her lies a brutal, never-ending climb of almost twelve kilometres that rises more than 4000ft as it approaches the finish line near the top of the Palomar Mountain.

Some call it the Alpe d'Huez of elliptical cycling. Yet unlike the Tour de France there are no crowds of fans for this rather quirky event. Instead, Mary and her fellow competitors grind up the narrow and twisty road in lonely fashion with only a handful of curious, early-morning onlookers for company.

More than thirty years have passed since she sped to a golden double on the track in Helsinki and tangled with Zola in the Los Angeles Coliseum. Back then the eyes of the world followed her every stride. Now, she competes in relative anonymity.

One thing remains unchanged, though. Mary still has a desire to push her body through the pain barrier and she retains the hunger to win for winning's sake. This, for example, is the fourth time she has raced an elliptical bike up the Palomar Mountain and she vows to keep coming back until she wins the women's title.

So far, Mary has had a series of near misses and the 2015 event is no exception. She finishes runner-up to Sarah Brown, a twenty-nine-year-old international middle-distance runner from nearby Solana Beach who smashes the course record by eight minutes despite being in the early stages of pregnancy. Behind, as Mary charges through the finish line and into the arms of her husband, her consolation is a personal best on the gruelling Palomar Mountain course and a silver medal.

Mary does not look disappointed with second place. She looks exhilarated and a little relieved to have made it up the mountain in a good time and happily poses for post-race photographs with fellow competitors, most of whom are excited to have their picture taken with an athletics legend.

Later, everyone meets at the nearby headquarters of ElliptiGO, the leading outdoor elliptical bike brand, for the presentation of prizes. Mary is in a relaxed mood and even admits to being a little tipsy after a couple of glasses of champagne to celebrate her earlier performance. "The alcohol won't change anything I say," she smiles, as we prepare to take a jog down memory lane.

For someone who was so tricky to track down for an interview, Mary is incredibly friendly and generous with her time. She is chatty, has a good sense of humour and talks about her past exploits more than expected. Like most great athletes, she has a considerable air of charisma. If she has a reputation for being hot-headed and at times a little difficult to deal with, she does not show it. On the contrary, I find her to be charming, likeable and more than a little emotional as she stifles a few tears at least twice during our interview.

Most sports legends are a disappointment when you see them in the flesh and meeting them can be an anticlimax. They are sometimes rude and often aloof. Pleasingly, Mary is neither and welcomes me cheerily.

Physically, she looks as lithe as she did during her heyday on the track and admits to being only 4lb heavier than she was during her peak. The pigtails and braces that characterised "little Mary Decker" in the mid-1970s are long gone. Her hair is lighter these days, although it is not quite the bottle-blonde look that her nemesis in Los Angeles '84, Puică, famously sported, while her warm smile is one of a confident middle-aged woman at ease with herself.

Up close, though, there are plenty of signs of the ravages of time. Her lower legs and feet are covered in an incredible lattice of tiny white scars from her multiple surgical operations. Her hands, meanwhile, are riddled with arthritis and her fingers are twisted and gnarled.

Not that Mary seems self-conscious or vain about it. She makes a point of showing me what the arthritis has done to her hands and takes her shoes off to reveal her tapestry of scars and withered calf muscles. Naturally, there is regret in her face over what the disease and surgeons have left her with, but she has no qualms about letting me see her battle wounds and with a shrug of her shoulders tells me she is determined it will not stop her doing her new sport.

"Before I discovered the elliptical bike I was at a point where I was able to go out jogging," she says, looking back to 2012, when she was first introduced to the world of outdoor elliptical biking. "But I hate jogging. I really hate it. Shuffling along at seven or eight-minute mile pace is not satisfying. But that's all I could do because I could not get up on my toes anymore when I ran.

"So I got to the point where, for a few years, I didn't even want to do that because I felt if I could not run properly then I wouldn't want to be out there at all. But now, after training on an elliptical bike, I am fitter than I have been in ten years. Jogging slowly was more hurtful to me than doing nothing at all, but getting on this bike and riding and realising that I could push myself up a hill and push myself on the flat, I got 'that feeling' again. And I thought I'd never have that feeling again."

Looking back on her catalogue of injuries, the common theory during most of Mary's career was that the same biomechanics that helped her break world records were also to blame for her body continually breaking down. She was like a highly-tuned but incredibly fragile racing car.

"You know, that's what they say," she sighs, before proposing an alternative theory that culminates with the suggestion that most of her multiple operations were probably not even necessary. "Over all the years I was always accused of over-training and I don't believe I over-trained. I was not a high-mileage athlete," she explains.

"My high-mileage weeks were seventy to eighty miles but I couldn't do a lot of those because if I did do them then I would be hurt the following week. So when I performed at my best on the track in the middle-distances I was training right around fifty to sixty miles a week."

This compares to the estimated 140 miles per week that British distance runner Paula Radcliffe ran in the build-up to her world marathon records. Emphasising quality over quantity, Mary adds that most of her own training miles were at a brisk pace. "I rarely ran slower than six-minute pace so it was always good quality training."

Rather than her injuries being related to over-training or wonky biomechanics, Mary believes it was all due to an inherited condition. "In retrospect I have this gene, which I only found out about when I was diagnosed with arthritis in my hands. It is HLA-B27L and it makes you predisposed to inflammation in all parts of the body. I've had an unusual form of colitis. I have arthritis. I've had sinusitis. I've had all the itises you can imagine."

Mary reckons her first operation for a running-related injury took place soon after she left high school and started college. Another one almost killed her, she adds, after the area that was operated on got infected. With hindsight, much of the surgery was probably unnecessary as well.

"The only thought at the time was that 'she over-trains because she runs and runs at a high level', but it is a proven fact that if you have this gene then you can have an Achilles problem without doing much or even any running," she explains. "So I feel like I had a lot of surgeries that may not have been necessary if I'd been diagnosed earlier with this predisposition and treated for it with preventative medicine."

To combat her problems, Mary takes methotrexate and some other medications, mainly for her arthritis. "At first the arthritis was apparent in my hands," she remembers. "When you have other aches and pains, you don't think you have arthritis. But when I looked at my hands and they started doing all the twisty-turny stuff and it began to hurt, then I went to see a rheumatologist.

"I was tested for lots of things and that's when all this other stuff came out about the gene causing my problems. I was, like, wow – you mean all these years, all these thirty years, I may not have had to have half the surgeries I needed to have? And that I might still be running today?"

The frustration is evident as Mary looks back on what she now feels were unnecessary surgeries. Surely, in recent years, she must at the very least have quietly cursed the doctors responsible for making the decisions. In addition to preventing her from enjoying her running today, it thwarted an attempt during the twilight of her career to race in the 2000 Sydney Olympics.

Pointing to a particularly extensive surgery done to her feet, she says: "They rerouted the tendons in my toes to take pressure off my posterior tibial tendon, which I ruptured in the last track event which I got to compete in, which was a 5000m in my national championships in New Orleans in 1998. My goal at that time was to train long enough and hard enough to make the 2000 team to go to Sydney. So I went to have this surgery, which was the most horrible thing in the world because I had both feet in both legs operated on.

"The premise for having the work done was that it would take the stress off my lower legs, my Achilles tendons and my posterior tibial tendons. At the same time this doctor did a gastroc release (lengthening the gastrocnemius tendon to relieve pressure in the foot) and now I have absolutely no calf muscle and I never got it back after the surgery – ever – despite going to physical therapy for years and years.

"I did everything you can possibly try to do, but I couldn't get a calf muscle back and it won't fire anymore because of the operations. So even now riding the ElliptiGO, I think I'd be stronger on it if I had a calf muscle because right now I am strong here," she says, pointing to her heart and lungs, "but down here, in my calf muscles, there is no strength."

Without the surgery, there is a chance Mary could have lined up, aged forty-two, in the Sydney Olympics 5000m, a race won by Gabriela Szabo from Romania from Sonia O'Sullivan from Ireland. "Yep, etcetera," Mary interrupts with a laugh. "At this point it doesn't really matter."

You can tell it does, though. It rankles with her. Success at the Olympic Games always eluded her. Similarly, she would have loved to have run a marathon and reveals she made a private pact with Fred Lebow, the race director and founder of the New York City Marathon, to make her 26.2-mile debut in the Big Apple. "Before Fred died, I had a deal with him," she recalls. "I told him that when I run my first serious marathon I wanted to run New York. We had this deal but Fred is now gone and I never got to."

Mary's husband is sitting a couple of metres away, chatting to ElliptiGO enthusiasts about the aeroplane and engineering world he got involved in when his own sports career as an Olympic discus thrower and strongman competitor came to an end. At 6ft 7in, he is an imposing figure and reminds me of a Minotaur as he prowls around the ElliptiGO complex in bullish fashion. In conversation, though, he is every bit as affable as Mary and full of jokes and self-deprecating comments about his age. "I'm so old, I competed at the original Greek Olympics," he smiles, before reminiscing about his friends from the 1980s such as decathlon legend Daley Thompson.

After describing her injury nightmare and how she found salvation in the unlikely shape of an elliptical bike, I tell Mary that Richard described the machine as "a godsend" and I suggest that he probably had to put up with a relatively moody wife for many years if she was unable to do the one thing she loved more than anything else – to run. "It has, it really has been a godsend," says Mary, her eyes welling up with tears as she looks at her husband. "To have 'that feeling' again and to do events like this world championships and the California Coast Classic – a 525-mile fundraiser which I did recently on an ElliptiGO – is just great."

As well as the ElliptiGO World Championships and California Coast Classic, Mary has completed the Death Ride, Tour of the California Alps, a 129-mile challenge that sees riders tackling five big mountain passes.

Mary and Richard have little interest or contact with the track and field world today. "I don't follow the sport now. It didn't treat Mary very well," says Richard, referring to the struggle they endured to clear her name after she failed a drugs test on the eve of the 1996 Olympics.

She still makes occasional appearances at track events held in Hayward Field, Eugene. Otherwise, she has largely rejected the world of elite athletics and in its place she has embraced a community who gain pleasure from riding a machine that mimics the action of running.

It is slightly surreal, mainly because the elliptical bikes are still not very widespread and attract strange glances from traditional cyclists and runners, let alone non-sporting members of the public. ElliptiGO enthusiasts are also a little eccentric, with one rider even having an image of the machine tattooed on his chest.

Back home in Oregon, the focal point of Mary's day is her training ride on her elliptical bike. During these workouts, she completes anywhere between an hour and up to four hours with every session culminating with a one-and-a-half-mile uphill effort back to her house. "A short workout for me is one-and-a-half hours," she says. "I feel good if I do two-and-a-half and if I do fours I think 'woo-hoo!'"

She has three Weimaraner dogs and a couple of smaller dachshunds and is keen to show me photographs of them which she carries on her phone. Beautiful animals with long legs, bags of energy and unusually piercing eyes, the Weimaraners used to accompany Mary on long walks in the woods before she discovered the elliptical bike. For years it was her only exercise. "We have fifty-five acres and all I did, exercise-wise, for a while was go out hiking in the woods with the dogs," she says.

"Now, on the bike, I put in between 200 and 250 miles per week generally. Sometimes something comes up that gets in the way, but generally I am pretty consistent. It makes the rest of my life whole, because when you start running and competing from the age of 11 and all of a sudden it stops, there is a big void and I was left thinking, 'How do I fill it?' And this has done it."

Many top athletes stop running once they retire. In fact, some are relieved to hang up their trainers for good. Not Mary, though. "I wish I could still run," she admits. "If I could, I would love to. My big goal when I was younger was to run marathons when I finished racing on the track. I ran one marathon when I was twelve and I wanted to do them later when I was older."

If Mary's body had allowed her to step up to 26.2 miles and tackle the marathon, she would have been one of the first women to have the opportunity to tackle the distance in major championships. The first Olympic women's marathon, for example, took place in 1984, while the longest track distance for females at those same Games was Mary's ill-fated 3000m race. The 5000m and 10,000m for women were not introduced into the Olympics until 1996 and 1988 respectively.

Given this, women's long distance running was in its infancy and Mary was at the forefront of the revolution. The first big 'jogging boom' of the 1970s was dominated by men, but during the early 1980s there was a similar surge in the growth of women's running with Mary and Zola leading the way.

Despite the rise in popularity of running, even male runners were regarded as unusual and often jeered at. So what was it like being a woman runner in the 1970s and early 1980s? Did Mary feel in the minority? "Yes, absolutely," Mary reflects. "I started running when I was eleven and I remember going for runs and people pointing at me as I ran down the road like I had three heads or something.

"It was more male dominated and there were more events for men. I remember doing races like 800m at big track meets in the United States and they were exhibition events because there was a feeling that the women's races surely can't be a real event?

"Or they sometimes called the races exhibition events because I was too young. I had to be fourteen, so when I was twelve and thirteen they would let me run but they would have to make the event an exhibition event in order to let me run against the best in the country. Generally, though, the attitude was 'you girls can't run, you're just the entertainment!'"

The sexism within athletics merely made Mary more determined to demonstrate she was worth watching. "Most of the time I was simply focused on my training but I did notice that when I went to an event all the press and all the attention was centred on men's events. So in my mind I thought 'I need to run faster' so we got noticed and so that women got the respect we deserve because we've put the same amount of effort into what we're doing.

"First, you're running to win, but if you're winning easily then you're running for something else and for me it was either to be faster than I was before or to be faster than anyone's ever been before. I always felt I had to make it count."

Inevitably, Mary is a little jealous of modern female runners who are able to race not only 10,000m and marathon but also the 3000m steeplechase, which was an event which did not make its Olympic debut for women until 2008. "Of course!" she says. "I am envious because I wish I'd been running during this period today. But on the other hand I feel proud that I was part of what has enabled what is going on now. You have to be part of something at some point and my time was back then."

For old time's sake, I pull out a few vintage magazines featuring Mary as the cover star and it is interesting to gauge her reaction. Instead of gushing over her own press clippings, she excitedly turns to a friend and points out a photograph of Julie Brown, the 1975 world cross country champion and fellow Los Angeles Olympian. "That was who I was telling you about earlier," says Mary.

Then I reveal a recent issue of *Athletics Weekly*, featuring a two-page picture special of her famous 'Decker double' from Helsinki in 1983, and Mary is not sure how to react. "Oh my goodness, why?" she asks, almost embarrassed that her victories are still being covered several decades later. "People love nostalgia!" I reply, adding that her Helsinki double gold was one of the greatest middle-distance performances in history and surely her finest achievement?

"Yes," she says, "I was very proud of myself during that World Championships because going into it everyone in the athletics world was saying 'she can run well against the Americans and she can run fast by herself but she can't win anything'. So I was out to prove a point and I was very proud to do so."

Was it her proudest moment? "I think as far as an international competition, yes. I mean I've had some amazing races, runs or events, but as far as an actual competition, then yes."

Which gave her the most pleasure – the 3000m victory or the 1500m triumph a few days later? "The first one took the pressure off for the second," she says. "The second made it even sweeter, but the first one was that I had done what I went there to do.

"Going into the 1983 World Championships I originally wasn't going to do the double but I ran both events at our US Championships and I remember having Richard on the phone when I first knew him and he said 'why not run both?' I said 'well, I guess I should!' So that's what happened."

Mary does not look like the kind of athlete who spends her evenings replaying old races and, sure enough, she confesses she has only watched her victories in Helsinki once since 1983. It was a more pleasurable experience than she imagined, too.

"The first time I watched the World Championships – the whole event, either race – it must have been the 1990s when Galen Rupp was in high school and Alberto Salazar was coaching his team," she recalls, "and I invited their cross country team to our house for spaghetti the night before the state championships.

"Alberto thought it would be a good motivating thing to show them these races from the World Championships. And it was the first time, I swear, that I'd watched it from start to finish. I hate watching myself. But I made myself watch it because we had these kids watching it and it was kind of cool, because they cheered at the end and it turned out to be pretty special. I thought 'wow, because I did that I get to watch these kids do this now' and it was a nice moment."

Noticeably, Mary brings up the topic of the 1984 Olympic 3000m final without being prompted. "Of course, when it comes to the '84 Olympics, I have never watched that," she says dismissively.

Not at all? "No, not at all," she insists. "The only thing I see is the clip they show over and over again."

As an athlete with so many world records and world titles under her belt, it must be frustrating to be primarily remembered for a race she didn't finish. "Of course it is," she admits. "I hate the phrase 'it is what it is' but the LA Games is what it is. And, you know what, the Olympics just never worked out for me and I have a lot of things to look back on which are better and more positive.

"When I meet people they often look at me and say, 'Oh, you're that runner' and some of them who don't know a lot about track and field say, 'Oh, LA. Oh, I cried,' or that kind of thing. But people who know the sport do not really bring it up ever and they just respect me for what I've done and the career that I've had and I certainly don't base my athletics career on what happened in LA."

From Munich to Montreal and Moscow to Los Angeles, Atlanta and Sydney, Mary was destined never to show her true ability at the Olympics. She is not the only world-class athlete to suffer from this curse, though, and as I mention great athletes like marathon legend Radcliffe, Australian runner Ron Clarke, British miler Roger Bannister – all of whom failed to win gold at the Games – Mary's eyes begin to water again and she is noticeably flattered to be put in such esteemed company, albeit as part of a dubious club of super-athletes who failed to succeed on the greatest stage of all.

"It's because it was here, in LA, and it was very dramatic and of course I was expected to win and that's just the way it went down," Mary says, trying to make sense of it as her voice tails off.

There is no longer any animosity between Mary and Zola. But there is no close relationship either because they have barely seen each other for years. The pair met when they raced over a mile on the roads in Sydney in 1992 and got together briefly for a television documentary at the LA Coliseum in February 2016. But apart from that, their paths have not crossed in the last quarter of a century. "As for Puică," Mary adds, "oh goodness, no. I don't travel much these days. Not overseas at any rate."

Given her immense history in the sport – from her early period as a child prodigy to a veteran athlete who is still testing her body today – what is Mary's advice to young athletes who are both blessed and burdened with a similar talent? "You need to love what you're doing and don't just do the sport because your parents have a vision for you," Mary replies. "I think it's something that you have to feel inside and that you want. Whether your parents care or not, it's got to be somewhere that you want to go."

Her words are heartfelt as she continues: "A lot of kids are pushed into different sports and it's often the sports that the parents used to do. So I believe it has to come from within the athlete because as the athlete gets older then they realise this is not what they want to do."

Using the example of her own daughter, Ashley, she continues: "Our daughter did not want to do competitive sports. We introduced her to everything and every sport. We didn't push in any direction. When she was at college she did salsa and ballroom dancing and now she lives in the Chicago area and goes to the gym every day doing spinning classes and that's what she's happy doing as she doesn't want to be competitive.

CHAPTER TWELVE

UNSUNG HEROINES

"When we competed against each other, flames would fly."
Maricica Puică

MARY AND ZOLA achieved more fame and fortune for their collision in the Coliseum than the athletes who made the actual podium in the women's 3000m at the 1984 Games. It is ironic. Some would go as far as to call it an injustice.

The one-two-three of Maricica Puică, Wendy Sly and Lynn Williams were largely ignored by the media after the race and they remain relatively little-known figures in comparison to Mary and Zola. Winning a medal in one of the most infamous races in history was bittersweet, as their achievements will forever be overshadowed by Mary's fall. Yet the facts are that they have gold, silver and bronze from the Olympics in their trophy cabinets, while Mary's best position in the Olympics was a mere eighth in 1988 and Zola's highest place was seventh in 1984.

All three medallists seem content with their position in history, though. There is no bitterness and barely any regret. Away from the controversy of LA '84 their careers contained many other fine performances and they have gone on to enjoy successful and healthy lives.

Over in Romania, Puică is currently easing into retirement in the small city of Câmpulung. Nestled on the edge of the Carpathian Mountains, about two hours north-west of Bucharest, she spends her days pottering around her fruit garden making jam, marmalade and sometimes plum tuică, the national drink of her country. Now well into her sixties, she jokes that the only exercise she does these days is running errands to the local shops. Helping look after stray animals is also a key part of her life and she is an avid supporter of dog shelters and other local animal charities. Such is her involvement in animal welfare, in fact, she has been dubbed 'the Brigitte Bardot of Romania'.

Outside Romania she is vaguely remembered by some as the blonde-haired athlete who won the Olympic title when Mary and Zola fell. Within her own country, though, her reputation is different. Considered one of Romania's greatest sportswomen, she is bona fide athletics royalty and, among other things, has served as Romanian ambassador for sport, tolerance and fair play with the Council of Europe.

A fascinating character, Puică was tempted many times during her athletics career to defect to the West. But she endured the violent Romanian Revolution of 1989 and her incredible durability saw her racing on the international scene until she was almost forty.

Friendly, approachable and easy to get hold of, Puică returns my phone call in prompt and cheery fashion. "Hellooo! It's Mari-cheeka Pweeka!" she says, simultaneously reminding me how to correctly pronounce her name. Soon after, though, our conversation stutters to a halt as she speaks only Romanian, fluent Spanish and barely any English and, while I speak basic Spanish, it is not enough to cut it in a serious interview and I revert to using a translator.

"I still remember the events of Los Angeles 1984 as if it happened just yesterday," says Puică. "I remember how Mary Decker fell and I wanted to help her get up, but if I would have done that, stepped off the track to help, I would have been disqualified so instead I focused on the race. It's unfortunate that she fell. All of us wanted to give their best in this race. If I had fallen I would have continued to run, but for Mary it was beyond her strength."

On the hype surrounding the race, Puică continues: "The journalists were interested in playing out Decker-Budd as a duel. They made an icon out of Decker and kept going on about the fact that Zola was from South Africa. When it came to me, I was a Romanian, our country was very small and there was also the fact that it was behind the Iron Curtain. I'd say seventy to eighty per cent of people I met at the Olympic Games did not even know where my country was located on the map."

Born in July 1950 in Iași, eastern Romania, as Maricica Luca, she was one of the youngest children in a large family dominated by brothers who excelled in a variety of sports like boxing, volleyball, handball and archery. Their father owned a wood deposit and mother was a chef at a local restaurant and from an early age Puică took an active interest in sport and first showed her talent by running well in a regional race in 1966 when, aged fifteen, her talent was spotted by the director of the Iași sports centre, Ion Puică.

As the surname suggests, the two would later get married. The coach was twenty years older, but their partnership has endured and in 2015 they celebrated forty-five years of marriage. Also coached by her husband throughout her career, she says: "I've had brilliant performances on the track, a good husband, an extraordinary man who has been everything for me – dad, teacher, coach, everything I needed."

With 800m and 1500m bests of 1:57.8 and 3:57.22 going into the 1984 Games and the stamina that had earned her two world cross country titles, some experts had tipped the robust Romanian to win gold even if Mary had not fallen. Not surprisingly Puică is also convinced she would have won, whatever the circumstances.

"Even if Mary would have continued the race, she wouldn't have won it either way," insists Puică. "Mary wasn't in good shape. She wasn't prepared. I'm convinced that she did not rise up to continue because she understood that she couldn't do anything about the final outcome. I was in such good shape that I was ready for a 3000m world record and was very well prepared.

"In 1983 I had to pause for a few months due to injury and this break gave me an opportunity to recharge my batteries, focus my energy for the Olympics. In March 1984, I won the world cross country title in New Jersey and in the summer came the victory at the Olympics. Nobody can say that I won because the Russians boycotted the Games, because at the World Cross Country Championships I beat the Russians who could have competed against me in Los Angeles."

Looking back, Puică adds: "Zola was very young, very modest, nice girl, very open, very good, while Mary was excessively confident, wanted to do everything she liked, behaved like a spoilt child."

After Los Angeles, Puică ran her fastest times close behind Mary – and ahead of Zola – in the great series of 1985 clashes on the grand prix circuit.

Then, in 1987 aged thirty-seven, she won silver behind Samolenko in the 3000m at the IAAF World Championships before competing in her fourth and final Olympics in 1988, where she exited in the heats.

Summing up her longevity, George Vecsey wrote in the *New York Times*: "As a marvel of durability, Puică ranks with Billie Jean King, who was terrorising people at Wimbledon at the age of thirty-eight, and Dino Zoff, the 1982 goalkeeping hero for Italy at the age of forty, and Kareem Abdul-Jabbar, an all-star at the age of forty."

One year after the 1988 Olympics, the Romanian Revolution erupted with a period of torrid civil unrest ending with the trial and execution of the country's long-time leader, Nicolae Ceaușescu, and the end of forty-two years of Communist rule. Rather than avoiding the conflict, though, Puică was drawn into the situation when she appeared on Romanian television to praise the youthful revolutionaries, urging: "If we have to die, let us die together."

The comments led to death threats, but the political turmoil quickly ended and the country emerged as a more stable and happier nation. Subsequently, Puică turned to coaching and guided fellow Romanian Violeta Szekely to Olympic 1500m silver in the 2000 Olympics, although ironically the coaching success led her to finally quit athletics.

"When I was watching Violeta run in Sydney, I thought I would die with a heart attack at the side of the track," she recalls. "As an athlete and as a coach, I was very emotional. It was then that I decided to quit, thinking I'd better stay healthy and calm, instead of falling ill because of all this tension."

As for regrets, she adds: "I would have loved to have had a child, but it was impossible during the career days. We did not have anyone who could help us with a child. I spent my days between Iași and the capital, Bucharest, and deciding to have a child would have meant taking a career break for over a year and, back then, you couldn't come back from such a break. My biggest regret in life is the fact that I did not have a child. I love children very much and I would have loved to have had five, but we were not meant to have it all."

Of all the athletes from the 1984 Olympic 3000m final, silver medallist Sly remains closer to the sport than most. While the British public had been brainwashed into thinking Zola was going to win a medal for them in Los Angeles, it was the teenager's more established and streetwise team-mate, Sly, who slipped under the radar to make the podium and today she works full time in the world of athletics as a magazine publisher and team manager for British cross country running squads.

As managing director of Great Run Publishing based in London, she looks after a family of publications that includes *Athletics Weekly*. Prior to this, her busy career in the industry has seen her work for *Reader's Digest*, while outside the magazine business she often passes on her athletics expertise to the next generation of up-and-coming athletes, especially junior women. With a teenage son of her own, she is also adept at handling youngsters of the opposite sex.

Sly is known for her charming, gregarious personality, but beneath the smiling exterior is a gritty, determined character. It is these latter traits that drove her to the runner-up spot at the 1984 Games and also helped her recover from a serious injury to her head sustained after a mugging incident in 2004.

Fending off a thief who tried to steal her briefcase, Sly was knocked to the ground during the scuffle and suffered a brain haemorrhage that needed surgery. Easing back to health, she soon returned to work and in 2014 was awarded an MBE for her services to athletics – exactly thirty years after her medal-winning run in LA.

IAAF president and double Olympic champion Coe is among those in awe of Sly's career. "Her two fifth places in the World Championships in 1983, in 1500m and 3000m races won by Mary Decker, were performances of the highest quality," he wrote in the *Telegraph*. "A year later Decker was to play a prominent but prostrate role in Sly's finest moment, when a mid-race collision between the American and Zola Budd left Decker lying on the track clutching her hip and making a noise familiar to every kindergarten teacher. Sly, unruffled by the histrionics, got the silver behind Romania's Puică."

Born as Wendy Smith in Hampton, Middlesex, on bonfire night in 1959, it was some years before she would find her stride as a runner. No one in her family was particularly sporty, with her father smoking cigarettes heavily and unusually, for a British Olympian, she failed to win a medal at the English Schools Championships – an event often dubbed the "kids' Olympics".

A bit like Zola, she was initially attracted to the sport of netball. Unlike Zola, however, her tall, slender frame meant she was good at it. Soon, though, inspired by watching the Munich Olympics on television, she joined Feltham Athletic Club – coincidentally the same club that Olympic and world champion Mo Farah joined when he moved from Somalia to Britain in the mid-1990s – and she began to make her mark on the teenage running scene.

By 1977, Sly was winning national titles in England and along with athletes like Chris Benning and Chris Boxer helped drag British middle-distance running out of a malaise that it had sunk into during the 1970s. She was also not afraid to follow an untrodden path when she became one of the first European women to move to the United States to train in the altitude of Colorado, or heat of Florida, while earning money on the lucrative US road racing circuit.

"I just loved running – I still love running," she says, looking back, "and I was lucky that from an early age I trained with men and treated it as normal and I looked up to British male runners like Dave Bedford, Brendan Foster and Ian Stewart, in particular, who at the time were world record-holders and Olympic medallists. They were heroes to me and I wanted to run as hard as them, train as hard as them, be as hard as them."

To emulate one of her heroes, Sly even wore the same style of long, red socks which were popularised by world 10,000m record-holder Bedford. "It's quite embarrassing now to think about it," she says, "but for ages I ran around in the hope some of his magic would be transferred into these red socks I was wearing."

Sly was also inspired by Lillian Board, the 1968 Olympic 400m silver medallist and 1969 European 800m champion. With a touch of irony, Board was born in Durban, South Africa, but competed for Great Britain with distinction before she tragically died from cancer in 1970 aged only twenty-two.

The amazing Grete Waitz struck a chord with Sly, too, as the Briton was emerging onto the world scene. "I admired Mary but I wasn't built of the same stuff that Mary was built of. Whereas I was built more of the stuff that Grete was," says Sly, referring to the Norwegian's rugged stamina compared to the American's speed and fragility.

"Grete was probably the most influential in changing people's perception of female distance runners," she adds. "I guess single-handedly she wouldn't have been able to get the marathon in the Olympics (in 1984) but there must have been a perception change at some stage in the early 1980s that women could handle the marathon and Grete was at the forefront of this by running times on the roads which were quicker than anything anyone had dreamt of previously."

Some of Sly's best performances came on the roads, too. As well as beating Zola in the Olympics, Sly defeated her over 10km in Phoenix in March 1985 and smiles at the thought of her superior win-loss record against her more famous rival. In addition, she beat her role model, Waitz, most notably over 15km in Tampa, Florida, in February 1983. Pulling 12 seconds clear in the final mile, Sly ran 48:18 and recalls: "I ran something like 4:50 for the last mile as I was absolutely scared out of my brain that she was going to come back at me. It was a big deal for me because as well as being my idol she had been finishing about half a lap ahead in the World Cross Country Champs! The race 'made me' as a runner because I had the confidence after that run and I beat her again at the Crescent City Classic 10km in New Orleans in 1985."

Like many female runners during the era, Sly's natural endurance was suited to 5000m and 10,000m, or even the marathon, but 3000m was the longest track event for women at the major championships in 1983 and 1984. "It's only now when you see how far women's athletics has come that you look back and think, 'blimey, that was archaic'," she says.

"I didn't make any money on the track – at all," she explains. "The money for me came on the roads and I used that money to fund my track season and be a full-time athlete."

The gamble of moving to America paid off for Sly, but everything was a learning process. For starters, knowledge of how to use altitude training was in a primitive state compared to today and her first sports massage did not happen until the 1983 World Championships. "He wasn't even British, but Australian," she says of the masseur. "How times have changed."

On the altitude factor, she adds: "I'm perhaps talking wildly with rose-tinted glasses, but I think I could have broken four minutes for 1500m and got close to 8:30 for 3000m if I'd understood how to train a little better. But injuries also play their part and I suffered from a few."

One of these cropped up in spring 1984, just as the countdown to Los Angeles was starting to get serious. "I picked up an injury in my ankle which I was told was a stress fracture," she says. "I was distraught because to lose six to eight weeks at that time of year and have to build back up again meant I might as well have said 'forget the Olympics'. But then I got on a plane to Boulder and saw a sports injury expert Andy Pruitt who told me it was my anterior tibialis muscle. He treated it with ultra sound and I was back running within two days."

With the injury healing, Sly's preparations for Los Angeles were then hit with a new challenge. "Zola had come to the UK and my mum and dad had naively given the press the number for where I was staying in the States. There was no social media, internet, or mobile phones back then, so I had heard of Zola but I didn't really understand the impact her arrival had in the UK and neither did I understand the impact it would have on me.

"So I came back to England in May, which was what I did every year once it had got too hot in Florida to run, and suddenly my phone was ringing non-stop. Journalists wanted me to go on TV. I had press non-stop sitting outside my flat and, to be honest, I just could not cope with it."

In training, Sly was flying under the guidance of her coach Neville Taylor. But she was unable to reproduce her form in races in the run-up to the Games. "I was emotionally drained because there was so much focus on things that I didn't want to focus on. Unlike 1980, when I missed out on qualifying for the Olympics by one second, I started 1984 knowing I was going to the Olympics because I reached a level where I was fifth in the world and it was almost a given. But it was in danger of going horribly wrong and then Zola appeared and I could not produce a decent race and it was all in my head. There was nothing wrong with me physically but my emotional energy had gone."

After seeing a sports psychologist, Sly decided she needed to take control of the situation and travelled back to the United States to prepare for the Games. "I knew if I stayed in England, I was never going to produce anything," she says, adding: "I got myself in such a state I watched the British Olympic trials on TV and had a temperature of 102. I had made myself ill. Today, there's an expectation that athletes will have to speak to the press but back then, unless you were Seb Coe, Steve Ovett or Steve Cram, as a British athlete you weren't used to getting much attention. So to suddenly get it and for it to all be negative was hard."

Sly even avoided the official British holding camp in San Diego. Instead she stayed with her coach and the British runner Eamonn Martin in a house rented by her kit sponsor, Brooks, in Manhattan Beach in Los Angeles. "I ran up and down the beach every day and we found a good track nearby. I just focused on my running and it was the best thing I ever did. Then, in the final big session, we cut it short because I was running so well and my coach said 'you're ready'."

Ironically, Sly had been unlucky enough to trip up in races a few times in her career. As a teenager, she fell in the European Junior Championships in Donetsk and finished 11th despite losing a shoe. On another occasion, she fell at the start of a New Year's Eve race in New York's Central Park and was trampled by fellow athletes as they scrambled to get past her and into their running. "It was terrifying," she remembers.

In Los Angeles, though, she was always smartly positioned and well poised to capitalise on the melee caused by Mary's fall. "It was just a really tough race that was extremely physical," she recalls. "A couple of people dropped out – not just Mary falling over – it was a hard run."

Does the lack of recognition for medallists like herself annoy her? "I'm a great believer that if you hang on to negative stuff then the only person you are hurting is yourself," she says. "So I put it behind me very quickly. The most hurtful thing at the time was when I came off the track in LA and the first question was, 'did you see what happened?' No one said 'well done' after I'd run 8:39 to win silver."

Sly continues: "So after that you just move on. I knew how well I'd run. When you are with people who know and understand the sport, they value what you did and that means more than anything. If your peers appreciate what you did, that's probably as good as anything."

On Zola's youth and inexperience, Sly says: "She was put in a situation that she was naturally going to be uncomfortable. If you're used to running on your own, you are going to find it hard when you find yourself in a physical race. It takes time to learn how to hold your own and it was always going to be difficult for her when she got into a race like that which she could not control.

"My whole tactic going into that race was to not let Zola or Mary control it. I always wanted to be there or thereabouts and not let them 'own' the race. I don't think Zola was comfortable being behind and being tactical. Mary always ran like that – hard from the front – and it suited me to be honest."

Sly's career finally ended after the 1990 Commonwealth Games when a nerve-related problem hampered her running style. She still runs these days, but only three or four times per week and is just as likely to be found in the gym doing the kind of strength and conditioning work that endurance runners barely did in the 1980s.

"I would have loved to have been born ten or fifteen years later because the opportunities to race the distance which I felt I was better at would have been there," she concludes. "But I also feel extremely proud to be part of that initial burst of women's distance runners."

Battling her way into bronze in Los Angeles was Canadian runner Williams and, like Puică and Sly, she is thriving in middle age. As well as her Olympic medal, she won Commonwealth 3000m gold in 1986, world cross country bronze in 1989 and smashed national records from 1500m to 10km on the roads. Her 1500m mark, in fact, of 4:00.27, still stands as her country's all-time best.

From 1983-2003, she was married to Canadian distance runner Paul Williams but the mother-of-four has since reverted to her maiden name of Kanuka. She lives in Penticton, British Columbia, but still travels widely on athletics-related trips.

Today, she coaches runners of all levels, even beginners who employ a mixture of jogging and walking. An effervescent character, it is hard to imagine any of her runners failing to be inspired by her words. Many elite athletes have a slightly snooty view of mere 'joggers', but Kanuka is just as happy giving advice to novices as she is to potential world-beaters.

Linked to this, she promotes aqua running and was among the first athletes to use the technique in the 1980s. Again on the cross-training theme, she is a qualified Nordic walking coach, where poles are used to help you cover the ground, while she also promotes the use of StreetStrider machines – an outdoor elliptical bike similar to the brand that Mary uses.

"I love to paddleboard – it's my Zen," adds Kanuka, who clearly is not letting age restrict her physical activity. "And any time I can sneak away for a hike in the mountains, I'm gone."

Looking back on her career, I expect her to name her Olympic medal as her best achievement, but she says: "Honestly, my number one moment was my bronze medal at World Cross in Stavanger, Norway, in 1989."

The race was won by Annette Sargent of France with Nadezhda Stepanova of the Soviet Union second. "I couldn't believe how easy I felt actually finding myself leading, in front of the Russians and Romanians and with Rosa Mota of Portugal on my heels. I will never forget when with about 1km to go they took the lead and I was thrilled because I figured I'd be able to outkick them, as I had so much energy, but there's where my strategy didn't work. The mud was so deep I couldn't get any traction and had to settle for bronze, which I was thrilled with anyway. Cross country was what got me into the sport in the first place and I loved it."

On her cross-training techniques, she says: "I was a pioneer with deep water running. My coach at the time was Dr Doug Clement – a world renowned sports medicine doctor – and it was his observation that horses are tossed into deep water for both recovery and strength, so why not runners? I had many frustrations with injury and being unable to handle much mileage, so for me it was the answer. I still water run now and certainly have all my athletes including at least one session per week as part of their programme."

On her elliptical bike, she says: "I was having a severe bout of plantar fasciitis a few years ago and was having to go on an elliptical trainer inside the gym. Then I saw a girl go by me on a StreetStrider and I didn't even need to try it. I bought one, recovered from my injury and since then just love to go out on it."

She adds: "I actually bumped into Mary on a run in Eugene a number of years ago and we discussed the frustrations of various aches and pains. I told her about my StreetStrider and some time later I heard she was amazing with an ElliptiGO. Either way it gets us runners moving outside without impact in a way that is the closest thing to actually running, which is awesome."

Finally, Kanuka offers an opinion on the controversial Olympic final. "I was an 'unknown Canadian' in the field, but knew I could run with anything dished out after the training I'd experienced leading up to the Games," she explains. "So I was thrilled with the results."

She adds: "Many people would have said at the time, 'well, Mary fell, the Eastern bloc countries weren't there, the Canadian was lucky!' Perhaps all of this was the case, but I did go on to place well and consistently in grand prix events and championships for years afterwards, so was able to dispel those thoughts.

"My fifth place in the Seoul Olympics 1500m in 1988 – only one tenth of a second from a silver medal – was a superior performance given the competition in Seoul. It was viewed as a disappointment but only for those that don't know the sport."

On Mary's fall in Los Angeles, Kanuka says: "Well, Mary and Zola went predictably to the front and the pace was fast with lots of bumping and jostling. Mary was definitely uncomfortable being unable to run confidently in front of the field. We all knew she was not going to run away with the win after the way the earlier rounds went – she was vocal about not being happy with the bumping in the heats – and in the final she somehow locked ankles with Zola and she went down.

"I thought she'd be up and would rejoin the pack, but apparently she fell down hard on that railing. I don't think she was going to win that day, but we will never know."

When the 1984 Olympics took place, it was hard to imagine South Africa being allowed back into the Games anytime soon. Even more difficult to foresee was the fact that the country's track and field medal drought at the Olympics would be brought to an end not by Zola but by her former teenage rival, the relatively unheralded Elana Meyer.

As the sporting world re-opened its doors to South Africa on the eve of the 1992 Olympics, Zola was once again representing the country of her birth. But after being knocked out of the heats at the Barcelona Games, she was subsequently overshadowed by Meyer as the twenty-five-year-old ended South Africa's thirty-two-year wait for an Olympic athletics medal and earned her nation's only track medal of the 1992 Games when she won silver in the 10,000m.

Despite hitting her peak almost a decade after Zola was at her best, Meyer was actually born in the same year as Zola – 1966 – and is only five months younger. Given this, the duo found themselves in a number of races as teenagers growing up in South Africa and the rivalry helped push Meyer to a higher level.

"I grew up racing Zola from the age of thirteen or fourteen years old, so I had this world-class phenomenon that I had to deal with," Meyer remembers. "Obviously she beat me by a long way as a junior but as the years went by the gap got smaller and smaller and ultimately I managed to beat her."

Meyer was hardly short of ability as a child and aged thirteen won a half-marathon outright. She adds: "Zola was a world-class athlete from the age of fourteen or fifteen and even though I ran pretty good times – 4:18 for 1500m at age fourteen or fifteen – Zola was just so much better. Then she had the opportunity to pursue an international career at eighteen and because of our political situation I didn't. So our racing paths totally split.

"She came back to South Africa much later and was never the same. She had a tough career and was very ill-prepared for the political situation. She was not well managed as a young athlete, coming from a very conservative family and being thrown into the international world and being asked to answer political questions. It's a real pity that someone so talented was denied the chance to compete and was instead used as a political pawn internationally."

Like most South African athletes, Meyer was frustrated at being unable to compete on the international stage and unlike Zola did not have an obvious family link that would enable her to run for another nation. "What was a saving grace, for me, was that Zola was in South Africa until the age of seventeen or eighteen, so in that period I improved every year because Zola was still in front of me," Meyer adds. "So within South Africa, there was world-class competition for me. But during the period that followed, I missed out."

Meyer was good enough to run at the Los Angeles Olympics but missed out. "Then 1988 came and we (South Africa) were still in isolation," she continues, "so for eight years it was very hard and by the time I got to the early 1990s the frustration was really starting to kick in and from a personal perspective I just wanted to race the international girls. At that stage I wanted to race against athletes like Liz McColgan and Lynn Jennings and even though I couldn't race them physically, I raced them on paper."

When Meyer's opportunity finally came, she grasped the moment in memorable style. After a 25-lap battle with Derartu Tulu of Ethiopia, Meyer won a symbolic silver medal for South Africa as Tulu also created history by becoming the first black African woman to win an Olympic medal as she took gold. Together, draped in their national flags, they then went on an emotional lap of honour.

"When I walked onto the Olympic track in 1992 it's hard to describe just how much emotion was captured in that moment," Meyer remembers. "It was a mixed bag of emotions. It was a special moment for me and something I will remember for the rest of my life."

After Barcelona, Meyer broke the world record and won the world title over the half-marathon distance. "I have no regrets," she says. "As someone who came from a small town with no athletics history and from a country that was banned for thirty years from international competition, athletics gave me a life beyond what I could ever have expected."

Today, Meyer runs for fun and fitness and says: "A day that starts with a run is a better day." She is also a busy mother of two children, helps organise the Cape Town Marathon and is the figurehead for an academy called Endurocad which aims to find a new generation of South African distance runners to follow in the footsteps of herself and Zola.

Stretched by Zola during her early years, Meyer had to raise her game to keep up with her rival. Similarly, British athletes were forced to improve when Zola arrived in England in 1984. Initially, Zola faced opposition from athletes who were worried she was going to take their spot in the national team. Ultimately, though, her impact was positive as she helped to raise standards which had slumped during the previous decade.

"Zola did a lot for women's athletics in this country," says Susan Tooby, who along with twin sister Angela was one of Britain's leading distance runners in the mid to late 1980s. "She made us aware of what we had to do to reach the top."

Zola's move to England arguably acted as the catalyst for a renaissance in British female distance running, starting with runners like Liz McColgan and Yvonne Murray in the late 1980s and early 1990s through to world-beaters such as Paula Radcliffe and Kelly Holmes at the turn of the millennium. As for the Tooby twins, they are both teachers today but during their athletics careers Susan went on to run a 2:31 marathon to place twelfth in the 1988 Olympics, while Angela also made the 1988 Games over 10,000m and won silver in the 1988 World Cross Country Championships behind Ingrid Kristiansen in Auckland.

Due to spiralling threats from anti-apartheid groups, Zola was forced to pull out of the Auckland event. But Angela remembers: "Zola wrote me a note before the championships saying, 'Good luck, Angela, thank you for being my friend', which was quite touching. People use this cliché of her being a political pawn, but deep down all she wanted to do was run, she wanted to have friends and she wanted to be liked. Plus, she was an absolutely phenomenal runner."

Murray agrees with the fact Zola inspired better British performances. "Zola was a big factor in my progress," says the Scottish runner who, in addition to winning European and Commonwealth titles was a room-mate of Zola's at major events. "She was a figurehead. She provided a standard of excellence for me to aim at. She was also misunderstood. She was great fun to share with – once you got her talking she wouldn't stop, but she was understandably wary of strangers."

Another Scottish athlete, Lynne MacDougall, ran the race of her young life, aged nineteen, to finish runner-up to Zola over 1500m at the UK Championships in 1984 and later made the Olympic 1500m final in Los Angeles. She has more reason than most to bear a grudge, as she held the British junior records for 800m and 1500m and lost the latter to Zola when the South African moved to England. But she says: "I felt sorry for Zola. She was just a young girl who wanted to do her running and ended up being used as a pawn. In the Athletes' Village at the 1984 Olympics she was very quiet but was a great runner."

Like many of Zola's and Mary's contemporaries, MacDougall still runs for fun and is enjoying life as she combines motherhood with a job as a researcher at the University of Glasgow. Given that more than a quarter of a century has passed since the 1984 Games, though, Father Time has not been kind to everyone. Unlucky athletes like Mary can barely break into a jog without pain due to the ravages of injuries and sports-related surgeries. Others have entered the athletics afterlife and left us completely.

They include some of Mary's coaching team from Athletics West – with Bill Bowerman dying in 1999 and Dick Brown in 2016. Ravilya Agletdinova, the Soviet runner who finished fourth in the 1983 world 1500m final and took European 1500m gold in 1986, died in a traffic accident in 1999. Another Russian, the 1992 Olympic 3000m champion Yelena Romanova, died in 2007 aged forty-three after having suffered from heart-related problems, while the Norwegian great, Waitz, died in 2011 from cancer aged fifty-seven.

Many of the *Daily Mail* men who brought Zola to Britain are also long gone, such as Ian Wooldridge, Brian Vine and the paper's editor, David English. Ditto most of the British politicians involved in Zola's nationality switch in 1984, like Leon Brittan and Denis Howell, plus of course Margaret Thatcher, have died.

Other athletics icons from the 1980s have gone on to lead colourful and fascinating lives. Coe, the Olympic 1500m champion in LA, went on to organise the London Olympics in 2012 and is now, in his position as IAAF president, the most powerful man in athletics. Carl Lewis, who won four gold medals in Los Angeles and an incredible nine Olympic golds in total, has had unsuccessful stabs at acting and politics before going on to be an ambassador for LA's bid to stage the 2024 Olympics.

The inaugural Olympic women's marathon champion at the 1984 Games, Joan Benoit, is one of the world's top veteran runners and in 2008 clocked 2:49 for 26.2 miles at the age of fifty at the US Olympic Trials, 2:47:50 in Chicago in 2010 aged fifty-three and in 2015 ran 2:54:03 in Boston at fifty-seven. Another American marathon legend and Mary's mentor and coaching advisor, Alberto Salazar, has gone on to coach top runners like Farah and Galen Rupp. Nawal El Moutawakel, a Moroccan who in 1984 became the first woman from an Islamic nation to win an Olympic gold when she took the 400m hurdles title in LA, has gone on to be an IAAF Council and IOC member.

For some, their life since the 1970s and 1980s has been more fantastical than anyone at the time could have imagined. Take decathlete Bruce Jenner, the 1976 Olympic champion and world record-holder, for example, who became a television star and, more recently, the most famous openly transgender woman in the world under the new name of Caitlyn Jenner.

As the current voice of the sport on the BBC in the UK, Steve Cram is tasked with reporting on a world of athletics in which there is rarely a dull moment. As runner-up to Coe in the 1984 Olympic 1500m final and gold medallist at the 1983 World Championships, he is also well placed to offer an opinion on the colourful careers of Mary and Zola.

Cram, who broke world records for 1500m, one mile and 2000m in the space of nineteen days in 1985, got to know Mary well during the 1980s as they shared the same shoe sponsor, while Zola once stayed at his house in the north-east of England before a race in Gateshead in 1984. Then, in 1992, he won the men's race at the same Sydney road mile where Mary met Zola in their last ever race.

"Mary was a prodigious talent," says Cram. "She was a tough cookie and not just a nice young girl who was running well. She was renowned for being hard on herself and training hard, but that was part of the era – where everyone was coming out of the '70s and into running high mileage. Given the frame that she had, though, it was perhaps not surprising she kept breaking down."

On Zola, Cram says: "When she came to England it was a massive story. I was very aware of two or three very good South African middle-distance runners who were not allowed to compete on the world stage and it was frustrating that the sporting boycott wasn't always backed up politically or from a business perspective. We were in a 'boycott environment' and culture at the time. It was part and parcel of being in world sport back then. You always felt sorry for the athletes who weren't able to compete during that period but as a principled person you thought, 'That's the right way to go'.

"So when the fast-tracking of Zola's citizenship happened, most people and myself thought, 'That's not right and not the correct way to go about things', but that was countered on a very personal level by thinking, 'Here's a great athlete and she should have the chance to show how great she can be'. And it's always difficult to reconcile those two things."

Cram met Zola in the summer of 1984 when the promoter Andy Norman asked him if she could stay with him before a race in order to avoid the media attention that might descend on her if she was in the official meeting hotel. "When I met Zola, I did feel sorry for her," Cram remembers. "She was still just a kid, really. She was very shy and withdrawn and had not been ready for the media frenzy of that year. She was very quiet and polite and that's when you saw the human side of it all – and her side of it.

"It was incredibly difficult for her to be thrown into that melee and you could see why she struggled with it. She was quiet anyway but it made her retreat into her shell even more. She was not unintelligent – I got that straight away – but she was not worldly-wise and had been brought up in a relatively remote area. So to her running was this outlet and she was fed a story that she would come to Britain and run well without knowing what would come with it."

On the fall in Los Angeles, Cram says: "There was no fault or intention. It was just one of those things that happened. For Mary it was a massive Games and it was so bizarre how the whole thing panned out. It was more to do with the American media than anything. Here you had this all-American girl and the US media only really turned to athletics in Olympic year and this pushed Mary into the spotlight in 1984.

"Because of Zola's infamy at the time, half (of the spectators) were against her actually being there so you had the perfect villain and heroine. So perhaps we shouldn't be surprised that it made such good box office."

On the fallout to the fall, he adds: "Mary's reaction afterwards, for me, was all wrong. I could understand her emotions at the time but two or three days later you should be saying 'these things happen'. But Zola became the villain of the piece and I don't think Mary helped that. The incident was all over the news but you often get these things at the Olympics where they deflect from the gold, silver and bronze."

Cram agrees that Zola and particularly Mary played a big part in showing that Western women could defeat the dominant Eastern bloc athletes during a boom period for female running that saw, among other things, the advent of championship marathons. "Mary showed that someone who wasn't from East Germany or Russia could run quick times," says Cram, although he adds: "Drug testing was just beginning to become more organised and was targeted around major championships and that would have helped Mary. Some of the performances of some of the Eastern bloc athletes were partly because of hit-and-miss drugs testing during the 1970s.

"Up until Mary and Zola came along, the best female athletes were from Eastern Europe and not very marketable. Athletes like East German sprinters Marita Koch and Renate Stecher were very fast but you couldn't really build a meeting around them. So when Mary came along and began breaking world records regularly, she became one of the sport's biggest stars."

Former *Athletics Weekly* editor Mel Watman had the best seat in the house during many of Mary's and Zola's races. Long before mobile phones – let alone the internet – became commonplace, he had to rush away from the Coliseum to post his 1984 Olympic reports back to England, where the words were typed in again by linotype operators. And today he is as busy as ever, still writing about athletics and keen to give his thoughts on one of the most controversial Olympic incidents in history.

"It was a gross injustice to Zola Budd that most of the 85,000 spectators became hostile towards her, for my view at the time – and it remains so – is that it was Mary who was at fault," he says, remembering the incredible scenes inside the Coliseum in 1984. "Shortly after the halfway mark Zola was slightly ahead, running in the inside lane, when Mary made a determined bid to pass her on the inside. There simply wasn't room, particularly in view of Zola's wide arm carriage, but Mary persisted … and paid the penalty, tripping over in a tangle of legs and out of the race. It was effectively over for Zola too; in tears as she was so unfairly booed, she was reduced to going through the motions and did well to finish the race in seventh place."

But Watman adds: "Who could say that either Mary or Zola would have beaten an inspired Puică that day? And from a British point of view, how deserving of her silver medal was Wendy Sly for her gritty run."

So often overlooked, perhaps the final word should go to the 3000m gold medallist from Los Angeles, Puică. Despite now being well into her 60s, the Romanian still sports the same striking blonde hair as she did during her sporting heyday and she smiles contentedly as she looks back on her famous clash with Mary and Zola. "When we competed against each other," she says, reminiscing on the summer of 1984, "flames would fly."

EPILOGUE

"Mary Decker stood alone in the 1970s and early 1980s as the Western world's single reply to the powerhouse of Eastern European running. But for injury, she could have been the Muhammad Ali of women's athletics."
John Rodda, *Guardian*

FOR AN ARENA that bills itself as 'the greatest stadium in the world', the Los Angeles Coliseum is badly in need of a lick of paint. Large cracks caused by an earthquake that damaged the arena in 1994 are still visible. Many of the seats used by spectators at the 1984 Olympics remain unchanged and look battered and weather-beaten after absorbing several decades' worth of intense Californian sunshine. Today, they are mainly used by fans watching American football, most commonly the University of Southern California Trojans and the Los Angeles Rams.

"Hardly any of the people who live nearby are aware of its immense history and the fact it held the 1984 Olympics, let alone the 1932 Games," Coliseum tour guide Sheree Pitts tells me. Like lots of local residents, Pitts was not even born when the LA Games took place, but as an ex-sprinter she appreciates the Coliseum's amazing athletics history and, as we stroll around the arena, we remember the great events of the 1984 Olympics and the most memorable moment of all in the women's 3000m.

Given the commercial success of the Games, it is ironic that the stadium has slid into a mild state of disrepair. Soon this will change, though. As part of a long-time lease on the Coliseum, the University of Southern California is planning a $270 million renovation project. New seating and other facilities will be installed but the USC is keen to retain what it calls 'the historical integrity' of the venue. Built in 1923, in addition to two Olympics it has held two Super Bowls, a World Series, a Papal Mass and hosted visits from three US presidents.

Not surprisingly, therefore, the Coliseum reeks of history. The Olympic cauldron at the east end of the stadium is still lit on special occasions. Puică's name is etched into the perimeter walls alongside fellow Olympic champions from 1932 and 1984. After finishing outside the medals, Mary and Zola have not left their mark, although a bronze plaque paying tribute to Nelson Mandela acts as a vague link to the impact the South African waif had here in the summer of 1984.

While there is no permanent reminder in the Coliseum of Mary and Zola's clash, their legacy runs rich and deep beyond the boundaries of the famous track that staged their encounter. Record-breaking performances from the duo in the 1980s have stood the test of time and some of their marks survive as national records today. Such achievements helped them become trailblazers for women's athletics and they were pioneers of a movement that would see the quantity of female runners increase so dramatically that they have grown from being in a total minority in the 1970s to outnumbering men at many modern running races.

When Mary and Zola were born, female runners were considered a curiosity and a rarity. The longest distance women could run in the Olympics was 800m and the marathon was considered 'impossible' for the so-called weaker sex by the patronising, male-dominated bodies that ran sport. Organisers of the Boston Marathon, for instance, forbade women from running their event from 1897 to 1972 and their determination to maintain this rule led to Jock Semple, a Boston race official, attempting to physically remove Kathy Switzer from the 1967 event, an incident that was dramatically caught by photographers and led to newspaper headlines around the world.

Nowadays, the Boston Marathon features an almost equal split of male and female runners. Switzer helped achieve this by gate-crashing the all-male event, but Mary and Zola also undoubtedly played a major role in popularising women's running. Whereas characters like Jim Fixx and Frank Shorter inspired the general running boom in the 1970s – the former thanks to his best-selling book *The Complete Book of Running* and the latter due to winning the 1972 Olympic marathon – the buccaneering exploits of Zola and especially Mary changed the perception of women's running.

"The American public, watching on television, raved over 'little Mary Decker' and, rather like another adolescent sports heroine of the period, Olga Korbut, she inspired hordes of other young girls," reported *Athletics Weekly* in November 1983. "The rapid growth of women's running in the United States must owe much to the massive publicity accorded Mary in 1973 and

1974. Thanks to her it suddenly became 'respectable' for white, middle-class American girls to run. Astonishing as it may seem now, until that time it was largely considered unbecoming for young ladies to run – it just wasn't deemed socially or physically acceptable."

Neither Mary nor Zola felt restrained by pre-conceived notions of what women were – or were not – capable of and they ignored the popular opinion at the time that athletics was 'unladylike'. There was an uninhibited freedom to their performances and they ran without barriers in their minds with the belief that anything was possible.

Illustrating her fierce determination to break barriers, Mary told Bob Wischnia of *Runner's World* in 1982: "Women don't push themselves hard enough. They don't know how to – and this applies to me also. When I look at pictures of myself hitting the tape, there isn't the agony on my face that you see on men's faces, which indicates I'm not running fast enough."

Mary even spoke several times in the 1980s about the prospect of women one day running a sub-four-minute mile. To most people it is an outrageous, fanciful idea, yet such an open-minded attitude drove her to an American record for the mile of 4:16.71 which still stands today. Similarly, Zola's best mile of 4:17.57 has survived as the UK record, while the original and unofficial 5000m world record which caught the attention of the world in January 1984, when she was aged just seventeen, was born out of pure innocence.

It is not just their outdoor mile marks that have endured either. Mary's best times for 2000m and 3000m outdoors, plus the mile distance indoors, remain the US records and she held the American record for 1500m for thirty-two years until 2015. As for Zola, she continues to hold South African records for 1500m, one mile and 2000m. When it comes to junior – or under-20 – all-time rankings, Mary still has the US indoor 800m best and Zola is world record-holder for 3000m and the mile. Not surprisingly, Zola also retains a multitude of British and South African junior records.

Of course Zola's records were achieved without footwear as well. Growing up alongside many similar shoe-less children in South Africa, she did not think it was unusual. Yet her barefoot performances in the 1980s led to her becoming the most famous shoe-less runner since Abebe Bikila, the 1960 and 1964 Olympic marathon champion, and her rejection of traditional trainers and spikes happened thirty years before the running world was consumed by a recent craze for 'minimalist' footwear with almost all the major shoe brands offering runners shoes that provided 'barefoot feel' which would promote a 'natural running' technique.

The barefoot factor enhanced Zola's aura and helped her, along with Mary, to become the first female athletes to overshadow their male counterparts when being the star attraction at televised track and field meetings. The Los Angeles Olympics, for example, included superstar athletes such as Coe, Lewis, Moses and Thompson, the gymnastics sensation Mary Lou Retton, a future basketball legend by the name of Michael Jordan and a young rower called Steve Redgrave who was destined to win five Olympic golds. Yet the Decker v Budd showdown outshone them all.

Linked to this, Mary and Zola's ability to generate financial reward was ahead of its time and smashed the perception of what female athletes were commercially worth. In this regard, their 'revenge rematch' at Crystal Palace in July 1985 was the prime example as Zola took the lion's share of the proceedings – an unprecedented £90,000 – to take on Mary over 3000m.

"The revelation that she had received from television £90,000 to race Mary Slaney at the Peugeot Talbot Games, unleashed a variety of emotions," said Tony Ward, the British Athletics spokesman during much of the 1980s, "from genuine anguish about the sport, mock horror, sordid opportunism and may yet activate a few suspect anginas."

It is often said that Zola was badly advised, but her team did pretty well for her on that occasion to negotiate such a gigantic fee. They also arranged a lucrative three-year deal with Brooks despite the fact she raced so infrequently in shoes. Then there was the large sum of money the *Daily Mail* threw at the Buddwagon as it rumbled its way through a summer of discontent in 1984.

The huge part the *Daily Mail* played in creating the Decker v Budd story cannot be underestimated. If the newspaper had not lured Zola's family to England, the athlete would probably have carried on plying her trade in relative anonymity and isolation in South Africa. Without the *Mail's* imagination, initiative and money, there would have been no race against Mary and no collision in the Coliseum.

Yet one of the big ironies in recent years is that the *Mail* has conveniently forgotten, or ignored, its role in bringing Zola to England during a period where it has waged a relentless campaign of criticism against so-called 'plastic Brits'. A number of its sportswriters have lambasted British Athletics for embracing athletes who were born outside the UK but who have British relatives. In 2012 one of the *Mail's* writers even asked Tiffany Porter, a sprint hurdler who was born in the United States but whose mother is British, if she knew the words to 'God Save the Queen' at a press conference where she had been named captain of the British Athletics team.

Porter politely declined the question and the reporter was subsequently banned from British Athletics press conferences. The *Daily Mail* was angry at having their reporter barred, but imagine if Zola had been asked a similar question in 1984 when the same newspaper proudly unleashed her upon the British sporting public.

Finally, there are a few myths that should be dispelled. Most of all, the Decker-Budd head-to-head in Los Angeles was not a close, deadly rivalry. Instead, it was something of a mismatch created by journalists looking for a juicy story in Olympic year.

Firstly, there was no genuine animosity. Prior to 1984, Zola idolised Mary, whereas the American was simply a little irritated – nothing more – by every interview on the eve of the LA Games involving questions about a South African teenager she had barely heard of and whom she did not rate as a serious threat. Then, after the Olympics, they were neither enemies nor friends as they lived in different parts of the world and rarely found themselves in healthy, racing condition at the same time. What's more, to further illustrate the lack of hard feelings, they were all smiles when they enjoyed a rare meeting in Los Angeles at the start of 2016 to film a documentary.

As for their relative running abilities, Zola was undoubtedly a fantastic runner who won two world cross country titles and set world records during her prodigious and primarily teenage years. She hit her peak aged eighteen and arguably never fulfilled her true potential which, given her huge reserves of stamina, was possibly over the marathon distance.

Mary, though, was a class apart and is, in my view, quite simply the most talented female middle-distance runner who has ever lived. It is hard to think of a more injury-prone athlete than the American, but she built up an incredible collection of national and world records, won world titles in memorable style and it is a travesty she did not win Olympic gold.

Merrell Noden of *Sports Illustrated*, the great US magazine that followed Mary's career so closely, wrote in 1991: "Her career has been epic, a trip so long and strange and fraught with hard luck it could almost be broken down into periods, like Italian art or English literature."

In the same year, John Rodda, the long-time *Guardian* sportswriter and Olympic historian, said Mary "stood alone in the 1970s and early 1980s as the Western world's single reply to the powerhouse of Eastern European running. But for injury, she could have been the Muhammad Ali of women's athletics."

Amby Burfoot, the 1968 Boston Marathon winner and former editor of *Runner's World*, says in his 2016 book *First Ladies of Running*: "In her competitive prime, Mary established herself as the greatest runner, male or female, in American history."

In his book *The Silence of Great Distance*, Frank Murphy adds: "Mary is the one person who carried the sport from infancy to age, crashing through social barriers, economic hurdles and competitive challenges as quickly as she confronted them. In the course of her progress, she acquired fast friends, attracted detractors and left a great many people simply confused and confounded. No one, however, can deny her greatness as an athlete and few people will deny her influence. She is popular, talented, unpredictable, in turn aloof and protective, inviting and forbidding, endearing and infuriating, unavoidable and unapproachable."

Which brings us to another myth. Mary is often described as being difficult to deal with, or a prima donna, but I found her to be polite, charming and engaging. Although I suspect she has mellowed with age and in her athletics heyday she was a potent mixture of steely determination and emotional fragility, together with possessing the inevitable selfish streak which every athlete needs if they want to achieve the extraordinary.

Similarly, Zola is often described as painfully shy and naïve. This may have been true when she arrived in Britain as a seventeen-year-old struggling to get to grips with the English language, but her subsequent years spent in the fast lane of athletics caused her to grow up fast. A number of sources say Zola was quiet but certainly not stupid and over the last thirty years she has proved an astute and worldly-wise businesswoman and mother. Armed with a magnetic reputation as 'the former barefoot waif who tripped Mary Decker', it would be foolish if she did not occasionally use it in her favour.

The alternative is to dwell on the disaster of LA 1984. Here, neither woman has allowed it to negatively impact on their life. Initially, the fall-out from the fall threatened to destroy them. Mary was lambasted, after all, by her own national press for her unsporting behaviour, while Zola was subjected to death threats. Yet, in time, they gathered themselves, re-grouped and bounced back to run even faster than ever in the late summer of 1985.

If anything, their lives were hurt more by events outside the LA Coliseum. For Zola, this came in the shape of non-stop press intrusion, criticism from anti-apartheid campaigners and family tragedies; for Mary the controversial drugs test positive late in her career was a deep and painful cut, while her never-ending battle with injuries tested her sanity to the hilt.

Despite their problems, on and off the track, they went on to enjoy much longer careers than most elite athletes, both running at a high level into their forties and continuing to compete into their fifties. Outside running, they are proud mothers with strong, happy family lives. Likewise, the three women who made the podium in the 1984 Olympic 3000m have gone on to be healthy and successful, with Puică deservedly feted in her own country, even if the rest of the world has largely forgotten her.

No one will ever let Mary and Zola forget the fateful evening of 10 August 1984, though. As hard as they try to outrun it, they can never escape it. The race is destined to haunt them forever and it left them with invisible scars that will never fully heal. After all these years and despite their many achievements, it remains the event they are most remembered for and has come to define who they are.

As I wander around the Los Angeles Coliseum, I cast my mind back to the summer of 1984 and the Games of the XXIII Olympiad. With the fierce sun burning overhead, I sit down in one of the now-antiquated seats and I glance towards the top bend of the track.

There, I see this classic Olympic moment frozen in time. Mary and Zola are gliding around the track, battling for the lead, as the packed crowd firstly cheer, then gasp, then boo.

ACKNOWLEDGEMENTS

THANKS TO KEVIN Pocklington from Jenny Brown Associates for having the vision to get the idea for this book off the ground and to Pete Burns from Arena Sport for publishing *Collision Course* with such enthusiasm and skill.

I owe a debt to my father, too, for fanning the flames of my athletics interest as a child as he took me to every corner of the UK to watch Zola's races on the eve of the 1984 Olympics. Naturally, my wider family has also shown great patience and support, especially my mother and my two children, Leah and Emily.

In researching this book, a number of invaluable sources were consulted and they include Zola's 1989 autobiography written with Hugh Eley. Three short books on Mary's early career written in the 1980s by Matthew Newman, Cathy Henkel and Linda Jacobs were also useful when giving a flavour of Mary's early years.

Past issues of the US weekly magazine *Sports Illustrated* provided a comprehensive account of athletics in the 1970s and 1980s, especially when chronicling the career of Mary. The archive of *Athletics Weekly* was a similarly definitive resource – the British magazine is called 'the historian of the sport' for a good reason.

Then there is *Runner's World*, especially its in-depth piece on Zola written by Steve Friedman in 2013, plus the comprehensive, authoritative coverage in the American monthly magazine *Track & Field News*, not to mention excellent but now-defunct magazines such as *The Runner*.

Naturally, this book would have been hard to write without referring to newspapers such as *The Times*, *Guardian* and *Telegraph* in the UK and the *Los Angeles Times*, *Chicago Tribune* and *New York Times* in America – to name just a few. Above all, the *Daily Mail* offered a rich seam of articles due to the major part it played in bringing Zola to Britain. In this regard, the British Library's archives were vital.

The Silence of the Great Distance by Frank Murphy, chronicling the growth of women's endurance running, provided not only help with historical facts but inspiration to produce a book of similar depth and quality. Also inspiring was an ESPN documentary in 2013 on Mary and Zola called *Runner*, which was directed by Shola Lynch, who herself was a Decker-esque running prodigy in her youth.

In order to minimise errors, Mel Watman, a long-time editor of *Athletics Weekly*, provided a crucial safety net with his excellent proofreading assistance. There is no one more knowledgeable in athletics and he was also helpful in providing background information and quotes for the content of the book itself.

When it comes to interviews, I have drawn on twenty years' worth of work at *Athletics Weekly* – fifteen of which have been spent as editor – for this book. But more recent and relevant interviews include Elana Meyer, Wendy Sly, Lynn Kanuka, Steve Cram, Lynne MacDougall, Susan and Angela Tooby, most of whom have been featured in *Athletics Weekly* in addition to being quoted in this book and all of whom were generous with their time.

One athlete I did have trouble understanding due to the language barrier, though, was Maricica Puică. Given this, I was helped enormously by Natalia Donets from the National Olympic and Sports Committee of the Republic of Moldova. As the winner of the 1984 Olympic 3000m final, Puică was a crucial athlete to make contact with and Natalia proved an excellent interviewer and translator.

For details about Mary's and Zola's races, the National Union of Track Statisticians and Association of Road Racing Statisticians provided great background. David Wallechinsky's *Complete Book of the Olympics* and Mark Butler's *History of the World Cross Country Championships* are a further two titles that I frequently draw on during my work as an athletics writer.

Printed sources aside, *Marathon Talk* podcasts provided excellent background. Martin Yelling and Tom Williams only started their *Marathon Talk* shows as recently as 2010 but they spoke to Zola in 2012 and related figures in the Budd-Decker story such as John Bryant.

Finally, my thanks most of all to Mary and Zola for being such fascinating athletes to write about. I hope this book does justice to their amazingly eventful and complex lives.

STATISTICS

MARY DECKER SLANEY

Born: 4 August 1958, Bunnvale, New Jersey, United States

Personal best times
Outdoors

400m	53.84	Innsbruck	14 July 1973
800m	1:56.90	Bern	16 August 1985
1000m	2:34.65	Hengelo	14 August 1988
1500m	3:57.12	Stockholm	26 July 1983
One mile	4:16.71	Zurich	21 August 1985
2000m	5:32.7	Eugene	3 August 1984
3000m	8:25.83	Rome	7 September 1985
5000m	15:06.53	Eugene	1 June 1985
10,000m	31:35.3	Eugene	16 July 1982

Indoors

800m	1:58.9	San Diego	22 February 1980
1000m	2:37.6	Portland	21 January 1989
1500m	4:00.8	New York	8 February 1980
One mile	4:20.5	San Diego	19 February 1982

(Also, 4:17.55 on an over-sized indoor track, Houston, 16 February 1980)

2000m	5:34.52	Los Angeles	18 January 1985
3000m	8:47.3	Inglewood	5 February 1982
Two miles	9:31.7	Los Angeles	21 January 1983

Road

5km	15:24	Palm Desert	15 December 1996
10km	31:38	Eugene	6 May 1984

Best achievements

» IAAF World Championships – 1983, 1500m and 3000m champion
» Olympic Games – 1984, 3000m fell; 1988 1500m 8th and 3000m 10th; 1996 5000m 7th in heat 2. Also qualified for the 1980 Olympics but did not compete due to a boycott
» Set 36 American records and 17 official and unofficial world records
» The only athlete to hold the US record at every distance from 800m to 10,000m
» Continues to own the US record for one mile, together with national records for 2000m and 3000m outdoors, plus the mile indoors, and held the US 1500m record for 32 years
» Won 11 US titles between 1974 and 1997
» Pan American Games – 1979 1500m gold
» IAAF World Indoor – 1997 1500m silver (but later stripped of medal)
» Youngest ever US international aged 14 years and 224 days in 1973

ZOLA PIETERSE (NÉE BUDD)

Born: 26 May 1966, Bloemfontein, South Africa

Personal best times
Outdoors

800m	2:00.9	Kronstad	16 March 1984
1500m	3:59.96	Brussels	30 August 1985
One mile	4:17.57	Zurich	21 August 1985
2000m	5:30.19	London	11 July 1986
3000m	8:28.83	Rome	7 September 1985
5000m	14:48.07	London	26 August 1985

Indoors

1500m	4:06.87	Cosford	25 January 1986
3000m	8:39.79	Cosford	8 February 1986

Road

10km	31:42	Oslo	6 May 1984
Half-marathon	71:04	Tokyo	19 January 1997
Marathon	2:55:39	Jacksonville	16 December 2012

Best achievements

» IAAF World Cross Country Championships – 1985 and 1986 champion representing England (also 4th in 1993 and 7th in 1994 for South Africa)

» Olympic Games – 1984 3000m 7th (representing Great Britain); 1992 3000m 9th in heat 1 (representing South Africa)

» European Cup – 1985 3000m 1st

» European Championships – 1986 3000m 4th and 1500m 9th

» World records at 5000m (unofficially in South Africa in 1984 aged 17 and later, officially, representing Great Britain)

» Set 14 world junior bests from 1983-85 from 1500m to 5000m and a world indoor 3000m record in 1986

» Still holds the British record for one mile, South African records for 1500m, one mile and 2000m and world junior records for 2000m, 3000m and the mile

DECKER-BUDD HEAD TO HEADS

10 August 1984 – Olympic 3000m final
1 Maricica Puică (ROU) 8:35.96
2 Wendy Sly (GBR) 8:39.47
3 Lynn Williams (CAN) 8:42.14
... 7 Zola Budd (GBR) 8:51.53
Did not finish: Mary Decker (USA)

20 July 1985 – Peugeot Talbot Games 3000m
1 Mary Decker-Slaney 8:32.91
... 4 Zola Budd 8:45.43

21 August 1985 – Weltklasse Zürich, one mile
1 Mary Decker-Slaney 4:16.71 (world record)
2 Maricica Puică 4:17.44
3 Zola Budd 4:17.57

30 August 1985 – Brussels, Ivo Van Damme Memorial, 1500m
1 Mary Decker-Slaney 3:57.24
2 Maricica Puică 3:57.73
3 Zola Budd 3:59.96

7 September 1985 – Rome Grand Prix, 3000m
1 Mary Decker-Slaney 8:25.83
2 Maricica Puică 8:27.83
3 Zola Budd 8:28.83

16 October 1992 – Sydney road mile
1 Mary Decker-Slaney 4:22.68
2 Zola Pieterse 4:32.60